The Memoirs of
Giorgio de Chirico

The Memoirs of
Giorgio de Chirico

Translated from the Italian and with an Introduction by
Margaret Crosland

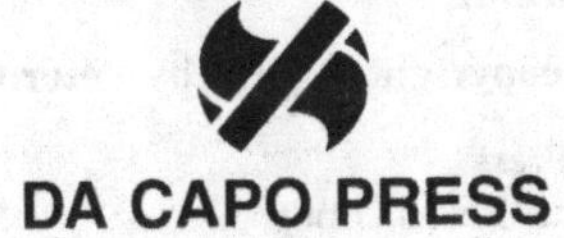

DA CAPO PRESS

Library of Congress Cataloging-in-Publication Data

De Chirico, Giorgio, 1888-
   [Memorie della mia vita. English]
   The memoirs of Giorgio de Chirico / translated from the Italian
and with an introduction by Margaret Crosland. — 1st Da Capo Press
ed.
       p. cm.
   Includes bibliographical references and index.
   ISBN 0-306-80568-5
   1. De Chirico, Giorgio, 1888-   2. Futurism (Art)—Italy. 3.
Metaphysical school (Art movement)—Italy 4. Painters—Italy–
Biography.   I. Title.
ND623. C56A2 1994
759.5—dc20
[B]
                                     93-21421
                                           CIP

First Da Capo Press edition 1994

This Da Capo Press paperback edition of *The Memoirs of Giorgio
de Chirico* is an unabridged republication of the edition published in
London in 1971. It is reprinted by arrangement with Peter
Owen, Ltd., and the Fondazione Giorgio e Isa de Chirico.

Translated from *Memorie della mia vita,* copyright © 1962
by Rizzoli Editore, Milan

English translation copyright © 1971 by Peter Owen Ltd., London

Published by Da Capo Press
A Member of the Perseus Books Group
http://www.dacapopress.com

Manufactured in the United States of America
10 9 8 7 6

Contents

Illustrations

The publishers wish to acknowledge with thanks Mr S. J. Allen and Dr Claudio Bruni for their assistance in lending and identifying some of the photographs and illustrations reproduced in this volume.

Introduction

No Italian painter of the twentieth century, with the possible exception of Modigliani, has caused so much comment, ranging from eulogy to dismissal or outright condemnation, as Giorgio de Chirico. Born in Greece and trained partly in Germany, de Chirico was stimulated by Italy and France alternately until he rejected all foreign influences and settled in his own country—first in Florence, later in Rome. The ever-perceptive Apollinaire was one of the first to write about de Chirico's appearance—on his own advice—in the Salon des Indépendants in Paris in 1913. Jean Cocteau was so impressed with the Italian painter that in 1928 he wrote an 'essay in indirect criticism' about him, entitled *Le mystère laïc* (The Lay Mystery), a piece all the more interesting because it appeared just when de Chirico's style was evolving from the early 'metaphysical' period and his novel *Hebdomeros* was in the press.

The appeal of the metaphysical paintings, with their mythological, philosophical and historical overtones, was more than purely visual, and the Surrealist writers valued the artist's reliance on imagery from the unconscious. These paintings had a 'literary' content which drew praise and interest from many writers, and as a result de Chirico has had close relationships with various writers for much of his life, even if these associations were not always friendly.

De Chirico himself began to write as soon as he began to paint, starting with poems which sometimes reflected aspects of his paintings and sometimes seemed to supply a key to the 'enigma' his canvases often evoked. He has written many articles and essays, often with the insight of a painter-poet, on artists of very different types—Boecklin, Derain, his favourite Courbet—and applied himself to larger issues such as the value of Surrealism, the problem of 'modernistic' art, and questions of technique.

His criticism has always been subjective and as he has grown older his expression and attitudes have become more subjective still.

He has even relished controversy and litigation on the authenticity of his own paintings, and has rarely missed an opportunity to denounce critics who discussed his work adversely, in particular his later painting. Since he had decided to paint in that style, why, he asked, should anyone question his decision? His self-preoccupation has become more apparent in the latter part of his life. In 1945, when he was in his late fifties, he published his first book-length work about himself, his experiences and his opinions, the *Memorie della mia vita*, which constitutes the first part of the present volume. The second part, covering the years 1945 to 1960, appeared in 1962, including the *Technique of Painting* (compiled by de Chirico), the Chronological Table and the Bibliography, all of which will be found in this English edition.

The Milan publishing firm of Rizzoli, who brought out the complete *Memorie*, claimed that the book belonged to the great tradition of autobiography in de Chirico's own country—Benvenuto Cellini, the goldsmith and sculptor, and Vittorio Alfieri, the poet-playwright, had already written their own life stories in a vein of militant egocentricity, giving their versions of 'the truth'. Most people writing about themselves claim naturally that they are giving an accurate account of events in which they participated. They claim they are telling 'the truth'—as they see it.

This autobiography may leave out a great deal, but it supplies essential clues to the author's character and his work. The passage telling of his father's death, while de Chirico was still a schoolboy, is perhaps the most moving page in the book. This event, and the subsequent years which he and his younger brother spent with their mother, had a deep, probably emotive influence on the man and the artist. His early painting reflects a world where direct human contact has been lost—all that remains of people are statues and shadows, while the only portraits, inevitably, are those of de Chirico himself, his mother and his brother. A thematic analysis of the imagery in his paintings and his imaginative writing reveals many striking links between the two and the classic, obsessional, sexually orientated symbolism of dreams. My own theory is that the early paintings were projections of his deeply concealed unconscious life at the time, which, as this autobiography shows, was not a very happy one. During his early middle age the 'metaphysical' painting stopped : the artist may have become aware of his inner conflicts and, since it seems they receded at the same time, he no longer expressed his unconscious feelings on canvas. At this crucial moment he wrote that impressive Surrealist novel in which Hebdomeros, the hero, finds that Immortality has his father's eyes. As life went on, another type of problem seems to have developed, leading to de Chirico's evident conviction that he was the centre of the universe and that everyone else, especially critics and other painters, was subsidiary, stupid, and hostile towards him.

Whatever his own views of his work, Giorgio de Chirico will probably always be identified as the 'metaphysical' painter, the painter of streets and squares full of 'enigma', 'mystery and melancholy', 'nostalgia of the infinite'. The most important message of his autobiography is, however, twofold: it states that his 'metaphysical' painting did not stop in the twenties and that all his painting, irrespective of its period, is of equal value. He refers in these memoirs to the occasions when he has been asked to 'authenticate' faked copies of his own paintings. Yet he does not clarify the mysteries surrounding certain copies he is known to have painted, and he has apparently made mistakes when 'authenticating' paintings supposedly by himself. Perhaps this is why in the mid-1940s he stated that he had in fact never given up metaphysical painting.

Anyone who examines closely de Chirico's paintings and his autobiography will become preoccupied with questions of absolute truth and absolute values in painting and literature. At the same time it should be remembered that de Chirico was one of the first artists in this century to achieve importance in what is now called dualmedia expression, as have Dali, Hans Arp, Picabia and subsequently many others. Since his painting is complemented by his writing, a study of both is essential if we are to understand de Chirico himself. Ideally these factual and sometimes repetitive memoirs should be read in conjunction with the poetic novel *Hebdomeros*, which in many respects is a *roman à clef*. From the *Memoirs*, for instance, we learn that the character in *Hebdomeros* who 'went shopping' for several days was no less than André Derain, and the strange personage who asked everyone what they had eaten for their last meal was based on a count who lived in Ferrara. Other links between the two books include the use of free association, dear to the Surrealists, the tendency to magnify natural phenomena until they become unnatural, and at the same time a nostalgic search for tranquillity.

In the notes at the end of the book I have endeavoured to fill in the background to some of the many names and references which may be obscure to readers outside Italy. I should like to thank Dr Mario Tassoni, Librarian at the Italian Institute in London, for his help in compiling these notes, and Mr Victor Reinganum for his advice about the notes on painting technique. And Mr Michael Levien has given me valuable editorial advice throughout my work on de Chirico.

The Bibliography, originally prepared by the publisher Vanni Scheiwiller, has been updated and anglicised for this edition where feasible. However, it has not been possible, in the time allotted, for me to verify all the entries in this section and bring it entirely up to date.

MARGARET CROSLAND

Part One

I

My most distant memory is of a big room with a high ceiling. In the evenings it was dark and gloomy in this room; the paraffin lamps were lit and the shades put in place. I remember my mother seated in an armchair; in another part of the room sat my little sister, who died shortly afterwards; she was a little girl of six or seven, about four years older than me. I stood holding in my hand two minute discs of gilded metal, pierced in the centre. They had fallen from a kind of Oriental scarf, completely covered with these little glittering discs, which my mother used to wear on her head. As I looked at the two little discs I believe I thought of timpani or drums, something that should have produced a sound, something that people played or played with, but the pleasure I felt at holding them in my inexperienced little fingers, like the fingers of primitive painters and those of modern painters, was certainly linked to that profound feeling for perfection that has always guided my work as an artist. Those identical discs which matched exactly and glittered, with the perfectly shaped holes pierced in the centre, appeared to me then as something miraculous, just as later Praxiteles' *Hermes* in the museum on Mount Olympus seemed perfect to me and later still the portrait of the *Daughters of Lysippus* by Rubens in the Munich Pinacothek, and a few years ago the famous canvas by Vermeer, *The Mistress and the Maidservant*, in the Metropolitan Museum of New York.

It is the quality of the material that determines the degree of perfection in a work of art, especially in painting, and this quality is the most difficult thing to understand. For this reason the so-called intelligentsia, led by the so-called painters, prefer to remain aloof from such questions and take convenient refuge in so-called 'spirituality'. Before I was twenty years old I had already understood the whole of classical music and classical literature, all philosophy, ancient and modern, but it was only much later that I really began to understand the mystery of great painting. Now, still later, I understand the sublimity of a painting by Rubens or Velasquez, Rembrandt, Tintoretto or Titian.

From that extremely remote memory of my infancy, from that dark and gloomy room which I see again as one sees a dream again within the mind, there emerges a symbol that is minute and tremendous, a symbol of perfection : the little gilded discs, each with a hole pierced in the centre, from my mother's Oriental head-dress.

At that time my little sister died, but I do not remember the occasion. Later my mother told me that at the time of the funeral I was sent out for a walk with a nursemaid, and that she, either from stupidity or spite, stopped with me at the very place where the cortège accompanying my sister to the cemetery was passing. At this time also my brother was born, but I do not recall this fact either. All this took place in Athens in about 1891. I had been born three years earlier at Volos, the capital of Thessaly, on a torrid July day, while the candles melted in the candlesticks and the heat of summer was intensified by a hot wind blowing over the city; it came from Africa and the Greeks called it *livas*.

Dark years passed. I have a confused memory of my brother : I remember him as small, very small, disturbingly small, like certain alarming people one sees in dreams. I see again as in twilight scenes associated with long illnesses, like typhus, and wearisome convalescence. I remember an enormous mechanical butterfly which my father had brought me from Paris while in fact I was convalescent. From my bed I looked at this toy, with curiosity and fear, as the first men must have looked at gigantic pterodactyls which in the sultry twilight and cold dawns flew heavily with fleshy wings over warm lakes whose surface boiled and emitted puffs of sulphurous vapour. I remember a house where we lived; a house as vast and gloomy as a convent. The proprietor was called Vuros. This house stood in the high part of the city. From my window I could see in the distance an artillery barracks; when the Greek national fête was celebrated a battery came out of the courtyard at a rapid gallop and

14

went towards a hill which stood some distance away. When they reached it the men got down from their wagons and horses, arranged the cannon in a row and then fired salvoes. White globes, like clouds which had fallen down on to the earth, rolled round a little, then broke up and faded away against the side of the hill. The explosion was heard shortly afterwards and made the window-panes shake slightly. This fact of seeing the flash first and then hearing the sound afterwards made a great impression on me. Later I knew the reasons for it, but even today I am still slightly impressed when I watch a gun being fired a long way off, seeing the flash first and hearing the report later.

In that remote period of my life I felt the first claims of the demon of art. I greatly enjoyed tracing prints by pressing a print against a window with a piece of paper over it. I was always very surprised and excited when I saw appear on the window the precise outlines of the print I so much admired. But my *amour propre* as a budding artist was not satisfied; I wanted to copy the print without pressing it on paper. I was then shown how to do it, but I had great difficulty. One day I remember I was trying to copy a figure which represented St John the Baptist as a young man with a naked breast and a sheep-skin round his hips. The saint's head was slightly foreshortened and inclined slightly towards the left shoulder, a pose which seemed to me insurmountably difficult. I was desperate. My father came to my help. He took my pencil and on the saint's head drew a cross, its centre being the centre of the head. Then he drew a cross of equal size on my drawing where the head was to be, showing me how, with the aid of these two crosses, I could find the position of the eyes, the nose and the mouth, and the height and location of the ear, the line of the head and the jaw, and in this way with much patience and much rubbing out I succeeded in drawing the saint's head fairly well. I was immensely satisfied at having learnt the two-crosses method.

My father was a man of the nineteenth century; he was an engineer and also a gentleman of olden times, courageous, loyal, hard-working, intelligent and good. He had studied in Florence and Turin, and he was the only one of a large family of gentry who had wanted to work. Like many men of the nineteenth century he had various capacities and virtues: he was a very good engineer, had very fine handwriting, he drew, had a good ear for music, had gifts of observation and irony, hated injustice, loved animals, treated the rich and powerful in a lofty manner, and was always ready to protect and help the weak and the poor. He was also an excellent horseman and had fought some duels with pistols; my mother preserved a pistol bullet, set in gold, which had been extracted from my father's right thigh after one of his duels.

This means that my father, like many men of that time, was the exact opposite of most men of today, who lack a sense of direction and any character, are unskilled, incapable and, on top of everything, are unchivalrous, highly opportunist and full of stupidity. If today, for example, a child is unsuccessful in drawing a head, his father will certainly be unable to teach him the two-crosses method. If a boy is unlucky enough to have an 'intellectual' father, the latter will not only be unable to teach him any system but will encourage him to draw badly and go from bad to worse, hoping that in this way he will one day become a Matisse and earn fame and fortune.

While we lived in the Vuros house various things occurred, all unpleasant, like almost everything in life. Among them I recall an influenza epidemic, during which all of us—my father, mother, brother and I, as well as the servants and the governess—were forced to bed with a temperature. The only one who remained on his feet, although he had a temperature, was the cook, who was called Nicola, and of whom my brother Savinio speaks in his memoirs of childhood, but I think he gives him a different name. Nicola, although running a temperature, went from one bedroom to another, waited on everyone, went out to do the shopping, kept the accounts, cooked, went to the chemist's. In fact he was everything : cook, manservant, maidservant, secretary and nurse. He was in a sense what Nietzsche's sister was for the author of *Thus Spake Zarathustra*; at least in Nietzsche's own verse dedication to his sister at the beginning of a book he declares that for him she was mother, sister, wife and friend and that he, who denied God, made the sign of the Cross as he sent it to her.

During that period when we were all ill with a temperature the most intolerant, the most angry of us, was a governess from Trieste whom we called *frailain*, from the German Fräulein. She would yell and shout that we wanted to let her die of hunger. In those days the old system for reducing a high temperature was still in use : first of all a purge with castor oil; then disinfection of the intestine with a good dose of salol; total fasting; after the purge had acted a very light broth with all fat removed; quinine, massage of the chest and the spine with hot oil in which camomile flowers had been boiled; mustard poultices, made with the French variety called Rigolo, applied to the spine and the chest; and application of *ventouses*, also called cupping, and linseed poultices mixed with powdered mustard. But the *frailain* didn't want medicines and wanted to eat well-seasoned *pasta asciutta* and cutlets with roast potatoes. In fact the governess from Trieste was a modern invalid *ante litteram*; yet if she had had what she wanted she would have been very ill, for in those days there were no marvellous sulphonamides and antibiotics which today allow a patient to eat roast chicken and ravioli with stewed meat while suffering from a temperature of over 100°.

Another unpleasant fact that I recollect was a series of earth-quakes which occurred regularly every evening after sunset. The whole house moved slowly like a big ship on a squally sea. The inhabitants of the district, including ourselves, carried their mattresses outside into a square in order to sleep in the open. On this occasion also the cook Nicola excelled himself in endless ways. He carried out mattresses, cases and even some furniture, and in the morning he took everything back into the house. He also looked after my brother and me like a real nursemaid.

After the Vuros house we went to live in another, which was called Gunarakis. It was a small palazzo in the neo-classical style, and had a fine garden with a eucalyptus tree. My father was often away in Volos, the small town of my birth, where he was supervising and directing the building of the railway which was going into Thessaly. My memories of life at the Gunarakis house are very vague. From the windows which looked north you could see a long way, as far as a range of mountains which in winter were covered with snow and from where there came an icy wind which froze the house. I remember a very beautiful book which was given to me as a present, called *The Jesting Dwarfs*. The illustrations in this book were magnificent. I remember also another book with reproductions in colour of whole families of cats. These cats were so well drawn and coloured, so alive, that they awoke in me a great desire to draw and paint. I thought how wonderful it would be to be able to reproduce the forms and colours of an animal with such perfection. My mother had bought me an album to encourage me to draw: this album contained examples for copying which represented flowers, some of which showed only the outlines, while others included shading as well. I remember that I copied two roses with great care. My mother helped me to write a little letter to my father and she also put the drawing of the roses in the envelope. My father replied, congratulating me on the progress I had made in the difficult art of drawing.

When the weather was fine my brother and I went into the garden and there, with a small hoe and spade, we built miniature terraces. But then it would rain and our work would be ruined.

While my father was away the cook Nicola kept a strange revolver under the pillow on his bed. It consisted simply of a cylinder attached to the stock; the cartridges were put in the cylinder and fired by a detonator consisting of a small tube which projected in perpendicular fashion on to the cartridge. The striking part of the trigger was flat rather than sharp and struck like a hammer against the detonator which went off and fired the shot. Later, in Italy, I saw revolvers of this type, but fitted with a barrel, on monuments representing soldiers and heroes of the Risorgimento. I was deeply impressed when I saw this strange mysterious weapon, which resembled the modern rifle as much as paintings from the catacombs resemble Rubens's *Kermesse* [Village Feast]; I mean in quality and not in subject-matter. The stupidity of many readers today is such that, in order to avoid misunderstandings, it is necessary to spell out everything.

We lived for only a short time in the Gunarakis house. My father had to stay at Volos for a long period because another branch of the railway-line was being built alongside the mountains which rose to the east of the town. Then, with all the furniture, trunks and cases, we left for the city of the Argonauts on a steamer which sailed for the Piraeus.

2

Meanwhile I was growing up. My curiosity about the spectacles of life, and the attention I gave to them, increased. In Volos my father asked a young employee of the railway company to give me drawing lessons. This first teacher of mine, called Mavrudis, was a Greek from Trieste who spoke a little Italian with a Venetian accent. He drew wonderfully well. When he taught me how to trace delicately the contours of a nose, an eye, a mouth, an ear, a curl, a knot tied in a bow, when he taught me how to shade and graduate shadows, carefully hatching with his pencil, he gave me such a profound sense of mastery that the impressions I had later when looking at the drawings of Raphael, copying and imitating the drawings of Holbein and Michelangelo, studying the drawings of Dürer through a magnifying-glass, seemed trifles in comparison.

When I found myself in the presence of Mavrudis I looked at him, and as I looked I wandered into a world of dream and fantasy. I thought that this man could draw everything, even from memory, even in the dark, even without looking; that he could draw the clouds fleeing over the sky and the plants on the earth, the branches of the trees moving in the wind and flowers of the most complex shape; men and animals, fruit and vegetables, reptiles and insects, fish swimming in the water and birds flying on high; I thought that everything could be portrayed by this extraordinary man's magic pencil. As I looked at him I imagined that I was him; yes, I would have liked to be this man then, I would have liked to be the artist Mavrudis. I found myself in the same state of mind as Dr Bovary when, towards the end of Flaubert's famous novel, he meets Rodolphe

Boulanger and sits down at the same table with him in an inn. Dr Bovary knows that Rodolphe has been his wife's lover, for after her suicide he had found some letters in a secret casket, but Rodolphe thinks that the doctor is still unaware of the fact and in order to disperse the gloomy atmosphere he talks quickly and a great deal about this and that, about country matters, crops, cattle, etc., but the doctor, overwhelmed by his deep sorrow, does not listen to him, looks at him intensely, looks at this man whom she has loved and, says Flaubert, *il aurait voulu être cet homme.*

Many years later, in different circumstances and for different reasons, it happened again that I felt like Dr Bovary *vis-à-vis* Rodolphe, and this happened to me and still happens sometimes when I meet my friend the painter Nino Bertoletti. The painter Bertoletti is a man for whom I have always had great esteem and sympathy; he is intelligent, cultivated, educated and normal, and in art he has had the courage never to get mixed up with the schemes of the so-called modernists. Furthermore, he leads a well-balanced and regular life : during the more than twenty-five years since I have known him he has only moved house twice, while during the same period I have moved house twenty-one times, without counting the more or less prolonged stays I have made in inns, *pensioni,* furnished apartments, furnished rooms and with friends and relatives, without counting changes of city, district, country and even continent. Bertoletti has always lived in the same city, has kept his furniture, books and belongings. Now I have always wanted a peaceful and well-regulated life, surrounded by my things. It happens that when I find myself with Bertoletti, at a café or somewhere else, while talking to him about painting, exhibitions, Biennales and Quadriennales, I sometimes forget to listen to him and in looking at him I think that this man who is talking to me has moved house only twice in more than a quarter of a century and that these divans and these armchairs where he is sitting in his place in the Via Condotti are probably the same ones on which twenty years earlier he would sit in his place near the Via Nomentana and thus, as I look at him, I lose myself in a pleasant dream and in fantasy I imagine myself to be this man, to be Bertoletti myself.

My master Mavrudis came three times a week to give me drawing lessons. He was the first to teach me the love of clean, beautiful lines, fine contours and well-modelled forms. He was the first who taught me the love of good materials : Faber pencils with good points, paper of first quality, Elephant-brand rubbers, which were very soft. He was the first to teach me how to sharpen pencils in a regular way, cutting round the wood with care and symmetry and not in the slovenly manner of many people, making the point of the pencil look like a big toe deformed by cold. Later I found all these fine things explained with great acumen and intelligence in a very fine book on drawing written by Ruskin. If my master Mavrudis were in Rome today he could show the way to all our modernistic 'geniuses' and teach them that before being imitators of Cézanne, Picasso, Soutine or Matisse, and before feeling emotion, anguish, sincerity, sensitivity, spontaneity, spirituality and other moods of the kind, they would do better to learn how to sharpen their pencils properly and try to use these pencils to make a good drawing of an eye, a nose, a mouth or an ear.

Life in the little city of Volos was full of metaphysical and provincial events. I used to make kites. I had become a real master of kite-making, for which I used coloured paper. When I went to fly these kites in a square in front of our house I was almost always alone. Children from another district also came to fly their kites in this square, but they stood a long way away from me and tried to send theirs higher in order to obstruct my kite by entangling their strings with mine and bring it down. In local slang this operation was described as *fanestra*. If I wanted to make a verb out of *fanestra*, I could say that when I was fanestrated I reacted violently and threw stones at the fanestrators.

I was very skilled in shooting stones with a catapult, an ability I have retained, and if I have no proper catapult I can do the same things with my trouser belt. One day, after one of my most beautiful kites with gorgeous colours had been fanestrated, a particularly violent stone-fight broke out. I believe that my brother was also with me as well as another boy of the same age, the son of a French engineer; but my brother was smaller than I was and my friend threw stones rather timidly. In fact it was I who did everything, I was the monomachist, the one who remained to fight alone, as I remain today in the camp of good painting, a camp which is less risky physically but much more difficult to lead to victory, for in fact it is much more difficult to paint a good picture than to win ten battles, either with stones or cannon, and even with atomic bombs.

When I think of my life at that time I see how certain events repeat themselves, in different circumstances, in different places, on different planes. Even at that time those Thessalian street-urchins were spurred on by hatred to bring down my kite, because it was more beautiful and bigger than theirs. In addition, they saw that I lived in a house that was more beautiful than theirs; that I was better dressed than they were and that I must be more intelligent and must know much more than they did about many things, and therefore I was anathema. In the same way now among intellectual, modernistic and asinine painters a kind of Holy Alliance has been formed for putting spokes in my wheels and causing me harm in my work as a painter; only today it is a question of other weapons and bringing down my painting is a little more difficult than it was for those urchins to 'fanestrate' my kite.

On that occasion the stone-fight came to a more dramatic end than the previous ones. I received a hard blow on the head from a stone, which was very painful. Fortunately I was wearing a kind of Basque beret pulled down over one ear and the stone struck me in a place that was protected by the thickness of the beret. Soon after I had been hit on the head the cook Nicola, who had left a tavern on the other side of the square to get me out of this mess, was struck on the mouth by a stone shot from a catapult and knocked down over a table that was standing outside. The cook's face was stained with blood. Nicola, a man of iron muscles who did not waste time, rushed furiously into the midst of the urchins and distributed blows and cuffs in all directions. Under this shower of hard punches the urchins dispersed as though by magic and Nicola, picking me up with one arm and my brother with the other, cursing and swearing, carried us into the house like dead weights. In the evening there was a kind of family council; I don't remember what was decided, I only recall that at a certain point my father concluded philosophically, 'Fortunately he was wearing his Basque beret.'

During the summer, when the weather was calm, we used to go fishing. These expeditions consisted of my mother, myself, my brother, and two railway employees, one called Messaritis and the other Calojeropulos, who were specialists in line-fishing. Messaritis was a dreamer and a romantic. He wore a little chestnut-coloured beard, was of medium height and was reminiscent of those people who, dressed as courtiers and gentlemen, in *Rigoletto* and other old operas pass across the back of the stage, while in front the principal singers are singing at the top of their voices about the sorrows and joys of the characters they represent. Messaritis was a specialist in the driving of locomotives, like the late King Boris of Bulgaria, and liked to be photographed, all dirty with soot, on the express, with his right hand resting on a lever. But in the evening, when his work was finished, he dressed with a certain elegance; he wore white linen waistcoats and went to have supper in the garden of an inn which was called the Auberge de France. This inn stood almost at the edge of the sea and Messaritis would order excellent pilaffs, exquisitely flavoured, and portions of roast lamb, rich, tender and almost sweet, like a tart. Messaritis was very sentimental and romantic. He was always in love with women and girls who were beyond his reach and when in the evening he was with us in the café by the sea, and his heart overflowed with suppressed passion, he would escape from himself by singing to me, as though for a joke, in a bass voice, scraps from popular Greek romances:

> those black eyes that gaze at me,
> lower them, O my light,
> because they slay me.

Calojeropulos, on the other hand, was a sceptic and a joker, but perhaps he was more profound and metaphysical than Messaritis. He played the violin and the 'cello and took part in concerts of chamber music in the house of the Austrian consul, who was called Minciaki. The Minciakis came from Trieste and in Venice I knew one of their nephews, the engineer Ehrenfreund, whom everyone in Venice called Frumi. Calojeropulos also sang in a low voice, but he did it as a joke. Through hearing Italian operas sung in Italian he had come to know a little of our language. When he felt like joking he would sing this song to me in Italian:

> *Ma in campagna è un'altra cosa*
> *c'è più gusto a far l'amor*
> *perchè là il cuor riposa*
> *vicino al suo tesor.*

But one day Calojeropulos recounted to me a very sad and mysterious thing, something profound and obscure, like the motif of

Dante's *Vita Nuova*. He told me that when he was a child there lived in his district a little girl of the same age, the daughter of their neighbour. He often played with this child and they became very good friends. One night the little Calojeropulos dreamt that he was in his bedroom and was looking at the canary in a cage near the window; in his dream this canary looked like his little neighbour. Suddenly the little canary began to swell slowly; it became like a big yellow ball and fell down dead at the bottom of the cage. Little Calojeropulos woke up crying, suffering terrible anguish, and remained awake in his bed until dawn. When morning came he heard loud voices from the house next door and shortly afterwards learnt that his little neighbour had died during the night.

The fishing expeditions were a great joy to me. It is certain that all these spectacles of exceptional beauty which I saw in Greece as a boy, and which were the most beautiful I have seen in all my life, made such a deep impression on me and remained so powerfully impressed on my mind and thoughts because I am an exceptional man who feels and understands a hundred times more strongly than others.

We got up very early in the morning to go fishing and when we entered the boat which was to take us out into the middle of the gulf, dawn was still breaking; the sea was a mirror. Never in other countries afterwards did I see a mirror of water so beautiful; however, on this shining surface a fish, a divine mullet, would leap out of the water. After so many years I see this spectacle as I saw it then, but if I tried to describe it completely, to represent it by means of a pen, a pencil or a brush, I would not succeed at all. Greece has inspired many artists at all times, but there are things so beautiful that they can only be imagined. There is much truth in fact in the words of the nineteenth-century Greek painter Nicolas Ghisis when he said : 'I cannot paint Greece as beautiful as I imagine it.'

During our stay at Volos in 1897 war broke out between the Greeks and the Turks. I witnessed many sights full of fear, anguish, piety and suffering, sometimes they were even revolting, and, multiplied by a hundred or a thousand, I saw them again during the First World War and later still during the Second. When the Graeco-Turkish War was declared there were, as at the beginning of all wars, moments of enthusiasm. Soldiers who had been called up passed by singing. Many middle-class people, who were not called up, went to the shooting-range to practise firing with the Gras rifle, which at that time was used by the Greek army. The Gras rifle fired one shot at a time and had a central percussion system. I believe it was invented by a French officer named Gras and was a perfected version of the old Chassepot rifle.

The first bad news came. The Turks advanced into Thessaly and the army of the Crown Prince Constantine was beaten. Panic broke out at Volos. Many people fled. Small steamers and also sailing ships, overloaded with refugees, moved heavily out of the gulf directly towards Attica. English, French, Russian and Italian warships came to protect the citizens of their respective countries. The Italian ship was called *Vesuvio*. It was an old ship whose principal armament consisted of an enormous breech-loading cannon, into which the complete shell was not loaded all at once, but the explosive, the projectiles and the combustible material were loaded separately. Furthermore, this cannon was fixed and in order to fire it the whole ship had to be turned round; in short, it was something which today would have given the commander of the American Pacific fleet an epileptic fit. The captain of the *Vesuvio* was called Ampugnani and was a gentleman for whom my father had a great liking. The captain of the French warship, called Pampelonne, was the classic type of nineteenth-century French naval officer. He wore grey whiskers and resembled Admiral Courbet as I had seen him in a print entitled *Admiral Courbet at the Siege of Fu-tchu*. Captain Pampelonne was an excellent pianist and came to play in our house; the preludes and nocturnes of Chopin were his speciality.

Dramas also took place during the occupation of Volos by the Turks. Among the inhabitants of the city was a Greek gentleman, a friend of my father's. He was a lawyer and was called Manusso. He was already elderly, a tall, strong-limbed man with a Herculean appearance. He wore white whiskers and eye-glasses. He had no family. He saw very few people, was taciturn and seemed to be obsessed by serious thoughts. Many years before he had killed a man in a fit of temper. He had been tried and condemned with attenuating circumstances, had worked off his punishment and on coming out of prison had taken up his profession of lawyer again. But he had become a different man. He was overcome with remorse. The thought of the life destroyed by his own hand gave him no peace.

One night, while the Turkish troops occupied Volos, some soldiers, wearing the uniform of the Ottoman army, knocked at Manusso's door. He got up and opened it. He was immediately surrounded and handcuffed under the threat of loaded rifles, then led out of the city by soldiers with fixed bayonets.

It was a sultry summer night. The soldiers, with their prisoner in their midst, passed beneath the window of another lawyer. He came out on to the balcony, for he could not sleep because of the great heat, and recognised his friend and colleague. He called out to him by name: 'Manusso, where are you going?' Manusso replied in a resigned voice: 'I'm going wherever they're taking me.'

The next day Manusso's body was found in a deserted field, slashed with bayonet wounds. Around it the ground was churned up by deep footmarks. The victim's handcuffs had been snapped. There were also a rifle in pieces, fezes and scraps of uniforms. The old Hercules, in spite of being handcuffed, had succeeded in breaking apart his handcuffs and had then defended himself as best he could, succeeding also in smashing the rifle of one of his murderers. But then, covered with blows, and suffering from loss of blood, he had fallen, never to rise again.

There was an inquest which came to no conclusion. Everyone was convinced, however, that relations of the man Manusso had killed so many years before had dressed up as Turkish soldiers to carry out their vendetta.

Another crime was committed at the same time. One morning a Catholic priest was also found dead in his bedroom from bayonet cuts. Fezes were found lying on the staircase. It appeared that the authors of this crime were also false Turkish soldiers; it was said that Greeks had killed the Catholic priest in order to attract the attention of foreign powers by making it look as though the crime had been committed by Turks and forcing them to make the Turks evacuate Greece.

During all this sad period my father had made every possible effort to save the railway equipment, and after the Turks had retreated he was decorated with the order of St George through the personal intervention of King George of Greece.

One day, during the Turkish occupation of Volos, I fell while playing in the garden and broke the bones in my right elbow. My arm remained bent and stiff and I could not move it in any direction. My mother asked an old Jew, who traded in empty bottles and said he was something of a doctor, to treat my arm. He massaged me with pig's grease, but my arm did not get better and we had to ask the doctor on board the *Vesuvio*, and he came and looked after me until I recovered.

This old Jew bought empty bottles and went round the town with a sack on his shoulders. When he came to our house and my father was there he always told the servants to give him all the empty bottles and not to take his money. The street-urchins of the district would appear behind the old Jew and sneer at him. One day, while he was going out of our house with his sack full of bottles, he began to complain, probably because some of the mineral-water bottles were not quite empty. On that day the crowd of urchins excelled themselves, seeing the old Jew in difficulties, and he stopped in the middle of the street to see whether the sack had finally given way behind his back. My father, who had been watching this scene from the house, became furious and sent the children away with threats and abuse.

Like all true gentlemen of the nineteenth century my father was pro-Jewish. Those boys teasing the old Jew, who was unarmed, alone and incapable of defending himself, represented in a small way the ignoble anti-Jewish campaign provoked by Hitler and which found fertile ground for development in the sadistic depravity of the German people, so many years afterwards. Anti-Semitism is no different from the sadism which ranges from the simple fact of saying that someone is a Jew, of 'revealing' the Jew, to the attacks made in the seventeenth century by the Marchese del Grillo and which later, through phenomena more or less serious, like the Dreyfus Affair, could reach the sadistic criminality shown by the Germans in systematic persecution and mass killings. Those urchins in Volos, perhaps through a subconscious need to justify their misdeeds, said that the old Jew 'did not believe in God'. I felt curious and one day I wanted to clear this matter up, so while the old Jew was going out of our garden with his sack full of empty bottles I came up to him and asked him what God was. He stopped, looked at me, carefully put his sack down on the ground and with his long wizened hand showed me the slopes of Mount Pelion which rose to the north, covered with white villages. He showed me the sky and the clouds which were passing on high and said, 'There you are, God is the hills, the sky, the clouds. . . .' I made no answer. I helped him to put the sack back on his shoulders and went back into the house, my mind full of confused thoughts.

The war came to an end, the Turkish troops evacuated Thessaly and the provincial life of the little town of Volos resumed its usual rhythm. The work which my father had had to supervise had come to an end and we then returned to live in Athens. It was the last year of the nineteenth century, that magnificent century so rich in art, thought, idealism, romanticism, virility and, most of all, talent. We had reached the threshold of the twentieth century, our century which lives under the ill-fated and destructive signs of pederasty, hysteria, impotence in the plastic and creative fields, envy, snobbery, mechanisation, agitation, stupidity, cruelty and the total lack of balance and integral thought.

We went to live in a house with a very noble aspect, named after the proprietor Stambulopulos. This house faced the royal gardens, in the most elegant quarter of the city. Beneath the windows, which faced east, was a magnificent avenue with rows of pepper trees, producing a fruit which resembled a small red ball. The ground was covered with these little balls which made it rather slippery. There was a strong, rather sweet smell in the air.

I had made progress in drawing. Apart from the classical models and studies for learning how to draw, which my parents bought for me in stationers' shops, I copied every face I saw. My father subscribed to the French periodical *L'Illustration* and I copied all the portraits of political, military and artistic personalities which were reproduced in it. Once, I remember, I copied in pencil a portrait of Jean Richepin as a young man. The copy was a great success and closely resembled the original. My father praised the way in which I had treated the hair, which was luxuriant and consequently difficult to draw. My father also took a drawing master for me. This was an Italian named Barbieri. He had come to Greece in search of work, but he had not found any and his financial situation was difficult. I believe my father asked him to give me drawing lessons more to help him than for any other reason. Barbieri came to the house and corrected my drawings. He was, however, less valiant than my first teacher Mavrudis. What was more—I don't know whether it was due to his eating garlic or drinking too much resinated wine —Barbieri's breath smelt so unpleasant that it needed all my devotion to art to last out the lesson. Once, for Christmas, Barbieri sent my mother a white card which he had engraved with a very sharp penknife. On one side was a bunch of pansies and by them he had written in impeccable handwriting: 'To Signora Gemma de Chirico, with good wishes and respectful greetings offered by', and underneath the signature, 'Carlo Barbieri'.

During the period when Barbieri gave me drawing lessons my parents had the idea that he should do a portrait of my brother in gouache. They explained to Barbieri that they believed the colours of gouache to be more suitable than oil paints for rendering the freshness and transparency of a little boy's colouring. While they talked, Barbieri had the expression of a man whose mind was elsewhere. At that time my brother had long hair curled in ringlets, like that of the Sun King. This curling involved a true ritual every morning and the maidservants and governesses carried it out by means of special equipment, a kind of small brown wooden cylinder, with a handle. It was hard and polished, rather like a British policeman's truncheon. When my brother appeared after this operation with his head completely covered with long ringlets our mother would say that he looked like a portrait by Van Dyck. My brother was the handsome one of the family and our mother was very proud of him. She made him wear big lace collars which stood out against his dark blue jacket. When my brother was taken out for a walk along the avenue with the pepper trees, he was seen by old women-servants resting on the public benches who, whichever the case happened to be, were housekeepers, nurses and nursery maids and even acted as procuresses. When they saw my brother they uttered cries of admiration, called him '*pulachimo*', my little bird, shouted to my mother 'May he live long!' and spat after him for luck.

Carlo Barbieri asked my father for an advance on the price agreed for the portrait, saying that he had not enough money to buy the necessary materials. My father paid the advance and Barbieri was not seen again. A little later my father was in a restaurant and saw fastened on the wall a plate blackened by fire, on which the head of a ferocious tiger, drawn in white, stood out. The drawing was signed Carlo Barbieri. When the owner was asked for information he said that a few days earlier an Italian gentleman had come, his clothes neglected and with a beard of at least six days' growth. He had sat down at a table and had ordered a splendid meal with a bottle of wine. When he had eaten and drunk copiously he asked for the bill to be brought to him, but then without looking at it he told the proprietor that he hadn't a penny in his pocket. But he offered to leave some work in payment and the proprietor accepted. Barbieri asked for a plate and a candle to be brought to him, carefully covered the surface of the plate with smoke and with the point of a large pin, which he had taken out of his tie, he drew on the part covered with smoke this tiger's head which, according to the proprietor, had been very much admired by everyone because of its impressively ferocious expression.

During this period my father became seriously ill. My father was often ill and his face was alarmingly pale. I always saw him looking old, pale and bent. Many doctors were called to his bedside, but they never succeeded in knowing what his illness was. The most famous doctor who visited my father then was Professor Karamizza. He was Professor of Medicine at the University of Athens and for this reason was highly esteemed by Athenian society. When he came to our house the servant who opened the door received him with deep and repeated bows, then, walking in front of him like an outrider and also moving sideways, like a crab, in order not to turn his shoulders round, he accompanied him up to the first floor where my parents' bedroom was and where my father was lying ill. I heard that afterwards, when he returned to the kitchen, the man who had accompanied him said to the other servants, in a voice breaking with emotion : 'A University Professor! He's a University Professor!'

My father survived this serious crisis and rose from his bed. At this time also my mother suffered from a kind of long nervous exhaustion which, from what I understood later, must have been due to her age.

We had brought with us from Volos a mongrel dog, a poor dog which had taken refuge in our house during the time of the Graeco-Turkish War. Originally this dog was called Leone, but then he was given the name of Trollolò, which stuck to him. He was extra-ordinarily gentle and intelligent and even now, after so many years, when I think of Trollolò I feel sad. We all liked him very much, but the one who liked him best of all was myself, for then as now I was the gentlest and most intelligent of all. During my father's long and painful illness Trollolò would sometimes go in the middle of the night on to a large terrace which stood at the side of our house and where a kind of long balcony had been added. There Trollolò would howl for a long time with his muzzle raised to the vast Attic sky, full of stars. My mother was very upset by this howling, but these lamentations did not presage the death of my father. They were only the expression of the sad heart of poor Trollolò who suffered because his master was suffering.

During this difficult period when my parents were ill the house was full of phials, bottles and little boxes containing medicines of all kinds. In particular, there were tincture of valerian and *l'alcool de menthe de Riclès*, a French product which carried a trade-mark on the box representing two angels in the act of lifting a bottle of the product and similar to those angels who, in Christian iconography, carry the bodies of saints to Paradise.

It was at this moment that I first saw an exhibition of painting and remained deeply impressed by it. Among the canvases that struck me most was in the first place an episode from the Graeco-Turkish War in Thessaly. Near a kind of poor-looking house was a detachment of infantry which, together with some officers on horseback, seemed to be waiting for the moment of going into action. Farther away the battle itself was visible. A file of infantry soldiers, some with one knee on the ground and some lying flat, were firing, and to the right a detachment of cavalry could be seen galloping along a wide and dusty road. In the foreground the body of a soldier who had been killed lay in the dust of the street. One critic, while speaking of this canvas, tried to be witty—which was, moreover, in bad taste —and wrote, alluding to the dead soldier's body, that he did not understand why the painter had included a 'still life' in his picture of the battle. In his article he used the French, *nature morte*. The painter of this picture was called Roilos and he was later my drawing teacher at the Polytechnic School. Roilos had specialised in military subjects. He had a great deal of talent, drew well and possessed a gift for composition. If he had lived in Paris, Italy or in another country more Europeanised than Greece he would have been able to acquire a high degree of fame. Publishers would have reproduced his work in substantial monographs and if he had been in Italy he would certainly have been compared by the critics and intellectuals to Paolo Uccello. He was in no way inferior to Giovanni Fattori, who was considered by our critics to be the genius of nineteenth-century Italy. Roilos was superior to Fattori.

Another painter who impressed me very much was called Rallis and lived in Paris, where apparently he was noticed by those who frequented the salons. Rallis painted with unusually bright and vivid colours and his draughtsmanship was very precise. His subjects for the most part were Oriental scenes.

I remember that at that time these pictures seemed to me very beautiful and much better than all the ancient pictures which I had seen at home reproduced in colour or in black and white in art books about old painting. These old pictures gave me less pleasure, and these famous works seemed to me less natural, less obvious. I think I felt like this because I had come to understand the greatness, the mystery, the joy of great painting and I think that nearly everyone sees great painting during their lifetime, even if they live for a hundred years, just as I saw it then, and if afterwards, with education and instruction, they learn to express respect and admiration for the works of the great artists of the past, this respect and admiration are purely mechanical facts and correspond to no sincere feeling, nor to any true and profound comprehension and conviction.

During our stay in the Stambulopulos house the first Olympic Games took place. Athens was *en fête*. Arches covered with flares from gas-jets spanned the streets in the centre, where the lights were as bright as sunlight. The winner of the marathon was a Greek named Luis. I remember Luis's arrival at the stadium. He was completely black, like some students of the École des Beaux Arts in Paris, when they dress up for the famous 'bal des Quat'z Arts' which is held every year. The Crown Prince Constantine went down into the arena and embraced Luis. The public was delirious. Another Olympic winner was an infantry corporal by name of Tofalos, who was the victor in the contest for weight-lifting. When Tofalos was a boy little more than ten years old he was rather short but was as plump as a whale and weighed 240 pounds. He was the son of a wine-grower in the Peloponnesus and in his father's shop he used to lift on his own enormous cases full of wine that four men together were unable to move.

In the stadium in Athens after the Olympic Games there were some performances of *Iphigenia in Tauris*. The famous tragic actor Sylvain had come specially from Paris, accompanied by the Franco-Greek Parnassian poet Moréas, who had translated the tragedy into French.

While the spectacle of the Olympic Games had been fine and heartening, giving rise to great enthusiasm, *Iphigenia in Tauris* was dreary, tedious and above all artificial. A destructive atmosphere of intellectualism lay over the public and the actors. It looked as though everyone was stifling huge yawns. It was an atmosphere in fact that was akin to the one which exists today in concert halls when modern music is being played, or in theatres during performances of plays with intellectual pretensions, or when modern works are shown in exhibitions of modern painting, in fact during all those gatherings, in all those places where the snobbery and stupidity of our contemporaries meet. I have always had a strong aversion to open-air spectacles. People in costume who speak and gesticulate beneath a real sky in the midst of real nature have always given me the impression of something as stupid as it is false. But the organisers of open-air spectacles do not want to understand and continue, more through stupidity than through obstinacy or conviction, to give these clumsy performances in all countries, and even film directors refuse to accept that in films people in costume cannot move about in the midst of real nature, beneath a real sky, among real trees, by a real sea, and that the older the people's costumes, the more real nature appears false in comparison. A person in costume needs painted scenery, painted skies, trees and mountains, because he can then appear in his true aspect. To do what is done today is stupid. The theatrical device of the Fortuny cupola and of all those mechanical aids which make rain, clouds, lightning, storms and the sea appear genuine, succeed only in giving the spectacle an air that is immensely dull, ugly, antipathetic, stupid and above all artificial. Naturally the public does not understand these things and during the summer shows at the Baths of Caracalla loud applause always breaks out in the last act of *The Force of Destiny* where one can see a waterfall with water that looks real. Men take a long time to understand what I and, with greater acumen and depth than I, Isabella Far, the greatest philosophical mind of our century, have written many times, explaining and re-explaining and demonstrating in every possible way. I remember again what Ernest Renan said, that nothing gave him a greater sense of infinity than the stupidity of mankind.

From the Stambulopulos house we went to one whose name I do not remember. People often moved house in Greece. The move would come about every two years. I have been destined throughout my life to move house continually. In the new house, which was a long way from the centre, I continued my melancholy existence. My father was often in the worst state of health. The house, which stood on the outskirts of the city towards the north, looked on to a wide stretch of uninhabited and uncultivated ground. There was a garden attached to our house which contained a pool of stagnant water, with water plants, midges, frogs, mosquitoes and reptiles of every description. I had malaria. During the night I had attacks of fever and felt so cold that my teeth chattered. When I was not too ill I would continue to draw and my father sent me to a Swiss-French painter called Gilleron who had a kind of school for drawing and painting

in his house. We copied a lot of prints in this house. The painter
Gilleron was a specialist in drawing the Acropolis, ruins of temples
and ancient monuments. He was a tall, robust man with a thick white
beard trimmed to a point. He wore eye-glasses. He resembled
Boecklin a little, but lacked that profundity and luminosity of
expression which characterised the great painter of Basle.

During the Greek Holy Week, when the procession which the
Greeks call the Epitaph passes through the streets at night, this
remote house, in the suburbs of the city, was particularly popular
with people who wanted to throw firecrackers and small explosives
at the walls. The Epitaph is in fact a true funeral in which the
Crucifix is carried in the same way as the bier with the deceased
person is carried at funerals. At the head of the Epitaph procession
come detachments of infantry, marching slowly with their rifles under
their arms and their bayonets lowered to the ground. A military
band plays funeral marches, among which those of Chopin and
Beethoven are outstanding. During this funeral the crowd makes a
great din firing rifles and pistols, and exploding firecrackers by
throwing them on to the ground or against the walls of the houses.
In Greek the firecrackers are called *varilotta*, probably from the
Italian word *barile*, or *varili* in Greek, and in fact they look like
barrels fastened with small pieces of rope. When the cortège passed
in front of our house there was a great noise of *varilotta* exploding
against the walls. I could not sleep on these nights because of the
loud noise, and the dog Trollolò, who had a mortal fear of
explosions, would hide beneath an armchair and pass a sleepless
night of terror. The reason for this particular persistence in exploding
firecrackers against the walls of our house came from the fact that
since we were foreigners, Catholics and above all Italians, we were
regarded as undesirable inhabitants of these districts away from the
centre, 'Franchi', as it was said in Athenian dialect.

An Italian came to the house to give my brother and me lessons
in Italian, arithmetic and history. He was not really an engineer,
but a kind of foreman, and his name was Pistono. Like Carlo
Barbieri he was one of the many Italians who had come to Greece
in search of work. My teacher Pistono was a short, muscular man
with a greying beard and side-whiskers. He always appeared in black
clothes which were worn and shiny and wore a black cravat tied in
a flowing bow. He was the classical type of democrat, socialist, liberal,
republican, that is a man who, acting on the principle of our century,

had the illusion that he was bringing his brothers new ideas, equality, liberty and comfort. In fact, he was the type of man who wears a red carnation in his buttonhole and says, 'Citizen Mastai, have a drink.' But with all this he was extremely likeable and pleasing, full of ingenuity, good-hearted, hard-working, respectful and honest, and although adhering to the anti-clerical line he would not have harmed a single hair of a priest's head. How disillusioned the good Pistono would have been today if he could have seen what has happened, after so many years, as far as equality, comfort and especially liberty are concerned, both in his country and in the countries of so many other men!

Apart from his work as a teacher he worked from hand to mouth in hundreds of ways to provide necessities for his wife and his many children. He used to make lard, boiling bacon rinds and other things of this kind in an enormous pot, and then he would sell the lard, which once it was cold would set hard and resembled gelatine. He used to sell it to the Italian colony and would supply it in terracotta dishes which his sons took to clients. During the carnival he bought in bulk large quantities of coloured paper and then, with a special machine which he had procured, he would manufacture so-called confetti, those tiny circles of coloured paper which were still used so widely during the last years before the First World War in carnival celebrations and in fact are still used today. He would put the confetti in paper bags and send his sons to sell it in the streets of Athens. He was a man full of ingenuity. He was also a calligrapher and a poet.

As a poet he had written an ode to celebrate the virtues and labours of an Italian engineer named Serpieri who owned mines in Greece at a place named Laurio. According to what Pistono said in his verses, before the engineer Serpieri had occupied himself with making the mines work, this place had been a desert where desolation reigned :

> Now there are palaces, now there are gardens,
> where before there was only a forest of pine trees.

The poem ended with a question and the reply to it : 'To whom is due the merit for all this? To whom do we owe such metamorphosis?' Reply : 'To the brave Serpieri.' It could be said that the engineer

Serpieri was brave, but he was above all large, in fact absolutely obese.

He had a very beautiful house in Athens in the same street as the University. The interior of this house had been decorated with frescoes by a painter from Bologna named Bellincioni who had come to Greece to paint the entire cupola spanning the apse of the Catholic church dedicated to St Dionysius the Areopagite. In addition to the frescoes on the cupola Bellincioni painted some on the side walls. The principal painting represented the ascent into heaven of S Dionysius. I still remember this painting very well. It was certainly neither a Tintoretto nor a Tiepolo, but I believe that if all our painters, especially our modernistic geniuses, wanted to embark on something similar, they would risk dying of general paralysis before they even began the work.

In Serpieri's house the painter Bellincioni had represented a few scenes showing miners working underground, rather in the style of the seventeenth-century painters when they painted the forge of Vulcan and the work that was done there.

In the meantime we had moved yet again and one day a Catholic priest by name of Brindisi came to see us in our new house. He had with him the painter Bellincioni, because he wanted the latter to see my drawings and the studies I had made. My father asked me to come in. It was winter and in the room that I entered, which was my father's study and library, it was very hot because the study was small and faced south, with thick Oriental carpets on the floor and heavy curtains at the windows. In addition, the stove was lit all day because my father, on account of his bad health, suffered a great deal from the cold. On the walls of the study were portraits of King Umberto and Queen Margherita in oval frames of carved black varnished wood. For the last ten years the rulers of Italy had been King Vittorio Emanuele III and Queen Elena, but my father had a particular liking for King Umberto and Queen Margherita and therefore still kept their portraits in his study. On another wall was an oleograph under glass which showed an old Breton sailor lighting his pipe. The face and hands of the old fisherman were lit by two types of light : a cold light which came from a window and another warm light, orange-red in colour, which came either from the match which he was bringing closer to his pipe or else from some fireplace or lighted brazier which could not, however, be seen.

As I went in I first greeted Dom Brindisi. My parents had told me once that I should kiss his hand and I always lowered my head to complete this operation, but Dom Brindisi shook me firmly by the hand and lowered it with a determined gesture to make me understand that this act of reverence was not welcome to him. I remained for an instant with my head bent, uncertain of what to do, then order and calm returned as at the end of certain comedies by Shakespeare. But this little drama which occurred whenever I met Dom Brindisi upset me a little. When the meeting took place in the street I was even more upset, because I was afraid that this scene would attract the attention of passers-by, I feared that a crowd would form and that among it would be some people I knew, and that among the people I knew would be some girl or woman with whom I was more or less in love.

I feel apprehensive in the same way whenever I go to a barber's. It is my habit to have my hair cut without having friction, massage, shampoos or anything else of that sort afterwards; when necessary I wash my hair myself at home with warm water and soap. But as long as I remember going to barbers, in every country where I have been until now, there is no barber of any type or race who does not ask me near the end of the cutting operation if I want a friction. Consequently, the whole time I am at the barber's until the moment I hear the fatal request, I suffer, I suffer until that moment occurs, just as I suffered as a boy while waiting until Dom Brindisi took hold of my hand. Naturally I try to educate the barbers, I try always to go to the same one and have my hair cut by the same boy, but this takes a lot of time. It is incredible how long it takes to make a barber's boy understand *that I don't want to have a friction.*

Then it has always happened that when, after the many months, sometimes years, it has taken me to make the barber understand my wishes, when in the end I have succeeded in having my hair cut without the offer of a friction, I have had to leave, changing either house or town, or even country, and then, in the new town, I have had to start all over again. Now, for example, in Rome I am educating a barber in this way in the Via Veneto. We shall see, when he has finally come to realise that I do not want a friction, whether I shall for a while be able to enjoy quietly the fruit of my persistent labour.

When, then, I entered my father's study I found, in addition to my father, Dom Brindisi and the painter Bellincioni. The latter was a tall robust man, dressed in grey, with much elegance; he had a

rubicund complexion, wore whiskers and a short but thick white
beard. He seemed satisfied with himself and with other people and
there was nothing about him of the painter dying of hunger, the
neglected genius, the Modigliani type who, in a freezing garret
suffers in order to follow one of his sublime ideals, dreaming of the
masterpiece that should bring him fame and fortune and which
usually is a complete daub, as in fact are the figures and portraits
of Modigliani, whom the snobs call Modì.

I began to show Bellincioni my attempts at drawing. He looked
at them benevolently, but I noticed in his expression a marked
indifference mixed with a touch of irony. I saw the same expression
in the eyes and face of the French archaeologist Homolle, who at
that time was the director of the French school of archaeology in
Athens, when, on one occasion, in a French *lycée* in the city, during
the examinations for the elementary *brevet*, he was acting as
examiner. A girl had just been asked the destination of some river
in France, which overflowed in spring, and she replied simply that
the river went into flood.

At that time my parents made me go to a school run by Catholic
priests which was called the Lycée Leonino, after Pope Leo XIII
It was a school frequented by the sons of Italian inhabitants of
Athens, but also included many Greek boys, because there were
classes in the Greek language. I remained only a short time in this
lycée because once or twice at home, in the presence of my parents
a few scurrilous words and phrases escaped me and my father soon
took me away because he was afraid I would pick up bad habit
from my acquaintances at the Lycée Leonino. My father was very
puritanical and an atmosphere of puritanism and Jesuitism pervaded
our family. I recall that when I and my brother were present while
friends of my parents were there, my father and my mother, but
especially my father, were on tenterhooks and lived in fear that one
of those present might say something which, however remotely, was
connected with love or sex. Once, I remember, a man, an engineer
said that in a certain district of Athens they ought to build a
maternity hospital. He used the word *partorienti*, people about to
give birth, and no sooner did the word *partorienti* ring out than a
deathly silence fell over the room. My father, who was embarrassed
coughed and then at once tried to change the subject. This puri
tanical and Jesuitical system of education is, however, excellent for
the development and refining of boys' intellects. The worst kind

on the other hand, is that which consists in trying to educate them freely, making them understand more or less secretly, but too quickly, the things that they always end by knowing later. This latter system atrophies the intelligence and has a negative influence on the boys' mentality. In addition, it is a system linked to a certain mentality that belongs to nudists and vegetarians.

During the time I went to the Lycée Leonino I took my first communion. A priest catechised me, together with other boys of my age. He explained to us for a few days what communion was and why, after the first communion, it was necessary to go to confession. I remember a comparison made by this priest while he was instructing the communicants. 'If you knew that the King were coming to visit your house, what would you do? You would immediately take a broom and a cloth and you would start to give a good clean to the rooms and remove all the dust and dirt from them. In this way the Christian, before receiving within himself the body of Our Lord Jesus Christ, should confess in order to clean his soul from any filth, that is the sins that it contains.'

This comparison made the worst possible impression on me at that time. The idea of imagining my soul as a room full of dust and dirt did not meet with my approval and I thought that this priest could have used a less unpleasant image and comparison.

After I left the Lycée Leonino my father engaged as a tutor for me and my brother a Sicilian gentleman named Vergara. To teach us German and gymnastics he employed a German who rode a bicycle and was called Gheit. When I had finished my German lesson and Gheit was giving a lesson to my brother I would quietly take the bicycle the teacher had left at the entrance and go for a ride. It was my dream to have a bicycle and my mother was ready to buy me one, but my father was firmly opposed to the idea because, he said, he was afraid I would fall off and hurt myself. I think, however, that this opposition of his was somehow linked to his puritanism. Bicycles were for him one of the things that one must not even think of, like disinfectants, microbes and pistols. In our house the words dagger, pistol, revolver, gun, etc., were never uttered. The only one which could be mentioned by name was the cannon, probably because it was not usual to keep cannons in the house.

In addition, I went to take French lessons from a Belgian teacher called Bronnaire. An Italian 'cellist gave me lessons on the 'cello. He was called Guida. He was a Neapolitan and had won prizes at the

Naples Conservatory, but he often played wrong notes. During the summer in an open-air theatre which stood on the beach at Falero, near Athens, Guida played the 'cello in the orchestra which accompanied the performances given by French operetta companies. The conductor of the orchestra was a Frenchman. It sometimes happened that during the performance of *La Fille de Madame Angot* Guida played a wrong note. The conductor would then look at him fiercely, but Guida, without losing his composure, would reply in bad French, '*C'est pas moa, mossié, c'est le floute!*', meaning that it was not he who had played a wrong note, but the flute.

During the time that Guida taught me the 'cello his wife died. I saw him come afterwards all dressed in black and looking tired. One day, when the lesson was finished, Guida was preparing to go. The windows were open and from outside, with the disturbing scents of early spring, came the cries of the first swallows. Guida looked for a moment at the clear sky and the gardens that were beginning to turn green, and while he put on his cap and buttoned his rather tight black jacket over his robust chest, he said to me, 'Now I'm going to pay a visit to my wife.' I saw that he had red eyes and that his chin was trembling slightly. I felt moved and found nothing to say. I accompanied him to the door. From that day I felt much more sympathy and respect for the teacher Guida.

The 'cello lessons were interrupted. I did not feel a great vocation for music in general and for that instrument in particular. But the sound of the 'cello has always pleased me and I have always preferred it to the violin. I find that it is very true to say that the sound of a 'cello resembles that of a human voice, a virile, baritone voice, warm and pathetic. But the instrument whose sound moves me more than any other is the guitar. I don't know why there are no guitar concerts with only the guitar and nothing but the guitar.

On the other hand, my vocation for drawing and painting became continually stronger. My parents, overcoming their puritanism and the fear that I would find myself in contact with boys who spoke roughly, decided to send me to the local academy of fine arts. The academy did not possess this title, it was called the Polytechnic. It consisted of three very fine large buildings in neo-classical style, similar to many others in the same style which stood in Athens and which had been planned by Bavarian architects who had come to Greece during the reign of the first King, who was called Otto and was in fact Bavarian. At the Polytechnic were courses in engineering, mathematics, chemistry, geology, drawing, painting, sculpture, decoration and xylography.

I went into the first class for drawing. It was a large room divided into three parts and lit by large windows, through which came the even cold light from the north. There were large benches beside a long table on which stood a kind of long desk, and under glass with wooden frames were numerous prints, lithographs and etchings of all kinds. There were reproductions of famous sculptures, figures taken from famous old paintings and also details from faces and bodies. The teaching at the Athens Polytechnic was very fair and systematic. It was carried out by those very useful methods which afterwards, with the so-called evolution in matters of art, with the so-called modernism, gradually fell into disuse, with the result that today in an academy a student does not even learn how to hold a pencil, a stick of charcoal or a piece of clay in his hand. The method used today, where the young student is made to work directly from life, is very bad. At the Athens Polytechnic there were four years of drawing and studying black and white from prints and sculpture before working directly from a living model. In the first year we copied figures from prints; in the second we copied sculpture, but only heads and torsoes; in the third and fourth year sculpture again, but the whole body, or groups of figures. In this way, by the time the student, after four years of apprenticeship had reached the fifth year, during which he drew and did chiaroscuro work from real-life heads, he already had a modest all-round knowledge and knew how to draw a figure so that it looked human and knew how to draw a hand and a foot without these things assuming in his drawing the ridiculous aspect of a couple of forks or the keys of a house, as can be seen in the drawings of our modernistic 'geniuses'.

While I went to the drawing classes at the Polytechnic I wanted to try oil painting at home. At that time I was completely ignorant of matters of technique, I who today am one of the very few who have lifted the veil from methods and media which were dead and buried for almost a century, not only in Italy but throughout the world. I thought, as Renoir used to say, more as a *boutade* than to express a truth; I thought, as I say, that painting in oils was done with oil and I then took the bottle of olive oil which stood on the sideboard, poured a little of the contents into a tin and, dipping a brush into it, I mixed on the table some of the Lefranc colours which I had bought in a shop. My first painting was a silent life—I use this the background to some of the many names and references which be applied much better than the French term *nature morte* to paintings showing objects and inanimate things. This first silent life of mine represented three large lemons, with their leaves, standing on a table. The composition was a little too symmetrical and monotonous. I had put one lemon in the middle, seen from the front, and two others at the sides, seen in profile, facing each other. I was not successful in the modelling of the lemon in the middle and it looked more like a little yellow shield than a lemon. I think, however, that I was barely twelve years old at the time and the 'great' Cézanne when he was already old, after having painted all his life, painted apples which instead of being convex were perfectly flat and some-times even concave; and some modern painters by the time they are grown up and some of them are old, and they want to paint fruit or objects, only succeed in producing a mess which looks like animal excrement, or cold lava, or dried mud.

On the other hand the lemon leaves and the grain of the wooden table were very successful. This picture caused a tragedy, however— it never dried. A few months after I had painted it you had only to touch it to find your finger covered with paint. I decided to solve the mystery. Every week a very old painter called Bolonakis came to the Polytechnic to correct us in the drawing classes. He was a marine painter. Half-way through the last century he had painted pictures which were not without pictorial quality, had much atmosphere and were full of poetry. As subjects they showed Greek beaches near Athens, seen from the port of Piraeus. On the beaches could be seen ladies and gentlemen dressed in the fashions of the period, as in the paintings of Courbet. The painting was smooth but not servile and its quality was reminiscent of Induno.

When I knew Bolonakis he was already old, could not see very well and wore thick spectacles; what was more he had fallen into the vicious habit of drinking and passed most of the day in taverns in the company of carters and workmen. With him in the tavern there often sat an old sculptor, a friend and contemporary. The latter had lived and worked for many years in Rome. In his studio there was a kind of marble-mason's shop opening on to the street and the old sculptor could be seen working there with a paper beret on his head. In this studio-shop there were many beautiful pieces of sculpture, all in Pentelico marble. Unlike the sculptors of today he had a great aversion to wood, terracotta, ceramic and wax. His masterpiece was a large piece of sculpture called *Xilotraftés* (the wood-breaker). It represented a completely naked man, with an athletic but harmonious figure, bent over a large piece of wood which he was holding in his hands and breaking with pressure from his right foot.

The painter Bolonakis, whom I asked about oil painting, also told me that it was done with oil. 'But with what oil?' I asked anxiously, thinking of my lemons which never dried. 'With linseed oil,' added Bolonakis. For me this was a revelation : linseed oil was a revelation like that which so many years later, one winter afternoon in the Louvre, in front of a painting by Velasquez, came to me from the words of Isabella Far : 'True painting is not processed colour, but fine coloured material.'

After my apprenticeship in drawing and working in black and white I joined the painting class. My teacher was called Jacobidis, a Greek from Smyrna. He was well thought of as a portrait painter. When later in Italy I saw the portraits of Giacomo Grosse, Tallone and other painters of this period I remembered Jacobidis; he drew extremely well and one day in his studio he showed me some nudes drawn in charcoal which he had done when he was a young man at the Academy of Munich. I was impressed by the perfection of the drawing and by the relief and delicacy of the modelling. He was a very good teacher and was very demanding about execution and form. When my father asked him if he thought I had any bent for painting, he replied that he allowed me to work quietly. 'He's making impasto! He's making impasto!' added Jacobidis with a laugh.

He used the word 'impasto' to allude to the talent I had for mixing colours and applying them to the canvas.

Among my companions were many fairly gifted boys, full of talent and desire to work. Among others I remember one called Kanzikis. He was really exceptionally gifted. In addition, he had created a whole life for himself. He was almost always alone. He would stop in the streets to draw men, animals, carriages, trees, anything. He lived in a perpetual dream of art and work, made every effort to progress and as a result was the opposite of what so many of our modernistic 'geniuses' are. He also had an odd way of speaking. He gave everything a special name. He called hair 'tresses', and the lower part of the human body formed by the two buttocks the 'nicoli'. He called men 'satyrs' and women 'saucepans'. In order to say that he had seen a gentleman with his wife he said he had seen a satyr with his saucepan. Kanzikis could have become a great painter, perhaps he became one, but I have never heard him mentioned again. It is certain that circumstances of life and ambiance play an important part in the formation, development and career of an artist.

About twenty-five years ago I saw in Rome an exhibition of drawings by the son of the sculptor Dazzi. He was very young and I was astonished by the power, skill and assurance of these drawings. Roberto Longhi, who like all those who have not succeeded in doing what they want hate anything that contains real value, wrote at that time a stupid and envious review. I have heard no more of Dazzi's son either. He too must have been a victim of environment and circumstances, because it could certainly not be said of him that he lacked talent. He had talent, and to spare.

I also knew in Greece a young student named Pikonis. He was studying engineering and architecture, but outside the school he drew and painted; he had outstanding intelligence, the profound intelligence of a metaphysician. I met him later in Paris.

At that time I often went out of the city to paint landscapes. I recollect that some of these were very successful. I went out whatever the weather, summer and winter. One afternoon in July when I had gone to paint some rocks beneath a mountain called Lycabettus, on which rises a monastery dedicated to St George, I caught sunstroke. I felt ill while I was working, but somehow or other I succeeded in returning home, carrying my canvas and box of colours with me. At home I went to bed with a terrible headache. My mother was very frightened and called the doctor. Ice was placed on my head and I was given a sedative. I fell sound asleep. When I woke up I was exhausted, but happy because my headache had gone.

In summer we went to pass the holidays in a pleasant place about ten miles from Athens which was called Kefissia. We stayed at an inn where we ate heavenly meals, as in fact one does everywhere in Greece. I remember the taste of amber-coloured grapes, without skin or seeds and so sweet that after eating them you had to rinse your fingers because they stuck together as though they had honey on them. I remember the divine taste of young lamb, delicate and tender, melting in the mouth like soft pastry.

During our last stay in Kefissia I had a great sorrow. Our dog, our good Trollolò, whom we had left with the servants at our house in Athens, disappeared. Usually we took him to the country with us, to the inn, but this time, I don't know why, he was left in the city. While wandering round the house he was picked up by dog-catchers and then killed; and those wretched servants, on whose heads I called down the curse of heaven, did nothing to save him. When we came back from holiday and I did not find Trollolò I was overwhelmed with deep sorrow and despair and I spent a whole sleepless night weeping and thinking of that dear creature.

3

The stays at Kefissia were saddened by my father's health which deteriorated continually, while he looked even paler and more exhausted. I gazed with sadness and nostalgia at other boys whose fathers were still young and strong. What made me suffer acutely and also made me angry was when, on going for a walk with my father, I saw people look at him and sometimes, after they had passed near him, turn round to look at him again. Remarks by the passers-by would reach me : 'How ill he looks !' 'See how pale he is !' 'He must be very old !' In fact, my father was not very old, he had simply aged a lot and a less superficial observer would have seen in his intelligent and kind expression, veiled with melancholy, a glow and a liveliness that contrasted with the general aspect of his person. I encountered the same look later, in the Prado Museum, in the last self-portrait painted by Titian when he was over ninety. It includes also an infinite tiredness and in addition a certain resignation due to the painter's great age; but the eyes are alert and wide open, luminous and still young with a look of intensity, still full of love and vitality for the sights of the world.

My father felt that his end was not far away. One day, towards evening, a fine evening near the end of April, I was going along a street in Athens with my father. Between me and my father, in spite of the deep affection which linked us, there was a certain aloofness, an apparent coldness or, rather, a kind of reserve which prevented those spontaneous effusions found among people of mediocre birth. We walked in silence and the shadows of evening came down over the city. I was on my father's left; at a certain moment he took hold of me by the shoulders and I felt the weight of his large arm. I was upset and embarrassed. I tried to understand the reason for this unexpected gesture of affection, and then my father spoke to me: 'My life is ending, but yours is hardly beginning.' We returned home without his saying anything more, my father keeping his arm over my shoulder.

A few days later my father felt ill and went to bed. I did not think much of this because I was accustomed to his frequent bouts of illness, but nonetheless I remember that on this occasion I began to feel a strange anxiety. During the night I woke up and heard the sound of mice scratching at something and running about on the pavement in the dark. I don't know why this sound made by the mice in the silence of the middle of the night seemed a bad omen to me.

My father was still in bed and did not improve. One morning I had to go on an errand in a district a long way away. It was May and a most beautiful day in the city of Minerva. All at once, on my right, on the other side of the street, I saw on the first-floor balcony of a house a great black pall flying in the wind. It was like a flash of darkness in the bright light that flooded everything. I felt a sudden anguish and a terrible presentiment. I felt that something fatal had happened at the house I had left. I quickly turned round and went home. When I arrived I found the main door wide open and saw that someone had gone out in a hurry. I hurried towards my father's bedroom. On the stairs I met Dom Brindisi, who embraced me and tried to take me downstairs again to the ground floor. I broke free and ran again towards my father's bedroom. When I entered I saw first my mother and my brother sobbing. I rushed over to the bed where my father was lying; he looked tranquil, with his eyes closed and a serene, almost happy expression, like someone who, tired after a long and exhausting journey, was at last resting in sweet and deep sleep.

Then came the dark hours of preparation for the funeral. Friends and acquaintances of my parents came to the house continually. But in the evening, when everyone had left and the servants had gone to bed, my mother and my brother and I stayed up to keep vigil over my father. It was a beautiful mid-spring night, a clear, sweet and solemn night; the full moon lit up the city that was sunk in sleep; the song of amorous nightingales rose from the surrounding gardens and from time to time came distant chords of a guitar and songs sung in chorus by groups of young men accompanying a friend singing serenades beneath the windows of the girl he loved. Midnight struck. Beneath the weight of fatigue and sorrow my mother and my brother had fallen asleep and I remained alone to keep vigil over my father. I looked at him and then I looked outside, through the open window, at the beautiful, moonlit May night. His last night on earth, I thought. For this, nature offers him a night so beautiful. Then I tiptoed into my bedroom, took some paper and a pencil, and returned to draw by candlelight my father's profile as he lay in the sleep of kindly death. My mother always kept this drawing and I believe that my brother still has it.

Next day the funeral took place. An infantry band came. When the bier was taken out of the house the band played a funeral march, while the soldiers presented arms. Afterwards the cortège went towards the Catholic church of St Dionysius the Areopagite. Leading the cortège was a junior officer who carried in his white-gloved hand a red velvet cushion on which lay the Order of St George, conferred on my father by the King of Greece for his services rendered to the railways during the occupation of Thessaly by the Turks.

There followed days of sadness : condolences, visits, letters. I recall, however, that the boys of my own age, my constant companions until then, did not utter a single word of comfort to me on the occasion of my father's death. Only a young sculptor, a student at the Polytechnic, whom, moreover, I knew very little and had seldom met, behaved differently. When he saw me dressed in mourning he came up to me and spoke of my father whom, he said, he had always regarded with feeling, because of his noble appearance. 'I know that you loved him very much,' he said to me, as though he had read my mind, 'but I do not want to say very much to you, because I also know there are sorrows for which words are of no avail.' Then he embraced me and kissed me, and feeling very moved I returned his embrace.

About eight years ago, while I was in America, my mother died. On that occasion also none of those friends whom I had known for many years and with whom I had so much in common took the trouble to send me a word of sympathy, a word of comfort. The only two people who remembered me and, through my brother, expressed sympathy with some affectionate words, were two people whom I seldom saw and who had never been particularly close friends : the sculptor Romanelli and the writer Antonio Baldini.

After my father's death I continued to work at the school of painting at the Polytechnic, but I failed in the final examinations. The subject for the examination was an old man with a white beard who posed in the nude down to the waist, his head swathed in a turban, and his hand holding a long Oriental pipe. I believe that my failure was more or less justified. I worked badly for that examination, I was not in too good health. The emotional shock following the death of my father, frequent intestinal troubles and the sultry heat of the Athenian July had made me feel tired, melancholy and discouraged, which certainly affected my work.

But I continued to work at home as best as I could. I painted self-portraits, fruit and objects. I drew from life and the days passed. My brother, who was making rapid progress with his piano lessons, wanted to dedicate himself to music. Everyone advised us to go to Munich in Germany so that I could continue to study painting and my brother music. Munich at that time was rather similar to Paris today. My mother began to sell the furniture and the house gradually became empty. There was a fine library of my father's which contained in particular books on mathematics, engineering and mechanics. We had inserted a notice in the newspapers about the sale of our furniture. Also for sale were two fine saddles of English leather, one for a man and the other for a woman. One day someone came to see the saddles. He said that it was not he who wished to buy them but the son of the archaeologist Schliemann.[1]

This son of Schliemann's was a fatuous blond young man who had inherited the millions left by his brilliant and deluded father and lived a fine life, regarding himself as highly important. Seeing that the other man was not making up his mind my mother said that it would have been better if Schliemann and his wife had come personally to see the saddles, but their envoy replied with much self-importance that these people could not come because they were rich and haughty. When my mother heard this reply she was furious, brusquely telling the envoy that he could go and that she cared as little about him as she did about Schliemann.

In contrast to the envoy of Schliemann's son, there came a young student of engineering whose clothes showed that he was very poor. He spoke a little Italian. He was shy, respectful and wanted to buy the books which he greatly needed, but the price was beyond his means. My mother was moved and gave him the books as a present. The poor student tried to thank her, stammering with emotion and his hands trembling. He went out hugging his parcel of books to his chest. The following day my mother received a letter written in Italian that was somewhat incorrect but which contained phrases so noble, striking and lofty that it could have stood comparison with the finest letters of Goethe, Mme de Sévigné and other famous letter-writers of the past. My mother called me and my brother to her and read us the letter from the poor and grateful student.

4

The day of departure came. It was decided that before going to Munich we would stop to visit a few cities in Italy. We embarked on a Greek steamer at Patrasso. The steamer went direct to Venice, but after Brindisi the rolling and pitching movement became more marked and I began to feel very ill. When we reached Bari I begged my mother to stop the journey by steamer and proceed to Venice by rail. My brother, in one of his books, says that this steamship journey was interrupted because I suffered from seasickness. It is true that I insisted more strongly than he did to our mother that we should proceed by rail, but it is also true that my brother suffered just as much from seasickness as I did.

My mother consented to my request. We reached Venice and went to stay at the Albergo Luna. We took our meals, however, at a restaurant which was called Il Capello Nero. Then began the exhausting and interminable visits to churches, palazzi and galleries. In the evenings I was extremely tired, because all day I had to stand with my head raised to look at paintings and frescoes, with the result that in the evenings I had a kind of twisted neck and the back of my head was extremely painful. At that time I did not understand the masterpieces of Tintoretto, Veronese and Titian as I understand them today and I saw them as everyone saw them, that is as coloured pictures and illustrations, with the result that when I looked at them I only found a relative kind of pleasure. I think that this boredom which was imposed upon me as a boy is voluntarily self-imposed by many adult people in all countries and of all races, although they are independent and masters of their actions, which proves the infinite stupidity of the human race.

If I had been able to do what I wanted at that time, instead of going round palazzi and galleries all day and tiring myself in this manner I would have spent my days at the Caffè Florian eating cream cakes and chocolate ices.

From Venice we went to Milan. Milan was in the midst of celebrations and excitement because the exhibition celebrating the boring of the Simplon Tunnel had recently been opened. There was a great display of painting at the exhibition and a pavilion was reserved for the works of Segantini and Previati.[1] I was deeply impressed by this collection. The poetry and metaphysics of these two great Italian artists, especially the latter, struck me and moved me deeply. Thinking over these feelings again today, and about what I saw and understood at that time, it has become clear to me that an understanding of the mystery and beauty of the content of great painting is something infinitely more elusive and more difficult to grasp than the poetic and metaphysical side of a work of art. At that time I was barely seventeen years old but I had already understood, no less than I understand today, the depth and metaphysical quality of the works of Boecklin, Klinger,[2] Segantini and Previati, of all those who, independently of the quality of their painting, have narrated, as they painted, something poetic, curious, strange and surprising. But an understanding of pictorial content, perception of the infinite mystery of such quality, this is something I arrived at only later and only later was I able to experience the joy of this understanding. In fact at that time, in Milan, I was enthusiastic about the works of Segantini and Previati, whereas a few days earlier, in Venice, I had not been in any way enthusiastic about the works of Titian, Tintoretto and Veronese.

When I compare the two pleasures and delights, that of seeing and understanding the poetic and metaphysical side, and that of seeing and understanding the side relating to quality, I feel that the second pleasure and the second delight are much deeper and more complete. This truth, along with so many others, was discovered by Isabella Far; it was she who says in one of her writings : 'The joy given by the contemplation of a work of art containing the principle of revelation is a great joy, *but it is not complete.*'

5

We left for Munich. It was early autumn. I was curious about the appearance of countries I did not know. The pine forests, a few scents that were new to me, a certain type of order, a certain type of comfort to which I was not accustomed, gave me a strange feeling of well-being.

We reached Munich and went to stay in an inn called the Englischer Hof. It was overheated. Every part of Munich was overheated; this comfort and ease astonished me. The cafés were extremely comfortable and the best kind of drinks were served there. Shapely, blonde and full-breasted waitresses served thick, frothy beer in tankards resembling small cathedrals. There was no dirt to be seen in the streets or anywhere, nobody was dressed in ragged or patched clothes, you never met any beggars. Order and civility were much in evidence everywhere. It's paradise, paradise on earth, I thought.

But in this paradise, even at that time, a great calamity was brewing: modern painting, as I will explain later on. And about a quarter of a century later there was to be another calamity, much worse than the former: Nazism. Furthermore, my acumen and my exceptional capacity for observation, which were already highly developed at that period, made me see that in that paradise all was not so beautiful and above all not so good as I had thought at first. I observed among the people of Munich, in spite of their apparent cordiality and their kindness and obsequiousness, which were sometimes exaggerated, some signs of irritability, discontent, hysteria and in fact an uncouth ill-will. It was something I had already observed as a boy in Greece, in my German teacher Gheit. I often noticed how in Munich many individuals, both men and women, even though rough and lacking in irony, behaved in a way that was impertinent and mocking, uncouth in style, rather like the badly educated children of present-day intellectual and rather dim-witted parents. I remember, once in Munich, going with my mother and brother to a gentlemen's outfitters to buy an overcoat. My mother did not find the goods sufficiently pleasing and went out saying that we would go and look at other shops and perhaps we would come back. Then the owner of the shop, who was a middle-aged man with a serious appearance, wearing a large fair beard and eye-glasses, began to utter his thanks in an exaggeratedly ironical manner and bowing deeply. He accompanied us to the door with hysterical, derisive laughter, bowing, snorting and saying repeatedly without a pause, '*Danke. Danke, vielmals! Danke. . . .*' As we went out and walked away from the shop, I could still hear the hysterical voice of this energumen in the distance. He had come out into the street and continued to call out '*Danke, danke, danke, viemals!*'

On another occasion, a few months later, I went with a student of painting, a Prussian from Berlin called Fritz Gartz, to the central post office, because one of my Greek friends who attended the University had asked me to see whether it was possible to claim a parcel sent to him by his family. This Greek had a somewhat lengthy name, he was called Papadiamantopulos. When I went to the window to ask if there was anything for Mr Papadiamantopulos the employee's mouth twisted in mocking laughter. Furthermore, other employees who had heard this name behind him in the office, began to wink at each other, to look at me slyly, suffocating with laughter, while they pretended to look at the registers. Finally the employee at the window said to me with a mad grin : '*Nein, mein lieber Herr, so einen schönen Namen haben wir nicht!*'[1] Seeing that I was having no success I asked my Berlin friend to take over the matter and then he, with the authority of his near-Albino blondness and his Prussianism, and his capacity for speaking out when necessary, succeeded in calming the hysteria of these energumens and induced them to look seriously for the parcel in question.

About countries, as about people and also individuals, false legends are created. For example, Italy has the reputation of being a country full of sun and flowers, but on the other hand I saw much more of these in Holland, England and Germany. The Austrians have the reputation of being kinder, more educated and more human than the Germans, although less serious and more frivolous. On the other hand the worst delinquents, the most sadistic criminals of the Nazi militia, were recruited from among the Austrians and Hitler himself was an Austrian. Many people believe that the Bavarians are less German than the Prussians because they live in the south, that is closer to us, and are more cordial, less hard, less wicked. This is not true at all. I lived two years in Bavaria and I can say with conviction that the Bavarians are much worse than the Prussians and that in the two years I stayed in Munich the only Germans with whom I was friendly and in whom I found a little cordiality and understanding were in fact two Prussians: Fritz Gartz, and his brother Kurt, a medical student. Kurt was obsessed by the philosophical ideas of Nietzsche and I observed in him mental anomalies; at the same time I observed that he, in common with everyone who had read Nietzsche, had not in fact understood what constituted the true novelty discovered by this philosopher. This novelty is a strange and profound poetry, infinitely mysterious and solitary, which is based on the *Stimmung* (I use this very effective German word which could be translated as atmosphere in the moral sense), the *Stimmung*, I repeat, of an autumn afternoon, when the sky is clear and the shadows are longer than in summer, for the sun is beginning to be lower. This extraordinary sensation can be found (but it is necessary, naturally, to have the good fortune to possess my exceptional faculties) in Italian cities and in Mediterranean cities like Genoa or Nice; but the Italian city *par excellence* where this extraordinary phenomenon appears is Turin. I tried to make Kurt Gartz understand all these beautiful things; he listened to me very intently and made a great effort to understand, wrinkling his forehead and looking down, but I felt that he did not understand and would never have understood.

Early one morning when I was still in bed Kurt visited me in the bedroom where I lived and which also served as my studio; he looked wild. On the floor, leaning against the wall, stood a picture which I had recently brought back from the Academy. It represented a nude man seated on a stone with a shield at his feet, surmounted by a sword. Kurt looked at this picture fixedly for a long time and I thought that he was taking an interest in my work and in the progress

I was making at the Academy. He began to speak, however, in a strange and disconnected fashion, as art critics and intellectuals do today. He spoke about ancient battles, Homeric battles, told me that he would have liked to be a warrior of that period and hurl himself naked with sword and shield into the thick of the fight and then fall covered with blows. With a hoarse voice he began to recite some lines from Schiller :

> *Will sich Hector ewig von mir wenden*
> *Wo Achill mit den unnahbarn Händen*
> *Dem Patroclus schrecklich Opfer bringt?*[2]

Seeing that his agitation was increasing I suggested, in order to calm him, that he should accompany me on a walk outside the city. I dressed quickly and we went out; the streets and rooftops were white with snow. We crossed the suburbs and went towards the countryside. At a certain point we saw a wagon which had stopped at the side of the road. The wagon was full of big tubes of cast iron. Beneath the excessive weight the back wheels of the wagon had dug deeply into the muddy ground, and the efforts of the horses and the incitement of the drivers did not succeed in moving the vehicle. My companion stopped and began to look at this scene, just as shortly before he had looked at the nude warrior in my room. At a certain moment, while continuing to look at the wagon, he took hold of my wrist and, grasping it tightly, said in a low voice : 'Look, the wheels of that wagon have sunk down and stuck in the soil. A great weight prevents it from moving. My mind resembles the wheels of that wagon.'

A few days later Kurt, whose mental state had become still worse, was accompanied to Berlin by his brother and taken to a psychiatric clinic. Three years later, when I had already returned to Italy and was in Florence, the painter Fritz Gartz wrote to me that his brother had committed suicide in Berlin, in a public park, by shooting himself in the head with a pistol.

At the Academy of Fine Arts I attended for a few months a class in black and white, then I went on into a painting class. The students were of very poor standard. Unlike those I had seen at the Polytechnic in Athens, where there were many young men full of talent and full of romantic temperament and love for painting, at the Munich Academy I did not see even one who knew how to hold a piece of charcoal or a brush in his hand. The painting which had the dominating influence at that time was the painting of the Secession, the painting which afterwards set the style of the Salon d'Automne in Paris and then spread throughout the world, establishing modern painting. All these styles, or *genres*, which were made fashionable in Paris by the nefarious propaganda of the dealers, had their origin in Munich. But in Paris the activity of the dealers in valuing and imposing decaying and decadent painting began with the advent of the impressionists; the activity of the dealers, as I say, was more unrelenting and more insistent there than in any other place. The Secession of Munich was the source, during that first half of the twentieth century, of two events which were excessively harmful for humanity. The second was, as I have already said, infinitely more harmful than the first, since it cost the lives of millions of innocent men and women and caused indescribable physical and moral suffering. These two events were modern painting and Nazism. Let us hope that the Bavarian capital has stopped there and that at least this time the famous saying that there are never two without three will be proved wrong, otherwise, when the third thing comes, it will be every man for himself.

While I busied myself in drawing and painting at the Academy of Fine Arts my brother took private lessons in harmony and counterpoint from the composer and organist Max Reger, who at that time was the modern Bach. I accompanied my brother to the counterpoint lessons to act as intepreter in a small way because my brother did not know German well enough. When I did not have to translate the teacher's remarks into Italian I looked through a large album containing splendid reproductions of Boecklin's paintings. Occasionally the door which communicated with the adjoining room was open and I would then peer into that room where a young woman, I don't know if she was the wife or sister of the teacher, was doing the housework. This very blonde and shapely German woman awoke in me, the anti-pederast *par excellence*, romantic fantasies and appetites which were in fact normal.

From the window I could see a large space of open ground with a row of poplar trees at the end. In winter the ground was covered with snow and crowds of children wearing caps like gnomes in fairytales were amusing themselves by throwing snowballs at each other.

During that year Pietro Mascagni came to Munich. In a vast concert hall in the Türkenstrasse the Italian maestro conducted a few excerpts from his works. The result was delirium. The public seemed to have gone mad. When the last chord of the finale to *Cavalleria Rusticana* rang out Mascagni, in a moment of artistic exaltation, threw his baton into the midst of the orchestra, at the risk of one of the musicians losing an eye. One of my friends, a Greek, who was also a student at the Academy, clasped me violently and, looking at me with an expression of hallucination, said : 'He's like a demigod !' At the exit the police had to intervene because crowds of Bavarian matrons, with hair as blonde as full-grown corn and hands red from laundry work, besieged Mascagni in a dangerous manner asking him to sign photographs, pieces of paper, the concert programme, a restaurant menu, anything, provided that he signed it.

I have always remained perplexed by these moments of public excitement over music and musicians, and also by the infinite patience with which so many individuals, apparently sane in mind and body, sit in concert halls and listen, for hours on end, motionless but visibly tired and bored, to symphonies and very long-drawn-out compositions which are never-ending and, what is even worse, pieces of modern music. I have wondered why the same thing is not done for painting; why for example in a room, facing a public armed with binoculars and opera-glasses, pictures (naturally not modern ones) are not shown, and why the public is not forced to look at each picture for a time corresponding to the duration of a long symphony : that is, about sixty minutes. I do not believe that looking for an hour, with the eye of a painter and the mind of a philosopher, at a large and beautiful composition by Titian or Rubens, should be less interesting and more tedious than listening to a long symphony or a long concerto for the same period. Why is this not done? I believe that the explanation of the difference can only lie in human stupidity which, as I have already said, according to Renan and also to me, is as immense and infinite as the universe.

I don't know if my brother was advised to do so by our mother or by someone else, but he went to find Mascagni who was staying at the Vier Jahreszeiten inn. During the stay in Munich my brother had composed an opera with the title *Carmela*, for which he had written the libretto himself. It was a romantic and Neapolitan subject, rather like Lamartine's story *Graziella*. My brother returned enthusiastically from the visit to Mascagni. He said that the famous maestro had been very affable and cordial towards him, that he had listened with much interest to some extracts from the opera *Carmela* which my brother had played to him on the piano, that he had praised these excerpts, had encouraged him to persevere with composition and had insisted that he went to see him when he, Mascagni, was back in Italy. There was no time to lose. Mascagni was leaving for Rome in a few days' time, so my mother and my brother left Munich direct for Rome. I remained alone, waiting impatiently for news. It was late in coming and was not what I expected. In Rome my brother had not succeeded in seeing Mascagni. The man who had been so kind and cordial in Munich had become, in the city of the Caesars, a kind of elusive phantom and my brother had not only failed to speak to him, he could not even see him from a distance—which shows the worth of putting your trust in the promises of mortals.

I remained in Munich for a further year. I lived a colourless and boring existence. During the day I worked at the Academy; in the evening I went to the café to play billiards or chess with my friend Gartz. Sometimes Gartz and I went for long walks in the country round Munich and climbed in the neighbouring Bavarian Alps. Gartz was engaged to a young lady from Westphalia. About once a month this young lady, accompanied by her mother, would come to Munich to visit him. On these occasions, the day before her arrival, I would arm myself with a pair of shears which were lent to me by my landlady, and together with my friend Gartz we went in the middle of the night to a public park which lay opposite the palace of the Prince Regent. This garden was full of the most beautiful flowering plants. I would walk in front and without stopping I would make broad cutting movements to right and left, producing a cascade, depending on the season, of roses, carnations, chrysanthemums and other flowers. Gartz, who walked behind, would pick up the flowers as a dog collects wild plants behind a hunter. We had recourse to this stratagem in order not to attract the attention of any keeper by stopping in front of each separate plant. As a result, the next day Gartz would present himself at the station to receive his fiancée with a magnificent bouquet of fresh flowers which had not cost so much as a single pfennig.

At that time I was a great Wagnerian. I never lost an opportunity to hear Wagner's music either in the theatre or at concerts. Today

I have lost my love for that music in which I feel something mawkish and immoral, something which is also perhaps bad.

I decided to return to Italy. My mother and my brother, after the sudden fiasco in Rome when they failed to see Mascagni, had gone to Milan. There the publisher Ricordi was very interested in the opera *Carmela* and hopes revived. I also went to Milan. I believe it was the summer of 1910. We went to live in an apartment in the middle-class district of Milan, in the Via Petrarca. I was painting canvases of a Boecklinesque flavour.

My brother also drew and painted. We read and studied a good deal. We had a Latin teacher called Domenico Fava, the author of a slim volume of Latin synonyms published by Hoepli and much appreciated by students. My brother continued to compose music and write libretti. He had finished a long opera with the title *Poema fantastico*, which was something like Weber's *Oberon*, but it was based on Greek mythology and prehistory, strongly seasoned with burlesque spirit in the style of Pulci[3] and Rabelais.

My brother was unsuccessful in arranging anything with Ricordi. At first the famous publisher had encouraged him greatly, as Mascagni had done in Munich, and had even begun to print the opera *Carmela*, then, and we never understood why, he became more distant and increasingly impossible to see, until my brother realised that there was nothing more he could do. I said that we did not understand the reason for this change, but I attributed it simply to the operations of the usual envious people.

Then we left the apartment in the Via Petrarca and made for Florence. We went to Florence for no particular reason. We were a little discouraged by the failure with the publisher Ricordi. In Milan I had tried to show my paintings in a one-man exhibition and for this purpose I had tried to see a certain gentleman named Milus, or Milius, I can't quite recall his name, who was the proprietor or the administrator of a building where rooms were rented to artists for exhibitions. But I too did not succeed in meeting the gentleman Milus or Milius.

We arrived in Florence. I was very depressed physically because, while staying in Milan, I had had serious intestinal troubles, chronic pains accompanied by much weakness. I could hardly climb stairs and in the street I was afraid I would succumb to fainting and always walked close to the walls. I felt strange sensations. Sometimes I felt as though I were walking along on cotton wool. In my mouth I could taste something like phenic acid. I often felt a pronounced weakness in my stomach, as though I had not eaten for two days, but when I sat down to table I had no appetite. I consulted various doctors who prescribed for me a quantity of pastilles, powders, compresses, drops, drugs to take before, during and after meals. My bedside table was always covered with little boxes and bottles bearing the names of Greek etymology—hepatina, hepatocrinisi, coreina, zimantrax, etc.—but this supply served no purpose and my condition did not improve. As a result I did very little work. I did more reading than painting. Above all I read books of philosophy and was overcome with severe crises of black melancholy.

In Florence my health grew worse. Sometimes I painted small canvases. The Boecklin period had passed and I had begun to paint subjects in which I tried to express the strong and mysterious feeling I had discovered in the books of Nietzsche: the melancholy of beautiful autumn days, afternoons in Italian cities. It was the prelude to the squares of Italy painted a little later in Paris and then in Milan, in Florence and in Rome.

We stayed in Florence for a little over a year. While we were there my brother had the idea of going to Munich to have his music played in a concert hall. He left with our mother. The music was played in the same concert hall in the Türkenstrasse where, a year before, a hysterical public had acclaimed Mascagni. My brother was not acclaimed by a hysterical public, but I believe the concert was not what is termed a fiasco. But he felt that even in Munich there was not much to do. I had stayed in Florence because of my health. I did not feel strong enough to make such a long journey and go as far as Munich. My mother returned to Florence alone; she told me that my brother had been advised to go to Paris which, at that time, because of the so-called 'artistic revolution', was beginning to be considered as the city *par excellence* that accepted new ideas and encouraged young people. Later I realised that all this exists only in men's fantasies and that in Paris people do not understand any more than they do in Rome, London, Madrid, Berlin or Pernambuco. My brother wrote, asking us to come to Paris. He said in his letters that it was in fact a city full of life, movement, intelligent people, and that it would be even in my interest to go there.

However, I was still very depressed. My health gave no sign of

improvement. I felt very weak and struggled continually with pain
and disturbances of all kinds. I consulted a medical celebrity of that
time, Professor Grocco. This outstandingly learned man told me that
I did not need medicines, but rest and good air, and he advised me
to go to Vallombrosa. In Vallombrosa it rained continuously.[4] A
terrible dampness penetrated into the bedroom in the *pensione* where
I had come to stay. The sheets were dripping wet. In the corners,
mushrooms grew on the floor and there was mould in the wardrobe
and the chest of drawers. My intestinal troubles, instead of diminish-
ing, increased, and my nervous depression increased too. I was overcome with a violent attack of melancholy and, since I could no
longer bear it, I ran away from Vallombrosa like a scalded cat and
returned to Florence.

I was not working and I had lost all faith in doctors, as in good
air and mountain cures. After that stay in Vallombrosa I was convinced that in certain cases mountains and pure air are definitely
harmful. Bruno Barilli told me once that when he was in Paris in
about 1930, a period when I was there too, he was sometimes invited
by a publisher he knew, Pierre Lévy, who was later the French
publisher of my novel *Hebdomeros*.[5] Lévy would invite Barilli to a
little property he owned near Paris. For a few days Barilli ate only
the freshest possible things : eggs barely laid by the hen, milk barely
taken from the cow, salads barely picked from the garden. It appears,
however, that after a short time all this extremely fresh produce
poisoned his system severely, so that in order to cure himself, as soon
as he returned to Paris, he would immediately go and eat in certain
horrible restaurants *à prix fixe* where food was served in a state of
advanced putrefaction. In this way Barilli brought his organism back
to a state of health by purging it of all the toxins which overfresh
food had caused to accumulate in it.

6

We decided to leave for Paris. We sold the house in Florence and took the train for Turin. I felt very unwell. It was July and the summer of 1911 was torrid. We stopped a couple of days in Turin to visit the exhibition which had just been opened. But with the heat and after the exhausting journey my condition grew worse. When we left Turin I felt very ill and had severe stomach pains. During the journey I felt worse, and when the train reached Dijon I begged my mother to stop there for a night, since I had not the strength to go on. It was late, about 1 o'clock in the morning. We went to a hotel and I went to bed, but the pains were so bad that my mother was alarmed and went out to find a doctor. She returned shortly afterwards with a military doctor, a captain, who immediately prescribed for me hot-water poultices and a sedative medicine with a laudanum base. My mother had no rest the entire night; she went into the kitchen to boil water and then continually changed the poultices on my stomach. She sent a waiter to have the prescription made up in an all-night pharmacy. When the waiter entered the bedroom and saw me lying there he said : 'That's all due to the heat!' He was right; throughout my life I have observed that heat and hot countries are very bad for people who suffer from intestinal weakness.

Towards morning the pains subsided and I fell fast asleep. When I woke up late in the afternoon I felt better and we decided to continue the journey. There was a train leaving for Paris that evening and we took it. We reached the Gare de Lyon in Paris in the middle of the night. My brother was waiting for us. When he saw me I could tell from his expression that I must have looked in very bad shape. It was the night of July 14th and Paris was celebrating; people were dancing on the pavements in front of the cafés where barrel-organs and orchestras were playing non-stop.

We went to the Hôtel Le Pelletier in the street of the same name where my brother had reserved two rooms for me and my mother. When I had undressed and got into bed I felt very relieved; I slept for a long time but my health problems were not over. From the Hôtel Le Pelletier we went to a *pension* close to the Champs-Elysées and from there to a small apartment which my mother furnished as best she could and which was in a building near the Etoile, in the Rue de Chaillot to be precise. My health was still bad, but in the apartment it gradually began to improve. I had become much worse through travelling and going from one hotel to another; the fact of having a home, being able to eat at home and rest a little was a good tonic in itself.

A doctor who examined me advised me to go to Vichy for three weeks. When I left for Vichy I already felt better. The cure provided by those health-giving waters, called by the Romans *aquae calidae*, where Julius Caesar cured his dyspepsia about two thousand years ago, and where my father had come about forty-five years earlier to cure the after-effects of malaria, did me a lot of good. When the treatment came to an end I returned to Paris completely cured. I had not touched a brush or even a pencil for some time. I went back to work and took up again the thread of inspiration which I drew from Nietzsche.

But I worked little and painted few pictures. The winter and summer passed. I heard confused talk about the Salon d'Automne, the 'revolutionary' painters, Picasso, cubism, the modern schools. I was advised to exhibit in the Salon d'Automne, but I knew that nine times out of ten an unknown painter who submitted work to an unofficial exhibition, subject to a jury, ran the risk, regardless of the quality of his work, of being rejected. From the reproductions I had seen and from the paintings which were being exhibited in the galleries of fashionable dealers, I had soon realised that what I was doing was completely different from what was being produced in Paris at that moment and that this was another good reason why my pictures would be rejected. A Greek gentleman named Calvocoressi came to my aid. He was a music critic and also a musicologist. A friend of Debussy, he had many acquaintances in the artistic and intellectual circles of the capital. He recommended me to the painter

Laprade,[2] whose name I had never heard mentioned, but he was a member of the jury for the Salon d'Automne.

During the night before my visit to the painter Laprade I dreamt that I saw a landscape somewhat similar to the banks of the lakes in Lombardy and Lake Garda. In the foreground were a few trees and some pink blossom; in the background was a stretch of water like a mirror. When I entered Laprade's studio the next day I saw, exactly opposite the door, standing on an easel, a painting which represented a landscape identical with the one I had seen in my dream. After I had been introduced to Laprade and had given him the letter of recommendation from Calvocoressi, I told him that during the night I had dreamt of the picture that was standing on the easel. Laprade smiled and said, *'Tiens, c'est rigolo.'* From which I deduced that the painter Pierre Laprade did not show the same interest in the metaphysics and mystery of dreams as someone like Pythagoras or Arthur Schopenhauer. Then he told me that he often travelled in Italy and that many of his paintings were views of the Lombardy lakes or Lake Garda. He was quite kind. He told me to send in three pictures, not too big, and that he would undertake to have them accepted by the jury. I submitted one of my self-portraits and two small compositions, one inspired by the Piazza Santa Croce in Florence and containing that exceptional poetry I had discovered in the books of Nietzsche, while the other, entitled *The Enigma of the Oracle*, contained the lyrical quality of Greek prehistory.

The three paintings were accepted and I felt very pleased and proud. It was the first time I had exhibited and that a jury had accepted my work. My three paintings were very well hung, all three together, in a room set aside for Spanish painters. The French are more impressed by and more curious about the Spanish than the Italians and also feel more respect and sympathy for the Spanish than for us. My pictures were a definite success and received some praise from the critics; but I did not succeed in selling any of them.

In the meantime, still taking the advice of people who knew the 'ambiance', I sought out Guillaume Apollinaire. He lived in a small apartment on the top floor of an old middle-class house in the Boulevard St-Germain. On Saturdays, from 5 to 8, he received his friends. Painters, poets and literati came, the so-called 'young' and 'intelligent' people who put forward the so-called 'new ideas'. On

Saturdays the atmosphere at Apollinaire's was rather in the style of Balestrieri's *Beethoven*.[3] Apollinaire pontificated from the chair at his work-table. Taciturn and consciously thoughtful individuals sat on the armchairs and divans; most of them, in line with the fashion of that time and that circle, smoked clay pipes similar to those which can be seen in the shooting-booths at fairs. On the walls were pictures by Marie Laurencin, Picasso and a few obscure cubists whose names I have forgotten. Later two or three of my metaphysical paintings were also hung there, including a portrait of Apollinaire, represented as a target-figure which, apparently, prophesied the head wound that Apollinaire received in the 1914–18 war.[4]

I nearly always went to these Saturdays of Apollinaire's, but I did so because I was still very young and therefore still fairly naïve and there were many things I still did not understand. But even then I did not have much esteem and sympathy for that ambiance and I was sometimes slightly bored there. Probably these feelings could be read on my face, because I observed that although Apollinaire and the others who made up the circle showed me some interest and cordiality, they were diffident towards me and detected in me an individual who was fairly different from them.

The famous Saturdays were also attended by the Romanian sculptor Brancusi,[5] who wore a long beard and would say from time to time, to anyone who cared to listen, that he felt 'much inner happiness'. His sculpture consisted of certain ovoid shapes which he polished and repolished with *roda di Berlino*, their surfaces resembling the sculpture of Wildt.[6] Derain[7] came too, sitting deep down in an armchair, smoking his pipe and never saying a word. Max Jacob[8] came, and, unlike Derain, talked continually in a precious kind of way, in a tone somewhere between irony and scepticism. His way of talking and dressing and his physical appearance made me think of certain *chansonniers* in Montmartre who improvised verses and songs and then circulated among the tables ridiculing the clients.

Guillaume Apollinaire advised me to exhibit in the Salon des Indépendants, and in fact during the following spring I submitted four paintings to the exhibition. That year two painters were on the selection committee : Dunoyer de Segonzac[9] and Luc-Albert Moreau.[10] Contrary to what has invariably happened to me in Italy, my paintings have always been very well hung in Paris. Before the opening I went round the Salon des Indépendants, while de Segonzac and Luc-Albert Moreau congratulated me on my paintings and told me that they were very 'decorative' and scenographic and that I would make a good stage designer; from which I deduced that although perhaps they were being slightly dishonest and wanted to be slightly unkind, they had in no way understood the exceedingly solitary and profound lyricism of these paintings. Moreover, nobody has ever understood them, either then or now. Usually people see these paintings as scenes imagined in the twilight, with the light of the moon in eclipse prophesying catastrophes, or great silences which precede cataclysms; a kind of atmosphere of terror, the air of a thriller or a suspense film. These interpretations belong simply to the surrealists, the leaders of modernistic imbecility; they are suitable for cheap literature. In fact the paintings deal with something quite different. . . .

During the same year I exhibited at the Salon d'Automne for the second time and sold a painting; it was the first time in my life that I had done so. The one in question represented a square with gates at the sides. In the background, behind a wall, appeared an equestrian statue similar to the ones dedicated to the heroes of the Risorgimento which can be seen in so many Italian cities and especially in Turin. The buyer was a gentleman from Le Havre; he was an elderly man called Olivier Senn. As to the price I think I had quoted to the secretary of the exhibition 400 francs.

One morning, while I was at home, the maid came to tell me that a gentleman named Senn wished to speak to me. I replied that he could come in and thus I met the first buyer of my paintings. However, he did not tell me at once that he wished to buy one of my paintings; he told me that he came twice a year to Paris to visit the galleries and exhibitions, that he was interested in painting and was a great friend of the painter Othon Friesz.[11] He asked me if I would like to have dinner with him and I accepted. During the meal he began to talk of the Salon d'Automne; he said that he had noticed my paintings and that he had also noticed their 'originality'. Finally he told me that he wished to buy the one with the rose tower,[12] but that he found the price of 400 francs was beyond his means and he asked me to let him have the painting for 250 francs. It was the first time that someone had offered me money in exchange for a painting; I was very moved and flattered, and M. Senn immediately seemed a sympathetic character to me. I also thought he was very intelligent and quite different from other men. I accepted the offer while thinking that M. Senn would have obtained exactly the same result without coming to seek me out and inviting me to supper, and even by offering me less. The reader will perhaps consider that there is a little cynicism in this line of thought, but if so he will be mistaken. I am not and have never been a cynic; but I have always been logical, possessing a great amount of observation and positive spirit and I have always been instinctively opposed to useless things. It is also true that if M. Senn had known that I would have immediately accepted his offer he would still have invited me to supper, because he would perhaps have been glad to spend a couple of hours with a young foreign painter, who spoke French well and painted things somewhat differently to those he was used to seeing.

These events took place in 1913. I did not see M. Senn again; only many years later, in about 1926, when I was in Paris again, I learnt that the painting of the red tower had been put on sale in a gallery in the Rue de La Boétie.

Meanwhile interest in the pictures I was painting, which I called metaphysical, was growing. A young dealer named Paul Guillaume,[18] who was also a friend of Apollinaire's, bought a few paintings from me. He also wanted to make a contract with me which would allow him to acquire my entire production. At that time a few of the dealers in Paris had begun to practise that nefarious habit of monopolising the work of a painter, and all that concealed and unsavoury underground work was enlivened with speeches and articles each more equivocal than the other, while the so-called art critics were hired to help. All these methods, combined with other factors, have brought art in Europe to the state of shocking decadence which prevails today. Naturally at that time I did not understand certain things as I do today, although instinctively I felt disgust and antipathy towards both the dealers and critics. I saw that the interest in my painting was increasing; I saw that the reviews and the newspapers were reproducing my works; I collected some money and some compliments; I was happy. But the fatal year of 1914 arrived; it was summer, hot and sultry. One fine day everything became confused and uncertain; people crowded into the streets; newspapers sold like hot cakes; the assassination at Sarajevo : war.

We remained in Paris amidst the great tension of the first days of fighting; the Germans were advancing on the capital. Every evening, towards sunset, isolated German aeroplanes flew over Paris, scattering manifestoes and streamers inciting people to surrender. But as I was going back home one morning about 11 o'clock I heard a shot. At first, I thought it was the cannon fired at midday and took out my watch to see the time; but then I saw many people running to a place nearby; I joined the crowd. An aeroplane had dropped a small bomb which had fallen on the pavement, killing an old gentleman and fracturing a girl's leg. An ambulance arrived at high speed; I heard people in the crowd cursing the *Boches*; there were bloodstains on the ground. We decided to leave Paris and my mother, brother and I went straight to a little seaside place in Normandy called Ouistreham. The train was packed with refugees; Paul Guillaume, who had been invalided out of the army and no longer had any military obligations, also travelled with us.

At Ouistreham we stayed for ten days or so in a hotel by the seaside. We drank cider and ate very well. The cooking at the hotel was very good; I remember certain roast duck which were real poems. Overeating and sparkling cider, together with the healthy sea air, gave Paul Guillaume eczema on his nose. The war seemed far away and forgotten, but the first wounded came to remind us of it : bandaged feet, arms in slings, soldiers walking with difficulty on crutches and wearing faded greatcoats. Fortunately the news was better; General Galliéni had requisitioned all the taxis in Paris and in one night had sent to a point in the firing-line a large number of soldiers whose arrival had not been anticipated by the Germans. The Battle of the Marne was won; the enemy retreated; the threat to the capital had vanished.

We returned to Paris. During the winter of 1914–15 I continued to work at my metaphysical paintings, but naturally, because of the abnormal state of things, all artistic activity had ceased. In other respects life in Paris had begun again; the cafés were full of people and the *boîtes* in Montparnasse were functioning normally. In these *boîtes* the *chansonniers*, in between a patriotic, sentimental song about the *grand général* (meaning Joffre) and other songs which ridiculed the *Boches*, made frequent allusions to Italy. *Que fera l'Italie?* What would the 'sons of Machiavelli' do? Would they go the right way? (Which meant, naturally, would they fight side by side with the Allies.) It was predicted, fairly correctly in fact, that Italy would enter the war in the spring; a famous *chansonnier* would sing himself hoarse in one *boîte* every night, bawling :

> When is Italy going to march
> with the Allied army?
> Easter-time or Trinity-time,
> Easter or Trinity?

Personally I have always thought that the 'sons of Machiavelli would have done better, both then and more recently in 1940, to keep quiet and concentrated upon their own affairs. In Italy everything will start to go better from all points of view, but especially in art and politics, the day when the Italians decide, once and for all, to stop being servile and provincial imitators and to stop kotowing to everything that comes from abroad and especially from Paris. Everything will go better the day when they decide to think and work seriously, to develop their own potentialities and loftily disregard what is being done and what is happening beyond their frontiers. Then, and only then, will Italians really begin to be *truly estimated by foreigners.*

It was exactly at this time, in 1915, that artistic and literary decadence began in Italy. Until that time, I remember, a certain style was still maintained in all camps. There had been and there still were literati, poets and writers : Carducci, Pascoli, D'Annunzio[1] and other minor figures who, however open they are to the attacks of a certain category of individuals, are real giants in comparison with the brainless molluscs who infest poetry and literature today, and then it was a question of cultured and even erudite men who continually perfected their culture and education; they were workers who passed whole days and nights at their work-tables, unlike those of today who are lazy and illiterate and spend their days and half their nights in cafés. The former were still men of much dignity, men who felt proud of being Italian and judged everything that was being done outside Italy with balance and good sense, without hypocritical envy and systematic hostility, as during the fascist period, but at the same time without ecstasy and ridiculous passion, as happens now. Whereas today you see our intellectuals who, simply on hearing the names of Paul Valéry, Claudel or Gide, simply on hearing people speak of the *Nouvelle Revue Française*, Picasso or Cocteau, wet their pants with excitement and are affected with a kind of quivering of the jaws as though they were suffering from malaria.

To give an idea of the extent to which this love or rather idolatory of foreign things can go today among our writers I need only say that a few years ago one of our painters went to Paris to have a taste of that calamity-city and see the originals of the 'masterpieces' by Braque, Matisse and other fabricators of pseudo-painting, in the sanctuaries of the Rue de La Boétie.

One morning when our painter was in Paris, he went with an Italian friend who had lived for a few years in the French capital to the Rue de La Boétie. They happened to meet Picasso who was on his way somewhere. The Italian who lived in Paris knew Picasso and stopped to introduce his friend to the famous Spanish painter. When our painter heard the name of Picasso and understood that this gentleman who had stopped to speak to them was really he, really Picasso in flesh and blood, he was overtaken by an attack of shuddering and nervous twitching; he opened his mouth but could not utter a single word; he emitted a few croaks while his jaw trembled; he had lost the power of speech : he had become dumb. Picasso left and afterwards our painter continued to utter hoarse sounds, trembled and remained incapable of speech while his friend, feeling upset, took him by the arm and led him to the nearest pharmacy. A doctor who was waiting there for patients examined him and said that he had suffered severe nervous shock, that he was probably a highly emotional subject (there are whole legions of these emotional subjects in Italy today), but added that it was not serious. The doctor asked the dumb man's friend if by chance the former had not received bad news of his family. The friend replied evasively, for he could not say that the situation was the result of a meeting with Picasso. The doctor advised a sedative with a base of bromide and tincture of valerian and told the dumb man to go back to his hotel, to go to bed and try to sleep. It was not until the evening of the same day, about 10 o'clock, that the painter from Milan recovered his speech and then his friend took him out, supporting him by the arm as though he were a convalescent, and led him to the Café du Dôme to eat something.

'But,' he would recall later, 'while we were there having supper I was very concerned because I remembered that Picasso sometimes went to Montparnasse in the evening and even came to the Dôme, and I was afraid my friend might see him again and lose his speech again, this time for the rest of his life.'

Events of this kind did not occur in the times of Carnovali, Fontanesi and Segantini, that is to say when Italian painters still knew how to hold a brush in their hands and had a little sense in their heads and a little pride in their souls.

Two men contributed to provoke this idolatory of anything foreign, with the consequent decline of all seriousness and all dignity in the field of art and letters: Giovanni Papini and Ardengo Soffici,[15] who, even today, are considered by many as the 'precursors' of the new spirit, like the men who made known in Italy the 'mysteries' of the modern French spirit, who 'purified' the air, who paved the way for new ideas and so many other asinine things of which we are suffering the final consequences today; to cure them we need many years of true intelligence, great seriousness and persistent work.

But let us return to memories of Paris. In the meantime friends and acquaintances would disappear from Paris one after the other, swallowed up in the war. Apollinaire had rushed to enlist, but he did this not so much for love of France as many ingenuous people believe, but because his origins were very complicated and obscure. He was of Polish origin; that is, his mother was Polish, but he was born in Italy, in Rome. Apparently his father was Italian. He had spent his childhood in the principality of Monaco and his youth in Germany; finally he had settled in Paris. As a result he was yearning to belong to one country, one race, to have a proper passport. This is proved by many people who come from one country but are born in another. Many of them feel that kind of modesty and shame due to being born in one country while possessing the nationality of another; in fact they are not, for example, Italians born in Italy of Italian parents, or Frenchmen born in France of French parents. Many people have this reserve, and even I and my brother had it and at that time we naïvely thought that in presenting ourselves for call-up, and doing our duty, as they say, we would change something.

We would not have been so ingenuous today, although even today, after living and working so many years in Italy, whenever I say that I was born in Greece, someone always adds: 'But you are Greek then!' And it is useless for me to protest and quote the cases of Ugo Foscolo, Matilde Serao, Arturo Graf and even add that although the French poet André Chénier was born in Constantinople nobody would ever have believed that he was a Turkish poet. . . . It is all to no avail and by now I am resigned to hearing often, when there is talk of where I was born: 'But you are Greek then!'

Apollinaire died on the day of the armistice, so that his gesture of fighting for France was of no use to him, but even if he had lived and become a French citizen, with all his papers in order, the Legion of Honour and the reputation of being a war veteran, it would have been just as useless. The fact of having been born in Rome, of a Polish mother and an Italian father, of having lived a little in the principality of Monaco, a little in Germany and then in France, would still have been there and nothing would have changed it.

Spurred on by the same impulse that led Apollinaire to enlist in the French army, I and my brother left for Florence where we reported for call-up in the military district in which we were registered.

7

The Italian consul in Paris had provided us with a pass, on which was written in French : *Please give permission to M. ——— to pass. Italian soldier called to the colours.*

At the call-up point in Florence I suddenly realised what delights I was going to encounter, and for the first time I observed certain 'beauties' of military life. First of all the smell : I had barely approached the call-up point, where there was a garrison and a military depot, when my nostrils were gradually assailed by a stench which reached me in waves, a splendid symphony of smells—greasy mess-tins, unwashed feet, carbolic, creosote and burnt coffee. As far as moral and intellectual pleasures were concerned here is a little episode, a little scene which I had occasion to observe in Florence when I went for my medical examination. The board of army doctors and army officers examined me and declared me fit for active service without taking the slightest trouble to ask me for my opinion, and I was the subject of a long discussion between a young medical lieutenant and an elderly colonel, who had probably been recalled from retirement. The latter was a fat man with flowing white whiskers and wearing summer uniform; it was his duty to select the corps and unit to which each individual declared fit should be allocated. When my turn came the medical lieutenant respectfully pointed out to the fat colonel that I had a receding chin. This young doctor must certainly have been an intellectual because he wore spectacles with tortoise-shell frames and behind those spectacles could be seen that stupid, pretentious and anxious look, characteristic of so many intellectuals.

Today he would have been a Freudian. In those distant days the snobbery of psychoanalysis, so dear to the surrealists and so many intellectuals and layabouts of our age, had not yet spread throughout the world. The surrealists were such fanatics about Freudianism that when their supreme chief, André Breton,[1] got married he did not take the usual honeymoon in Venice or Naples, where he could dream on the bridges over the lagoons or on the coasts of the Parthenopean Gulf together with his beloved, but went instead with his young wife to Vienna, not to savour the romanticism of the Austrian capital but to make the personal acquaintanceship of the master of libido and the Oedipus complex.

In those days that medical lieutenant in Florence could not have been a Freudian but he was very probably a follower of Lombroso.[2] In my receding chin he thought he saw definite signs of degeneracy and with admirable zeal he applied himself to talking about it in a low voice to the colonel in charge of selection. The latter, however, listened to him with a tired, bored expression, occasionally murmuring something without even looking at me, the object of the discussion. Finally, growing more impatient perhaps because of the heat and the stink of feet which was rising in the room, he suddenly made a sharp gesture with his hand, cutting short any further discussion, and in a hoarse, irritated voice called out loudly: 'Infantry! Infantry!' It was thus clear to me that this respectable senior officer considered the infantry as the one and only unit capable of taking to its bosom an individual of my type. He considered that unit, euphemistically called the queen of battles, as the one most suitable for receiving all rejects of society, including the worst degenerates and the most obviously deficient.

One sultry afternoon, provided with the pass which destined me to the 27th Infantry Regiment, the Pavia Brigade, whose base was at Ferrara, I boarded a train leaving for Bologna. In Bologna I changed trains and left again at once for Ferrara. The train went through the central part of the flat Emilian plain, which many people call the Romagnola. I have often noticed that in Italy there are reasonably well-educated people who believe the Romagnola to be a region, and then I have to explain to them that the region is called Emilia. The train was going through the middle of the flat plain; on both sides rectangles and squares of more or less cultivated soil flew past and the endless monotony of all these sections of colour, green-grey, yellow-grey, green-yellow, grey-yellow, yellow ochre or grey ochre, had a slightly soporific effect. Codigoro, Argento, names of places where the train stopped. I thought of Disraeli,[3] the famous Jewish prime minister during the reign of Queen Victoria. Disraeli : I think there are only two countries which, so far, have not practised various disgusting forms of anti-Semitism, such as 'observing' the Jews with indiscretion, ridiculing them and even insulting them as in the phrase *sale juif*, used by the French who remembered Dreyfus, or playing the kind of dirty trick practised by the Marchese del Grillo in Italy. The only two countries, I say, where so far at least, not even similar disguised forms of minor sadism and bad social education occur, are England and Turkey. Must we then for this reason deduce that England and Turkey are the two most civilised countries in the world? Pah. . . .

The train was approaching Ferrara. In my compartment were two very young volunteers wearing grenadiers' uniform. They were going somewhere into the battle zone. Both were brimming with enthusiasm, they had shining eyes and radiant expressions; they talked excitedly about the war; they hoped they would soon finish their officers' training course and leave for the firing-line. They sat together by the window, clasping each other tightly like a young couple on their honeymoon and gazing vaguely into the distance, beyond the monotony of the Ferrara fields, singing in a low voice, as though in secret, as though they both wanted to confess their infinite passion for their country. From time to time some verses from the song reached me above the roar of the train :

> Italy ! Italy !
> Austria crushes her
> But she does not turn back !

Opposite sat a plump bourgeois and a staff officer who wore the classic patches of dark blue velvet and had the dry forehead of the fifty-year-old trying to escape getting fat. These two men observed the two young volunteers and their juvenile enthusiasm; they observed it with curiosity and sympathy and also with a touch of sadness. But perhaps there was another feeling in their minds, a somewhat unpleasant one, a feeling of slight envy and pleasurable selfishness. Looking at the two young volunteers, the fat bourgeois and the staff officer must have been thinking of their own ages; they must also have been thinking that, unlike those two youths, they were not leaving for the front, they were not going to fight at the frontiers of their homeland; they were not therefore in that state which in all countries has always been admired and respected, and that for these good reasons certain satisfactions of life, above all those concerned with women and love, were fatally denied to them. But, in compensation, they were not being borne away by the train towards all those tasks, those sufferings and those risks of death, towards which the two young grenadiers were going, singing on their way.

I reached Ferrara and went to the depot to which I had been allocated, the Piastrini depot. This was certainly not an ideal place for a tired traveller. Imagine, reader, a kind of stable with walls covered in graffiti and writing of all kinds; up and down the stairs went recruits wearing filthy uniforms of grey cloth. The Tuscan accent predominated among these recruits: 'O Gigiii! Go awaay! Doan't play the foool!' From time to time there came from the courtyard, latrines and infirmary the classic combined stink of carbolic acid, burnt coffee and creosote.

In those distant days ether was not yet commonly used in hospitals and infirmaries; however, the more potent, more prosaic and less intellectual use of carbolic still predominated. I remember that fifteen years later, in Berlin, a lady who wanted to make me believe that she was seriously ill, while in fact she was completely fit, sprayed large quantities of carbolic acid not only over her bedroom and the entire apartment, but even on the landing outside the entrance door, so that the stink of carbolic overwhelmed me even down in the street, as I approached the main doorway. At that time ether had already come into use, but that dear lady naïvely thought that she had made a stronger impression on me through the good old.stink of carbolic.

I return to my memories of Ferrara. That evening I decided to remain in barracks. There was a captain from the reserve on supervisory duty who, in civilian life, I learnt later, had worked as an accountant in an exchange office in Florence. He was more severe and intransigent than an elderly appeal court judge. To all my respectful attempts to obtain a permit for staying out until 11 o'clock he replied with the inexorable words 'It is not possible', repeated in a tone of voice continually more irritable and peremptory. I realised, therefore, that I had to resign myself and remain in barracks. As far as food was concerned it was a bad evening; it was rice and I realised immediately that this grain, so dear to the children of the Rising Sun and so useful in the treatment of gastro-enteritis, was the great hate, the nightmare of all the infantrymen in the Piastrini barracks. In fact all those Tuscan peasants, in spite of their more than primitive habits and their robust appetites, unanimously declared a hunger strike. Although they went to the kitchens to have their mess-tins filled, they did so for the satisfaction of emptying out the contents. In fact, a little later the courtyard and even the latrines disappeared beneath an absolute flood of rice soup. In the latrines especially the spectacle reached a degree of horror that was truly Dante-like.

I refrained from going to have my mess-tin filled, because I did not want to be forced to empty out the contents afterwards in the barracks-yard. Although it was a very bad rice soup I objected to throwing it away, for after all it was eatable, something which in the absence of anything else could have satisfied the hunger of a man or an animal. This dislike of waste, together with my love for order and for simple things and habits, and the innate dislike I feel for insolent and exaggerated luxury, prove that my nature is that of a well-born man and a true artist. It is said that there are many affinities between an aristocratic man and a peasant because both the peasant and the true aristocrat are averse to waste and inclined to parsimony, even to avarice. This forced me to think that the mentality and habits of our peasants were declining, when I saw that my military companions, who were all peasants, had in fact no scruples about filling their mess-tins so that they could then empty out the contents without the slightest hesitation.

The intransigence of that reserve captain forced me to eat just bread that evening. This captain, in addition to being severe, insisted on saying '*voi*' and '*tu*' when he spoke to the soldiers. This is another thing that made me extremely angry during my three years of army life. I have never been able to understand why this offensive way of speaking had to be part of discipline and why, when giving orders, it should be necessary to be offensive. In the French army I did not find that the officers addressed the soldiers as '*tu*', and in spite of this the French army did not appear less well disciplined than ours. To emphasise inferiority when speaking to an inferior, by saying '*voi*' or '*tu*' to him, is a stupid and vulgar habit which is nonetheless used in Italy in various circles and in certain families when they speak to their staff.

In the meantime the shades of night fell gradually over Ferrara.

The sweet and solemn hour approached when Night, reclining on an invisible couch, seemed to empty with a gesture full of tenderness and grace, the contents of her horn, thus scattering sleep-giving kisses over the countries and cities of half the earth, as can be seen in that highly evocative painting by Arnold Boecklin, the *bête noire*, together with Rubens, of all the 'modernists' of today.

I returned to my room and after undressing as little as possible lay down on the straw palliasse which was allotted me. Fortunately I had been placed near two young men who were more civil than the others : one was called Rosselli, the other Corcos. Both came from Florence and both fell in combat. While waiting for sleep to overtake us the young Rosselli and I talked at length about the operas of Wagner, of whom he was a fervent admirer. I begged him to sing under his breath, while our companions snored in the dark, the leitmotiv of Lohengrin :

> Far from you
> In unknown land . . .

Then began the torture of rising at dawn, drilling and marching, all in the humid heat of July in Ferrara and in the company of peasants, many of whom were illiterate and stupid-looking and did not even know why they were there. I remember a young recruit from Puglie who believed he was at the front, where he was due to fight not Austrians or Germans but Turks; he was probably still thinking of the war in Tripoli in 1912. The more educated soldiers were destined to follow officer cadet courses; but before earning the right to join these courses one had to produce evidence of having studied and I did not possess even an elementary degree, although in fact I was more civilised and better educated than the others. As a result I saw myself condemned to be a mere soldier and to take part in a *tu-voi* conversation with the first sergeant who appeared. Further, due to the colonial heat of the Ferrara countryside, the extremely bad food and the forced marches, my intestinal upsets had returned. It was true that I could 'report sick', but it was merely a formality because the only illness that the medical lieutenant recognised was a high temperature which I had not got and therefore, in spite of my physical and mental exhaustion, I did not succeed in having even a single day of rest.

Fortunately one major who was attached to my regimental depot, a man of slightly more intelligence and psychological insight than the others, understood the case of my brother and myself and appointed us as clerks. In this way we could breathe and live more or less like human beings. Our mother came to Ferrara and rented a small furnished apartment; we could sleep at home, wash, change our linen, eat plain, good food and, in our free time, think a little about those aspects of art and thought which had always been the most important part of our lives. I began to paint again. The appearance of Ferrara, one of the most beautiful cities in Italy, had impressed me, but what struck me most of all and inspired me on the metaphysical side, the manner in which I was working then, were certain aspects of Ferrara interiors, certain windows, shops, houses, districts, such as the ancient ghetto, where you could find certain sweets and biscuits with remarkably metaphysical and strange shapes. To this period belong the so-called 'metaphysical interiors' which I then continued to paint, with some variations, and still paint now. At the same time I read a great deal and wrote some poems. I met the poet Govoni,[4] but rarely saw him. He lived in seclusion and did not welcome many people. I remember his house which seemed to be lost in the middle of the countryside. On the rare occasions when I went to see him the heat of the dog-days lay over Ferrara. The heat was suffocating, but in the poet Govoni's house all the shutters were closed. It was shady and deliciously cool and I was reminded of certain houses in Greece, in summer, during my childhood. There was also Govoni's wife, a very beautiful woman with a light brown skin, with that deep gaze, that 'nocturnal' gaze and those special eyes which are characteristic of some women of Ferrara. Since it was very hot and I was parched with thirst, Signora Govoni offered me a drink of tamarind syrup, but it was not the usual pseudo-tamarind which they put in coffee in Italy, tasting of hair-lotion, nor that which is sold in chemists' shops and is more or less a medicine; it was really made from tamarind fruits that had been squeezed and yielded their natural juice. This drink had a biblical taste, a taste of the Old Testament. I remember also the beautiful illustrations in an edition of *I Promessi Sposi* which Govoni kept in his library. The illustrations were by Gaetano Previati.

Later I also met Filippo de Pisis.

Meantime days, weeks and months went by in the city of the Estensi. I worked as well as I could, in spite of the little time at my disposal and my perpetually irritating way of life, due to the military surroundings, so alien to my nature. I knew a few people living in Ferrara. What struck me most of all among the Ferrarese was a kind of more or less latent madness which could not escape an acute observer, such as I have always been. Apart from this latent madness, a characteristic of the Ferrarese, is their mania for gossip and indiscretion; no sooner do they know someone than they want to know at once where he comes from, where he is going, where and when he was born, what is his civil status, who are his parents, what is his financial, emotional and sexual situation, etc. Furthermore, the Ferrarese are also terribly lecherous; there are days, especially at the height of spring, in which the libidinous atmosphere which hangs over Ferrara becomes so strong that it can almost be heard, like rushing water or the roar of fire. Professor Tambroni, the eminent phrenologist, who at that time directed the Ferrara mental hospital, and whom I knew, explained to me that this abnormal state of the Ferrarese is due to the fumes given off by the hemp and to the perpetual humidity. In fact, the entire city is built over ancient macerating vats.

Apparently the smell of hemp has a particular effect on the human organism. Baudelaire also mentions it in his *Petits poèmes en prose* :

During the hemp harvest strange phenomena sometimes occur among the workers, both male and female. It looks as though some vertiginous spirit rises from the harvest, circulates round their legs and goes maliciously to their brains. The harvester's head is in a whirl, at other times it is heavy with dreaming. His limbs grow weak and refuse to act.

Baudelaire then goes on to say that ever since he had been a child similar phenomena had happened to him whenever he played and rolled about on heaps of lucerne.

The countryside round Ferrara is covered with old macerating vats which are now pools full of fish, and if you cast a net into them you can pull it out so full of fish that it nearly breaks, just as you see in certain illustrations to the Bible. Among the Ferrarese whom I knew at that time there was a corporal who worked at my regimental depot. He was a highly original boy. He would sit in the storeroom of the depot, among pyramids of shoes, gaiters, cloaks, jackets, etc., and carry out, with the patience of a medieval châtelaine, the most beautiful and complicated embroidery. He had long finger-nails, which were lustrous and extremely well cared for; his hands often felt hot and then he would raise his arms over his head and move his hands, like certain dancers performing in the aesthetic style. He did this to cool his hands, he would say. He was obsessed by cleanliness, as I found when I went to his house. The bedroom floor was so highly polished with wax, so smooth and gleaming, that you had to walk on tiptoe and spread out your arms in order to keep your balance, like a tightrope-walker or someone learning to skate. If you did not take this precaution you were in danger of falling down at every step and ending up flat on the floor. He had bought from an antique dealer an old bed, an historic bed, which he had covered with a baldachin and with heavy, expensive hangings. The name of this individual young man was Carlo Cirelli. I painted his portrait and gave it to him;[5] some four years later this portrait was sold, probably by Cirelli himself, to the Milanese collector Adriano Pallini, who bought it for a large sum. Signor Carlo Cirelli never gave any sign of life. Naturally the portrait was his property and he could dispose of it as he wished, but I think that after the sale of that portrait, which had not cost him even half a lira, he could have remembered me and without paying me a high percentage of the price received, he could at least have sent me a little present—for example, well, half a packet of Tuscan cigars, which four years ago could still be found easily and cost relatively little. This has happened to me in fact with other friends who earned large sums by selling paintings of mine which they had acquired first for modest sums. These dear friends never had the slightest feeling of gratitude towards me; in fact I would say they are slightly irritated when any reference is made to the splendid profit earned for them by the fruits of the honest work due to my genius. As for Signor Adriano Pallini, he is an outstanding tailor in Milan and a perfect gentleman. He made my clothes for many years; the quality and durability of his fabrics are without equal and his impeccable cutting has since made him a master designer of masculine elegance and has brought him fame in all circles where fine good clothes are appreciated. I possess a winter overcoat which Pallini made in February 1931, and even today, whenever I wear it, everyone thinks it is new.

After Carlo Cirelli I knew Filippo de Pisis,[6] whose real name is Filippo Tibertelli. It cannot be said of him either that he was a champion and example of normality, but he was and still is full of ingenuity, and today he is one of the very rare European painters who have genius. When I knew him he was not yet painting, but he drew a good deal and was studying literature at Bologna.

In his family house in Ferrara, de Pisis lived in a strange room, full of unusual heteroclite objects : stuffed objects, strangely shaped bottles, decanters, flagons and earthenware pots of all sorts, old books which fell to pieces if you touched them. He lived in this magician's laboratory, a genuine surrealist *avant la lettre*. He wore a smock like Maxim Gorky and somewhat resembled the famous Russian novelist. Filippo de Pisis also had and still has a strange way of talking, observing, criticising and commenting on men, deeds and things. He has too his own personal irony, a sense of humour which is his monopoly; in fact, people can say what they like about him, but they certainly cannot suggest that he is an ordinary sort of man.

I also knew other highly original individuals at Ferrara. Among them was a count, but I cannot remember his name. He used to walk round all the streets in the city with a foolish, self-satisfied and absent-minded expression. Whenever he met a friend or acquaintance he would stop him, and as he stood there he would subject him to a stringent interrogation to find out what he had eaten for luncheon or supper. His fixation was to know what people had eaten at table and then he would always say that he liked rice and salami a great deal.[7] Late at night he would go round with a curious short stick which had a pointed end. In the small hours, when the city was deserted, you could see this strange count rummaging for ages, with the end of his stick, in the dustbins which stood outside the doors.

In this way, with a little metaphysical painting, acquaintanceship with a few more or less mad natives of Ferrara, a few walks with de Pisis and the interest aroused in me by the mysterious beauty of Ferrara, time passed. We wanted the war to be over; but once wars start they never seem to finish, just like the tragedies and suffering they cause. More and more men were needed at the front and all the soldiers allocated to sedentary work were given strict medical examinations. My brother was sent to Macedonia. At that time Carlo Carrà[8] came to Ferrara. I do not know whether he came there by accident or otherwise, but he came to the same regimental depot as me. We met later in a kind of hospital, or rather convalescent home, which was a few miles outside Ferrara. I took advantage of the relative quiet of the place to work a little more. This convalescent home was an old convent full of corridors, enormous rooms and a vast number of little bedrooms. I obtained the director's permission to install myself in one of these little bedrooms, where I worked quietly for several hours every day. When Carrà saw me painting the metaphysical paintings he went to Ferrara to buy canvas and colours and began to paint again, but with something of a struggle, the same subjects that I was doing, and all this with an effrontery and a *sans gêne* that were truly astonishing. Carlo Carrà then procured a longer period of convalescence and hastily returned to Milan, taking with him the metaphysical paintings he had done at the Ferrara convalescent home. In Milan he hastily organised an exhibition of these works, probably in the hope of persuading his contemporaries that he was the one and only inventor of metaphysical painting, while I in fact was one of his obscure and modest imitators. Naturally all these manoeuvres were incredibly naïve, because he knew that I had painted metaphysical paintings in Paris several years earlier and that they had been exhibited, reproduced and sold.

In the meantime came the defeat of Caporetto. Ferrara was full of soldiers; medical inspections became more and more frequent and strict; there was an urgent need for more and more men at the front. At Reggio Emilia there was a hospital, a kind of supreme court where certain unfortunate men who looked as though they would collapse at every step were declared fit for active service. The hospital was a dark and gloomy place where all those previously declared unfit for active service were sent for observation. The commandant of this delightful place, whose word was final, was a major in the Medical Corps and had lost two sons in the war. He had been sent there for delicate reasons. When I reached the hospital, where I had been sent for observation, my travelling companions told me that the commandant had pinned up on the office wall two large photographs of his sons who had fallen at the front. He would show these photographs of his sons to all the soldiers who came to him for a final decision, and say: 'Do you see those pictures? They show my two sons who have fallen at the front; you should go to the front too.' He did not add, 'You can fall there too', but *c'était tout comme.*

While I was posted at the Reggio Emilia hospital I was given such bad food that, together with the worst possible treatment and the destructive moral atmosphere, I developed so severe a gastrointestinal attack that when I went to the medical major I was really in a very bad state. In spite of the photographs of his sons who had died in the war, the major said that before I was sent to the front I should have a month of absolute rest and four months of sedentary service. I went back to Ferrara with the euphoria of a youth going off to stay in the country in order to meet a very rich and very month's absolute rest to take a furnished room and really rest. But beautiful girl to whom he is betrothed. I took advantage of the I also began to work: various paintings of mannequins, metaphysical interiors and Italian squares came to light at this period. In this way I reached the summer of 1918.

Yet our troubles were not over. Before the terrible calamitous war ended, other misfortunes came to afflict unhappy humanity. Spanish flu came. I had gone back to sleep in barracks. One night, in my sleep, I heard a loud noise and dreamt that I saw two hens as big as ostriches. I woke up and suddenly realised that the terrible disease had attacked me too. Remaining faithful to the old precepts I had known ever since I was a boy, I went to the nearest pharmacy and bought a good dose of castor oil and a packet of salts. After purging myself and disinfecting my intestine I thought I would get rid of the disease and remained in bed in my room; but my temperature went up and I began to spit blood. The following afternoon, along with other military patients, I was put to bed in an ambulance and taken to the same convalescent home where, about a year and a half earlier, I had been with Carrà and where Carrà had 'invented' metaphysical painting after having seen my metaphysical canvases.

The old convent had been transformed into a kind of vast hospital for those suffering from Spanish flu, and just to console us this illness was also called pulmonary plague. I was put in a very long corridor full of beds. I heard the patients coughing and moaning; from time to time someone would start ranting and die; I would hear a priest and two nuns rush up; I heard prayers mumbled in Latin and then the nurses would wrap up the body in a sheet and take it away quickly. As far as treatment was concerned, twice a day we were given liquid quinine in tins stinking of grease. Under my pillow I jealously guarded my wallet which had a little money in it. From time to time I would call an orderly, press a coin in his hand and arrange for him to make me poultices with linseed flour and put them on my chest and spine. In this way, thanks to the poultices, I spat less blood and my temperature came down. I began to feel better. I arranged to send a telegram to my mother, who was then in Rome. When she reached Ferrara I was already convalescent.

I left the hospital and went with my mother to live in the house owned by the mother of Carlo Cirelli, whose portrait I had painted

two years earlier. I felt much better. It was a great comfort to me
to have my mother close to me; she saw to it that I ate well and tha
I took medicines which would build me up.

At that time my brother returned from Macedonia; it was autumn;
we left Cirelli's mother's house and went to stay in a hotel. On :
evening, while I was painting a metaphysical interior in my hotel
bedroom, the canvas standing on a chair, I heard an unusual nois :
coming from the street below, like that of an agitated crowd. All at
once the door opened and my brother came in, shouting that the war
was over; Germany had asked for an armistice. I put down m /
brushes and ran to the window. The crowd was getting bigger :
groups of men went by singing; soldiers embraced each other and
danced in the middle of the street. Although I was still very wea :
I could not resist going down into the street. I put a woollen scarf
round my neck and wrapped up well in a coat, throwing one end
over the left shoulder, in case of disciplinary action, and went out.

The people outside seemed to have gone mad. I met companions
from my regiment; they were all beside themselves with joy; they
laughed and shouted in fits and starts as though they were delirious.
I also met some old senior officers, colonels whom I knew, com-
mandants of the depots and staff officers. Unlike the other soldiers,
these officers had funereal expressions and looked like whipped dogs.
The reason was clear; for soldiers of this type the end of the war
meant the end of a very good time; the war for them had entailed no
risk and no hardship, and with its end they would be saying good-bye
to high salaries, indemnities of all kinds and even to the prestige that
was more or less conferred on them by their uniform. For them, the
end of the war meant a return to bourgeois life, monotonous, colourless and dull, and also the threat of financial difficulties.

My mother returned to Rome and my brother left for Milan on
his way to a censorship office.

After the defeat of the Austro-Hungarian army, the military
authorities decided that my presence in the city of the Estensi was
no longer indispensable and as a result I was able to arrange a
transfer to Rome as a clerk in a military record office while waiting
for my group to be demobilised. After an interminable journey I
reached the Eternal City; but there I encountered another problem,
the problem of finding somewhere to live, a problem which I have
encountered many times in my life and still do. It is true that I
could have slept in barracks, but I had had more than enough of

them. In every hotel in Rome a well-displayed card announced in large letters the inexorable word 'Full'. This word removed all hope from the pilgrim who, as Pandolfo Collenuccio says, *weary of long wanderings, wishes to rest his weary limbs.* In that distant winter of 1918–19 there was no way of finding a room in Rome. Fortunately my mother, who had reached the capital before me, was living at the Park Hotel near the Via Veneto. Her room was rather small, and there was barely room for her bed, but we made an effort and after obtaining the permission of the manager we moved a wardrobe and had a mattress placed on the floor, where in the end I was able to *rest my weary limbs.*

In those days my pockets were nearly empty; metaphysical painting did not sell as yet, and at that time there were not yet any mystics of modernism, like Signor Carlo Belli today, to praise this painting in lyrical, hermetic and above all stupid terms, which only succeed in ensuring for the artist concerned, in the present and the future, a great success as a comedian. My pockets were nearly empty, but all the same I had made special arrangements to acquire in the grill-room of the Canepa restaurant certain potato croquettes which were exceptionally tasty, nutritious and cheap. Thus Corporal Giorgio de Chirico had his modest croquettes in the grill-room, while in the adjoining restaurant the rich and powerful, the profiteers of the war that was barely over, ate exquisite food washed down with expensive wines. Corporal Giorgio de Chirico, who was then the inventor of metaphysical painting, just as today he is the discoverer of great painting that has been buried and forgotten in the world for nearly a century, Corporal Giorgio de Chirico, I say, returned to the Park Hotel, holding under his cape his box of potato croquettes which at lunch he shared with his good mother, drinking a glass of good cold water. *Sic est et erit justitia mundi!*[9]

Those were heroic times, apparently. Big literary and artistic event
were maturing. There were stirrings destined to open up new avenue
and above all to show the Italians the right road to art and literature
Two reviews were in preparation : *La Ronda* and *Valori plastic*
Many people were heard saying that Italy needed a review. The
wanted one, they received two.

It was a question of 'winning the battle'. For my part I have alway
had serious doubts both about the heroism of those years and abou
the necessity of 'winning the battle'. Moreover, just as today, every
thing was based on a misunderstanding; the names of Manzoni an
Leopardi, Giotto and Masaccio were brandished on one side unde
the aegis of the Italian tradition, while *La Ronda* followed the styl
of the *Nouvelle Revue Française* in a provincial edition and *Valo*
plastici the style of the Paris art galleries in the Rue de La Boéti
and the Rue de Seine.

More than a quarter of a century has passed since then, the name
of the choirmasters have changed, but the music in Rome, and no
only in Rome, is still the same. Even in these lean times of today w
can see in the kiosks literary weeklies with plenty of paper, thei
principal articles are framed with bold rules of grey, red or blue
These weekly reviews are no more than provincial imitations of
few famous Parisian weeklies, such as *Les Nouvelles Littéraires*
Marianne and *Gringoire*. Our *Mariannes* and *Gringoires* suffer fron
Gallomania to the point of publishing articles titled *À la recherch*
du temps perdu.

At that time 'Proustitis' made more victims in Italy and in Rom than Spanish flu had made about a year earlier. 'Paul-Valéryitis', 'Gideitis' and 'Claudelitis' were still in process of incubation; later their germs acquired great virulence, which they still preserve today.

Let us return to myself for a moment. I was living with my mother at the Park Hotel. I had already met a few people from the artistic and literary circles in the capital. Anton Giulio Bragaglia, who at that time shared a photographic studio and a room for exhibitions in the Via Condotti with his brother, had offered to hold an exhibition of my metaphysical paintings, of which I had brought a number of examples from Ferrara. I had painted them during the war in the city of the Estensi, partly in barracks, partly in furnished rooms and hotels and partly in military hospitals. I accepted the invitation and exhibited a certain number of *Hector and Andromaches*, *Troubadours* and metaphysical interiors.

The exhibition was a mediocre success. Only one painting was sold, the only non-metaphysical picture in the entire exhibition, the portrait of a girl. The buyer was Professor Angelo Signorelli, who cautiously chose the least metaphysical painting in my exhibition. Professor Signorelli was the first Italian to buy one of my pictures, just as M. Olivier Senn was the very first man to buy one.

This was the time when Spadini[1] was much talked about in Rome. Spadini was considered the 'Italian' painter, the 'sanc' painter *par excellence*; the painter who painted what he saw, without complications, and who did not waste time in funambulism and cerebralism. When the critics and the intellectuals spoke of him they quoted the names of Titian, Veronese and Renoir, and since at that time Frenchitis and Parisitis were much stronger than nationalism or traditionalism, Spadini was mainly considered as the 'Italian Renoir'.

However, when I saw in Professor Signorelli's house a certain number of Spadini's paintings I suddenly noticed that it was not a question of Renoir and less still of Venetian masters, but simply of Munich. The Munich style of painting, although it was not spoken about as such, had quietly influenced several people all over Europe and also in Italy. The influence reached Italy through the German pavilions at the Biennale exhibitions in Venice, but above all by means of some German reviews. Among the most noteworthy was *Jugend*, which often reproduced by means of an accurate three-colour process work by Leo Putz, Leo Samberger, Rudolph Schramm Zittau and other famous painters from the Bavarian capital. The painter Sironi[2] also painted pictures in the style of the illustration in *Simplicissimus*.

It is not possible to criticise our painters for having succumbed to the influence of Munich painting, since it is at the basis of all modern schools of painting, starting with the famous École de Paris.

In fact, everyone is unaware that the painting done in Munich during the early years of our century, transferred to Paris, presented in a more skilful way, with the fat removed as it were, better seasoned in fact slightly *arrangé* and helped in particular by the universality of the French language and the astuteness of the Paris dealers, gave rise in Paris to all those genres which later spread throughout the world and caused Paris to be consecrated as the 'beacon of modern art'. What is more curious is that later, in the same city of Munich, the cradle of modernistic painting in Europe, the same people who had involuntarily created the Parisian movement were in the end influenced by the styles derived from their own style.

In 1908 the annual exhibition in Munich showed all that painting which later, more or less revised and corrected, or in certain cases made incorrect, appeared in Paris in the Salon d'Automne, the Salon des Indépendants and in the art dealers' shops. The French capital provided for this painting the ideal springboard to world fame which had been lacking in the Bavarian capital.

In those early years of our century the galleries and shops of the Paris dealers overflowed with impressionist painting. Large quantities of work by Renoir, Monet, Sisley, Luce, Pissarro, Bonnard, Signac and others less well known sought outlets to new markets. The dealers realised what splendid openings there would be in Germany and Central Europe in general; but in Germany, the country at which their main drive was directed, the cult of nineteenth-century German painters was still flourishing, and these were the pictures which sold at the highest prices. It is enough to realise that a painting by Boecklin would reach at that time a price of 60,000 marks, a vast price, and paid in gold. High prices were fetched also by the work of Feuerbach, Menzel, Leibl, Hans von Marées and Lenbach.[3] This was the situation governing the market created by the great collectors. The Munich painters were for the minor collectors. It was therefore a question of changing the ideas about painting held by the descendants of Teutobocus. The dealers in impressionist painting prepared this move very skilfully by secretly paying money to authentic German art critics who, in defiance of all morality and idealism as far as art was concerned, initiated in great style a vast campaign destroying nineteenth-century painting and the whole spirit inherent in it. I was in Munich myself at that moment, in fact, just at the time when the manoeuvre which had been initiated a few years earlier had reached its height. I remember that once, while I was at the Academy of Fine Arts, where I attended a painting class, an angry student arrived, brandishing a copy of the newspaper *Münchener Neuste Nachrichten*. In the paper was a long and extremely violent article attacking the painter Leibl. Now, everyone knew that Leibl had been a great friend of Courbet and that the French master thought highly of his German colleague and praised his work; this judgment was all the more important because the creator of *L'Atelier* was not as a rule very kind about the painting of his contemporaries. 'Is it possible,' said this student, justifiably enough, 'that our art critics can be better judges than Gustave Courbet?'

The indignant student did not know, however, what blind idiot had written these articles. They were also being written and still are being written in Paris and other capital cities when it is thought necessary to give a 'puff' to pseudo-geniuses such as Cézanne and Van Gogh as part of some dubious commercial deal.

Now that I have mentioned this unpublished aspect of the history of modern painting, which probably all art critics, in Italy and outside it, know nothing of, or pretend they know nothing of, I will resume the thread of my memories of Rome.

My exhibition at Bragaglia's was, in fact, something of a flop, at least on the sales side. On the other hand a fair number of people came to see it. Various Roman personalities of the day honoured me with a visit and the actress Diana Karenne also came. Since this was the first time I had ever talked to an actress, I was very excited; I went round with her, talking about my pictures, which she looked at one by one but without expressing any opinion. In the end, while she was already at the door and about to leave, she thought that before saying good-bye to me she ought to say something all the same, so she stopped for a moment, turned round to look at the walls of the exhibition and, with a thoughtful air, said: 'What a lot of work!'

The critics' reception of my exhibition was partly mute, partly hostile, as it has always been and in my opinion is now more so than ever.

Before the exhibition opened, Giovanni Papini, who was in Rome at that time, advised me to express myself through an article by

Roberto Longhi,[4] telling me that he was one of the people 'who understood more than the others'. Papini was in Rome to write a metaphysical novel; in fact, he went into isolation for some time. Friends remarked on his disappearance and said that he was working hard, but the metaphysical novel never saw the light of day. Papini returned to social life, but his face was distorted and his mood was that of a dog with hydrophobia. He plunged into Catholicism and whenever he saw me or my brother Savinio in the street he would cross over to avoid having to greet us. From that time onwards, and many years have passed, he nourished for Giorgino and Betty (the nicknames by which my brother and I were called when we were little)[5] a degree of rancour and envy which nothing will ever be able to cure. This is an unpublished piece of modern Italian literary history.

I took the advice given by the author of *Un uomo finito* and went to see Longhi. He came to my exhibition, looked at the pictures, said nothing, like Diana Karenne, then went out with me and tried to 'make me talk'. We reached Bussi's, a café-pâtisserie which then stood at the corner of the Via Veneto and the Via Buoncompagni. At Bussi's Roberto Longhi bought me a coffee, pronouncing the word in the English way. I, like a poor innocent, ignorant of everything naïve and confident, talked about art, expressed my ideas, my dreams, my hopes, opened my candid heart, told everything, confessed everything innocently and ingenuously to him, the man who was already preparing deep down in his mind, in a perfidious, devilish and horrifying way, the treacherous blow. In fact a few days later there appeared on the third page of the newspaper *Il Tempo* a savage article entitled 'To the Orthopaedic God'.

Longhi tried to write these articles in a style somewhere between the malignant and the brilliant, like that used by Barilli,[6] but since Longhi did not have the acumen and verve of our great national Bruno, he produced miserable stunted things, pretentious and hysterical pieces which had no sooner appeared than they yielded up their silly little souls to Satan.

From that day to this, namely over about twenty-seven years, Longhi's envy has mounted continually. When he meets me in the street he reveals a slight displacement of the jaws and an onset of facial paralysis. In addition, he possesses phenomenal magical and supernatural qualities, such as the gift of ubiquity and the faculty of disappearing when he wants to. I remember in this connection an occasion about two years ago when I was entering the Central Post Office in Florence, catching sight of Longhi coming towards me, about twenty yards away. He saw me, calculated the distance between us in an instant and probably deduced that if he had continued to go forward we would have met like two steamers in the fog. There was no time to lose and he resorted to an extreme method : magic. He stretched out his arms and dived into the pavement. I am not exaggerating or inventing : Roberto Longhi disappeared into the pavement. When I looked round to see where Longhi had finally gone, I saw his back far behind me by the doors, vanishing round a corner in the direction of the Via Strozzi. Now I wonder, dear reader, how one can do such things without possessing the gift of ubiquity and the faculty of being able to arrange at will the disappearance of one's own person.

Once, while I was living in Rome, Longhi came to my studio and bought a picture from me. It was a little masterpiece, painted from life in oil tempera, representing mandarin oranges on a tree, with the sky as background. Longhi bought this picture and the same day gave it to a gentleman who, I believe, was not even a great friend, and in any case there was no reason why he should give him such a gift. But this gentleman was one of my acquaintances whom I met almost every evening at the Caffè Aragno.[7] The diabolical purpose of this gesture was to give me striking proof of the low esteem in which Longhi held my pictures and how little he wanted to have them in his house.

Roberto Longhi began to bestow tremendous praise on other painters' work and even to buy it. Socrate, Sciltian, Morandi and Carrà were more or less patronised by Longhi who tried then, as he tries today, to express himself on every possible topic.[8]

On another occasion, while I was still in Rome, I had gone to Longhi's house about a painting of mine, representing melons and breastplates, which Longhi wanted to buy. However, he did not buy it, saying that the paint was cracking. It has cracked so much that the painting was reproduced in three colours four years ago and at present is one of the principal items in the Valdameri collection. While I was in Longhi's house there was a discussion between the two of us about the famous portrait by Raphael which is in the Pitti Gallery in Florence and is known as *The Pregnant Woman*. In 1920 I made a copy of this picture, which I still have. Longhi said that Raphael had drawn the woman's left hand inaccurately. I pointed

out to him that the drawing was not inaccurate, that the lack of
proportion in the hand, which can also be seen in certain works by
Albert Dürer, was due to a special quality, linked with the overall
nature of the picture. Far from reducing the value of the portrait
this quality in fact increased it. Longhi was incapable of producing
arguments and at one particular moment was seized with real
hysteria; he began to tramp up and down like someone who
desperately wants to urinate but cannot satisfy his need. While
Longhi was tramping up and down he repeated incessantly in a
strangled voice : 'Signor de Chirico, allow me to say good-bye to you,
allow me to say good-bye to you, Signor de Chirico!' The painter
Amerigo Bartoli was a witness to this scene.

I was once told that Longhi painted pictures himself, in great
secrecy. If this is true, the hysterical envy provoked in him by my
painting ever since 1918 could be logically explained.

A year before Longhi's attack appeared in *Il Tempo*, that is in
1917, Goffredo Bellonci, another prophet and seer in matters of art,
had expressed himself in highly sceptical terms concerning some of
my metaphysical paintings which were included in a collective
exhibition in the rooms of the newspaper *L'Epoca*, in the Via del
Tritone. Bellonci, with the confidence of a vaticinator who cannot
be wrong, declared to the Roman paper that the man who had gone
very far along the luminous ways of art was Carlo Carrà and not I,
because Carlo Carrà, according to the seer Bellonci, had been better
endowed by God than I had. These gentlemen are always infallible
prophets!

I am convinced that all these critics, intellectuals and others who
for more than twenty-five years boycotted my metaphysical painting,
speaking and writing ill of it, must now be biting their nails; not, as
naïve people may think, because this painting has not been the
ceremonial fiasco that they predicted with such certainty, but
because, having once spoken ill of it, they cannot now, without
infringing every norm of elementary decency, use metaphysical
painting, as so many people do today, to attack what I am doing
now. This is something which puts critics, painters and intellectuals
beyond the grace of God, since they see in it the achievement of
something which they would like to do and cannot; they feel they
must acknowledge the terrible proof of their mediocrity and impotence. But I should add that there is no lack of people who, having
said and written ill of my metaphysical painting, now praise it: in this

way some of those critics, like the eternal Roberto Longhi, after first attacking metaphysical painting, are now ready to break all rules of decency, and whenever they have the chance to attack me in a negative way, they uphold the metaphysical painting they once condemned.

9

During the collective exhibition held by the newspaper *L'Epoca*
there was a fight between one of the editors, called Recchi, and
Mario Broglio, who was supported by Roberto Melli. The cause of
the fight was, I believe, a difference of opinion on artistic matters.

I knew Roberto Melli, who at that time was very friendly with
Mario Broglio, in Ferrara during the First World War. I met him
again in Rome and it was he who introduced me to Mario Broglio.
Melli had recently given up sculpture in order to dedicate himself
to painting. He worked in a little studio in the Piazza Barberini and
one afternoon he showed me in that studio some small pictures
representing the Piazza Barberini seen from above, with the little
carriages waiting for fares.

Melli is a man of exceptional kindness. I remember how once
many years ago, although he was without means and his wife was
ill, he helped a poor young man who was suffering from tuberculosis
by arranging to pay for the treatment he needed. When Melli is in
the country he looks carefully along the ground and often jumps aside
to avoid stepping on the ants or other insects he finds in his way. He
is one of the *true Christians* who still exist in this old and dislocated
Europe.

While my one-man show was taking place at Bragaglia's gallery
I had begun to visit the museums. I experienced a particular liking
for the Villa Borghese, where I remained deeply impressed both by
the paintings housed there and by the classical beauty of the trees
and plants growing round the Villa. It was one morning at the Villa
Borghese, in front of a painting by Titian, that I had a revelation of

what great painting was : I saw tongues of fire appear in the gallery, while outside, beneath the clear sky over the city, rang out a solemn clangour as of weapons beaten in salute, and together with a great cry of righteous spirits there echoed the sound of a trumpet heralding a resurrection.

I realised that something tremendous was happening within me. Until then, in the museums of Italy, France and Germany, I had looked at the paintings of the Masters and I had always seen them as everyone sees them : as *painted images*. Naturally what happened to me in the Villa Borghese Museum was only a beginning. Afterwards, with study, work, observation and meditation, I made tremendous progress; in this way I now understand that painting is a phenomenon of such a kind that when others see it, those who do not yet know, those who are still in the dark, they wear themselves out in endless ways to save their faces, deceive others and also themselves. Since they do not succeed in any way they are unhappy, and being unhappy they do bad work. When I see this sad and painful spectacle, I am overcome with great pity for these wretches and I would like to offer myself as a sacrifice, I would like to be able to offer my naked breast to these outcasts and cry, 'Strike! Strike! Satisfy yourselves!' and I would like to embrace them and kiss them and weep and sob with them and, between sobs, to make them happy, swear solemnly I would *never paint again*!

It was the summer of 1919. It was very hot in Rome : there were days when a fiery wind blew over the city, one of those winds which come from Africa, like the one which blew on the day when I was born, where the ancient city of Jolcos used to stand. I had decided to copy a painting by Lorenzo Lotto at the Villa Borghese. I had never copied paintings in museums before; I mentioned my plan to colleagues and friends and they all smiled more or less benevolently to themselves. I, however, with that indomitable courage, that iron will and that total scorn for other people's opinions which have always guided me through life and which have now made of me the monomachist *par excellence* of painting, went to work. It was not very easy to begin, since I had neither diplomas nor permit, absolutely no entitlement to study, and it was precisely one of these entitlements that was needed for obtaining permission from the museum authorities. Fortunately Spadini, who knew the director, Professor

Cantalmessa, went with me to see him. Professor Cantalmessa was a very elderly gentleman who looked like certain artists, students and gentlemen of the previous century: he had a slight resemblance to Giuseppe Verdi; he also smiled at the idea that a 'futurist' wanted to make copies of old pictures and, since he could not tell from my accent, he asked me which region of Italy I came from. On learning that I was born in Greece he made a few unkind remarks, but then, after this little excursion, he became very kind and took me into the rooms of the Villa, explaining the works to me. While the director and I were walking round, respectfully greeted by the attendants, I noticed that like everyone concerned with art, both traditional and modern, he was much more interested in the subject and in anecdote than in painting itself. In this way I learnt from Professor Cantalmessa that Titian sometimes signed his paintings by writing in Latin, Titianus Vercellius, and that the painting *Blind Cupid* had been discovered after the removal of a picture which had been painted over it a long time after the death of Titian; the said painting represented a swan-hunt. We stopped in front of the painting by Lorenzo Lotto which I had decided to copy, one showing a bearded gentleman dressed in black. Professor Cantalmessa told me that this gentleman must have been called Giorgio because behind him to the left could be seen St George, on horseback, in the act of transfixing the dragon with his spear.

While I was copying Lorenzo Lotto's painting I often saw Spadini when he came to the museum and I talked about old painting with him. Spadini was a man full of character. A normal and intelligent man who appreciated and loved painting deeply, he had nothing in common with the majority of the painters of today, the 'modernists' who have one defect only, but a big one, that of being something in addition to painters. I have never liked Spadini's paintings, but it is difficult for me to like painting done today. Spadini's tragedy was that of being born in a period of profound artistic decadence which could not provide him with the means of carrying out what he felt, what he wanted to do. One century earlier, perhaps even half a century earlier, Spadini would have done much more, and he understood this. For this reason, in spite of praise from critics, in spite of the affection and solicitude of friends, and in spite of his sales to collectors, he was not happy. I could not help him then because it was only then that I was beginning to understand. If he had lived, if he were alive now, I could have done so. He was born too late and died too soon.

Many painters and men of letters met at Spadini's house. These gatherings often ended with big supper parties. Spadini and his wife, the charming Pasqualina, were very hospitable and generous. Naturally, since the moral decadence of the artistic and literary circles was already beginning to be strongly felt, I cannot say that these gatherings were particularly pleasant or interesting. The conversation was mostly kept going by gossip, lies and unkindness; the painters and intellectuals competed in order to appear acute, intelligent, wise, sceptical and superior. What is more, this attitude on the part of the modern intellectual is a phenomenon all too typical of our period, and its intensity increases from year to year. The people who are most likely to strengthen this phenomenon are those in whose works the intellectuals feel vigour and power. Moreover, as regards works of a particularly dangerous character like mine and those of Alberto Savinio, the intellectuals go to two extremes: feigned ignorance and tense silence. An impressive example of what I am saying is the relatively recent case of certain articles published over my signature in reviews and journals between 1942 and 1943. They were written by a lady, well known to almost everyone who knows me, who has recently adopted the pen-name Isabella Far. Many people knew the actual author of these articles, due to the simple fact that I myself had told friends and relatives both in Milan and Rome. However, nobody breathed a word; everyone remained silent and continues to remain silent, as though by command. Recently, Isabella Far's writings have been published in a book titled *Commedia dell'Arte Moderna*. It is remarkably odd to observe the hysterical reactions provoked by this book, *precisely over the writings of Isabella Far*. Why all this? Why this excitement? Because the strength of a great talent can be felt in these writings, and this is what intellectuals today cannot tolerate, cannot forgive and, most important of all, it frightens them. If Isabella Far wrote the usual colourless and pretentious rubbish of most modern writers, all would be well.

But let us return to Spadini, or else some readers, both men and women, might begin to suffer from locomotor ataxy.

The Spadini house, as I have already said, was very hospitable and much frequented. Among the regular guests were the entire members of the circle round the review *La Ronda*: Aurelio Saffi, Riccardo Bacchelli, Vincenzo Cardarelli,[1] Emilio Cecchi[2] and Lorenzo Montano, the pseudonym of Danilo Lebrecht. At a certain moment, and I do not know for what reasons, a young man who called himself Giusti appeared among the contributors to the review. He was extremely elegant, looking like a secretary from a legation or an ambassador, and there was absolutely nothing in his way of speaking or behaving which resembled the usual conduct of people from *La Ronda*. The others, the 'maestri', treated him in a condescending way and even laughed at him; they said he was not very intelligent. But this Signor Giusti once wrote a piece of lyric prose in *La Ronda* which, among the general murky pretentiousness of the review, had at least the merit of some emotion and feeling. Here is the ending of Signor Giusti's prose piece, an ending which I still remember: '. . . but the room where I shall sleep most peacefully will be the room of tomorrow, in the inn of tomorrow, on the way to the journey of tomorrow, because tomorrow is the sad epigraph to this deceitful life of mine. . . .'

The genius of *La Ronda* was Vincenzo Cardarelli; moreover, it was said that the review had been created entirely for him. Young people followed him about and were in love with him. At that time Cardarelli used to lunch in a restaurant in the Via Francesco Crispi which was frequented by writers and journalists. Cardarelli would always arrive with some manuscripts in his pocket; they were the prose pieces destined for *La Ronda*. Among the train of young admirers who accompanied him to the restaurant some ate with him and the others, who were less well off, ran off to their homes or to some modest *trattoria* where they hastily ordered a mouthful of something and then went back, that is when Cardarelli had reached the cheese course and there were already a good number of young people trembling with excitement at his table. Then scenes of this type would take place. At first he was respectfully asked if he would read something. When these young men realised they would have the benefit of some brand new Cardarelli prose their mouths began to water. Cardarelli would take a few pages of manuscript out of his pocket. The waiting became more anxious, the tension increased; the young people whispered to each other that it was going to be the Fables of Genesis; impatience increased; at a certain moment the Maestro's voice was heard : '. . . and then Noah looked at the Ark. . . .' A pause : Cardarelli had stopped reading, as though overcome with sudden sadistic feelings. The young men's eyes were fixed upon him and seemed to say : 'Go on, go on, we must have the rest; don't you see, Maestro, you're making us unhappy, we can't stand it any longer!' Then Cardarelli would read some more : '. . . and he found that it was good'. The reading was over; with a slow and solemn gesture Cardarelli would put the manuscript back in his pocket, tilting his head slightly backwards and grinning in Mephistophelian fashion while all around him the young men, stupefied with admiration, would remain silent.

Cardarelli's most ardent admirer was an intellectual from Bologna, a little over twenty, who had come from Rome to be secretary to *La Ronda*, but most of all, I believe, to be near Cardarelli and breathe the same air the Maestro breathed.

The admiration which resembles love and which some young men can feel for a master, or for someone they believe to be one, is a phenomenon encountered in all ages: from the young Alcibiades, who wanted to stay by the bed where Socrates lay in a fever, to the learned ephebes, the students of Plato, to the young men who would kiss D'Annunzio's hands (he himself mentions this when, having worked all night, he had looked at his hands in the lamplight: 'I thought,' wrote the poet, 'of all the young people who will kiss them, while I remain reluctant, in the dark.'), and so on, right up to the young men in love with Cardarelli. All periods have experienced this curious phenomenon in which, I think, there must be some underlying masochism and succubism linked with feelings of subconscious homosexuality. As for myself, I am proud of the fact that I have never given rise to wild passions in any young men and I have never been in love with a Maestro. In any case *I* would have been in love with a Maestra.

The gatherings in Spadini's house used to take place in the dining-room, which also served as a reception-room. On a wall of this room, to the left of the doorway, hung a picture by Carrà. This picture was entitled *The Metaphysical Muse*. Titles of this kind had been given by me to some of my paintings between 1912 and 1915 in Paris and afterwards, during the First World War, in Ferrara. Then the same titles, only half understood, or rather not understood at all, were plagiarised by Carrà in Italy and in Paris and applied at random in a shameful fashion by the surrealists to other paintings of mine which had nothing to do with these titles. So much for historical truth.

The painting by Carrà which hung in Spadini's house represented a kind of rubber doll which, instead of a head, had a kind of fencing mask and in its right hand held a kind of tennis racket, around which were roughly painted all the motifs which Carrà had taken from my paintings, without ever understanding much about them. I remember that behind this doll, on a kind of wall or portico, there was a cross painted in black. When I was at Spadini's I used to say jokingly that that black cross, which seemed to be rather a kind of cabbalistic sign or swastika, could cast a spell and that I would not want to have that picture in the house. Afterwards, Spadini's wife removed the cross by scratching it out with the tip of a penknife. When Spadini died and his body was brought into the dining-room, Carrà's painting, from which Spadini's wife Pasqualina had removed the cross, hung right over the dead painter's head.

Carrà's metaphysical painting had been sold to Spadini at the exhibition held by the newspaper *L'Epoca*. The sale at the time astonished many people and caused much comment in the artistic circles of the capital; there was also a rumour that the painting had been bought by Spadini on behalf of Angelo Signorelli. But the explanation is simple : Spadini believed he was persecuted by the modernists, the avant-garde and the cerebralists; he saw in Carrà a kind of supreme head of Italian cerebral painting and Italian avant-gardism, and I believe that this was not so much because of his painting but because of his rough manners, his brusque way of talking and his voice that was reminiscent of political meetings; he thought therefore that it was a good thing to buy a picture from him.

Spadini's purchase of a painting by Carrà makes me think of other, much more complicated cases. The influence that a person's voice and attitude can have, especially today, over a certain category of persons, is enormous. A large part of the success of certain painters, writers and other people too, is due to their attitudes. A man who treats another man badly can awaken in certain individuals an admiration which can develop into love. I believe there is a legend in which the vine turns to the peasant and says to him, 'Make me poor and I shall make you rich.' The vine in this case is referring to pruning. Some individuals, when faced with other individuals who treat them badly, seem to say, 'Strike me and I will love you desperately.'

In Paris I often had occasion to study a similar case in the relationship between André Derain and certain people. André Derain is a painter full of talent, but a great part of his success is due more to his way of behaving than to his qualities as a painter. He is the cantankerous man *par excellence*; he never speaks, and if someone addresses a word to him he replies with a grunt; in the street he pretends not to recognise the people he knows. Whenever he is invited for luncheon or supper he not only does not come but he does not even trouble to say that he is not coming; whenever someone goes to see him, an old maidservant replies in imperturbable fashion, 'Monsieur Derain has gone out shopping.' If some tenacious or fanatic person insists and says that he will wait until M. Derain comes back, the maidservant adds, 'Oh no, that's impossible, for when Monsieur Derain goes out shopping he sometimes stays out for several days.'[3]

However, Derain's admirers are without number. Those who fell most desperately in love were Adolphe Basler and Paul Guillaume.

Adolphe Basler was one of those dealers who in Paris are called private dealers because they buy and sell pictures without having a gallery. He was madly in love with Derain. One winter afternoon, while I was sitting on the *terrasse* of the Café des Deux Magots, the intellectuals' café on the Left Bank, I watched the following curious and diverting spectacle. Derain arrived, alone, as always, and sat outside on the terrace. In winter the *terrasse* was heated by braziers and protected at the sides with large glass screens. Derain sat down and ordered a *demi*, a pint of beer, and then bought some peanuts from an Arab street-vendor and filled his pockets with them. In this way, crunching the nuts and sipping his beer, he remained motionless, without looking in any direction, with the expression of someone profoundly disgusted with everyone and everything, while his elephantine eyes gazed at the doorway of the church of St Germain-des-Prés. Shortly afterwards, as though by magic, as though drawn by some mysterious call, Adolphe Basler appeared on the horizon. When he saw Derain he came closer and began to walk up and down in front of him, looking at him lovingly with shining eyes and making little gestures of greeting with his head and hands. Derain, motionless and imperturbable, continued to gaze at the church door. Since all the tables next to Derain were occupied, Basler continued walking up and down for a little time, but when a table on Derain's left became free Basler rushed towards it; but before sitting down he respectfully asked Derain's permission, as though the latter could have occupied two tables on his own. Basler, seeing that permission was not given, sat down timidly on the edge of the chair with one buttock drooping over it. Then he began another manoeuvre; he tried to speak to Derain: 'Good afternoon, Monsieur Derain, how are you?' and the other remained silent. 'Are you working hard at the moment,

Monsieur Derain?' And the other was more silent than ever. Then Basler, at the height of amorous intensity, stretched out a trembling hand and with the tips of his fingers barely touched Derain's shoulder. He should never have done it! A terrifying grunt, something resembling the trumpeting of a ferocious elephant, and a no less terrifying twitch of the shoulder where Basler's hand lay, were the sole response to this timid attempt at a caress. Basler quickly withdrew his hand as though it had been burnt and then, beaten and disappointed, gave up, sadly took out of his overcoat pocket a copy of *Gringoire* or *Les Nouvelles Littéraires*, I do not remember which, and buried himself in one of those utterly boring, endless tirades with which the Parisian literary weeklies are always abundantly supplied.

Paul Guillaume's love for Derain was no joke. One evening Paul Guillaume and his wife were having supper in their luxurious apartment in the Rue de Messine. They were alone, had decided to remain at home, and were expecting no one. Suddenly Paul Guillaume was overcome with a violent desire to see Derain. Desires of this kind are like the urges of pregnant women who all at once can demand strawberries and cream or lobster with mayonnaise and if their urge is not satisfied immediately they risk giving birth to a child with half a basket of strawberries or half a lobster on its face. Naturally in Guillaume's case there was no risk of giving birth to a child with half of Derain on his face, but since this urge was uncommonly strong, it was better to satisfy it at once. When the maître d'hôtel was informed, he rushed into the corridor and through the speaking-tube told the kitchen staff that Monsieur and Madame were going out immediately. The chauffeur, who was still eating, ran to the garage; an impressive Hispano-Suiza was driven out with all the care it deserved. Paul Guillaume had already come down with his wife and was waiting, trembling with impatience, at the doorway. He pushed his wife into the car and followed her. 'To Monsieur Derain's, quickly,' he shouted. The car started. Soon afterwards it stopped in front of Derain's house. Paul Guillaume ran up the steps three at a time, hurled himself at the bell and when the old maidservant, in her tattered slippers, came to open it, he did not even have the strength to ask for Derain. The servant looked at Paul Guillaume's worried face with some surprise and said, 'Monsieur Derain has gone to the cinema.' Disaster! Paul Guillaume went pale, uttered a kind of death-rattle and, in a voice strangled with anxiety, asked, 'Which cinema?' 'I don't know, my good sir,' replied the old servant without turning a hair, 'a local cinema.'

Without waiting any longer Paul Guillaume ran down the stairs, leapt into the car, shouted to the chauffeur to go immediately round all the cinemas in the district and stop in front of the entrance to each one, but to make haste, for the love of all the saints in Paradise. He did so. The car stopped in front of each cinema; Paul Guillaume leapt in one stride from the car to the booking office; he bought a ticket, throwing 50 or 100 francs to the cashier, and not waiting for the change. Clutching the ticket he would disappear into the auditorium; once there he anxiously asked for the director, the manager or the proprietor, he begged and prayed, told unlikely stories, handed out large tips, arranged for the show to be stopped and the lights switched on so that, trembling and fretting, he could look for Derain among the audience. Finally, at the fifth or sixth cinema, Derain was found sitting quietly in the middle of the auditorium eating nuts and enjoying a film with Tom Mix. Paul Guillaume uttered a roar of delight at the thought that his long-felt desire was finally satisfied and then, stepping on the toes of the spectators and bumping against their knees, almost falling into their laps, among curses, laughter and exclamations, joined Derain, seized hold of him and dragged him bodily outside, to the astonishment and hilarious curiosity of those present at the scene, who did not know whether it was something to do with a woman or the execution of a warrant for arrest.

10

Let us return to my memories of Rome. It was the time when *La Ronda* and *Valori plastici*[1] *battaient son plein*. For the information of readers, in case they are unaware of the fact, the French phrase *battre son plein* is of military origin and refers to the sound of the drums beaten hard with drumsticks; in fact, *son* here means sound and not *their*. There are even French people who when the subject is plural say or write *leur plein*.

The *terza saletta* at the Caffè Aragno also *battait son plein*. To enter the *saletta* was to be bolder than boarding an enemy ship with an axe in your hand and a dagger between your teeth. But to leave the *terza saletta* meant being bolder still. Seated all round the walls of that historic place were the rocklike legions of art and intellectualism. An indescribable hysteria, of which no instrument could have measured the power, caused the heavy marble tables to levitate, and they rose half a centimetre from the floor; a phenomenon, moreover, which I alone was able to observe. The *terza saletta* 'worked' hard all day. In the morning, at the hour when honest artisans and honest workmen are singing as they work, bent over the plane or the anvil, at those hours sacred, as I say, to work, there were already many visitors to the *terza saletta*. As friends arrived and greeted each other they tried to justify and exonerate themselves. 'I don't know,' said one painter, 'how I manage to work by this light, I can't see a thing! And how it rained last night!' 'I don't know,' said a writer, 'how I manage to write with all that noise coming from the floor above; the children stayed at home today and I've got such a headache!' His friends, who had already been sitting there some time, would listen to him and look at him in a surly manner.

In Rome you can't work when the weather is too good, either; so you have to venture forth and go to the Aragno. About noon Cardarelli would arrive, having risen from bed half an hour before. In order to avoid tiring himself by going as far as the restaurant he would often ask the waiter for two eggs with ham and a quarter-bottle of wine. Once when he was sitting near me and eating the ham and eggs with a good appetite, he began his usual talk, this time about Leopardi.[2] It was about the *Elogio degli uccelli*; Cardarelli quoted lines from the famous poem. '*Quantunque gli uccelli cantavano*,' he said, spacing out the words. 'Do you mean *cantassero*?' I interrupted. 'No, no, *cantavano, cantavano*,' Cardarelli went on, becoming animated and with the sly expression of someone who is thinking, 'This is just what I was waiting for!' : '*Quantunque* here means place and stands for *ovunque*.' 'But then,' I went on, 'Leopardi could have said *ovunque* : I don't suppose that in his day the adverb didn't exist.'[3] Cardarelli's reply to this second remark of mine was not very clear to me. He remained slightly taken aback, crooked the thumb of his right hand, holding the other fingers tightly together. He raised his hand curved in this manner to his ear and began to turn it round as though he were stroking an invisible surface, and in the meantime he said to me softly, 'There's music! There's music. . . .'

Now, still on the subject of Cardarelli, I must say something to satisfy my need for justice. All great men are anxious for justice and I more so than all of them. During last summer I found myself one day in a bookshop and opened a volume of poems by Cardarelli published by Mondadori. Having read a few lines I liked, I therefore bought the book and read all of it at home. Apart from the first poem titled *L'Adolescente* (which is in fact the one most highly praised by the author of the preface), all the others are very fine, and the poems *Ajace, Gabbiani* and *Sopra una tomba* are particularly fine. There is a strong lyrical inspiration throughout the whole book; an inspiration which is slightly reminiscent of Foscolo[4] and Leopardi but without any trace of imitation, just as a fine painting by Delacroix can be reminiscent of Tintoretto or Rubens.

The *terza saletta* at the Aragno was in a ferment. Now, if some people who came in the morning were discontented and angry, because they had not worked, some of those who came in the evening, after 5 o'clock, were contented, happy and satisfied. Some of them sat down and said loudly enough for everyone to hear, 'I've worked hard today and I'm rather tired.' They were content and much more tranquil than the others. They were more tolerant; they smiled benevolently at everyone, and treated the waiters with affectionate familiarity; there was something rhythmic and satisfied about each of their gestures. In fact, they felt fairly happy. Malice and hysteria, which often rose to 40° Centigrade and over, had gone down to 37° and even to $36\frac{1}{2}$°. Naturally there could be no mention yet of a complete cure, but they were better, much better; they were, in fact, like convalescents who had left their beds and were walking a couple of steps in their bedrooms; they were eating a wing of boiled chicken and a biscuit and drinking a drop of Marsala; actually they were feeling better, much better.

When the weather was fine, during those terrible Roman days which in October are called *ottobrate*, but which continue even in the midst of winter, great expeditions were organised from the Aragno to restaurants outside the town. One of the principal organisers of these expeditions was Mario Broglio. We would go and eat pork and lamb as cooked by Gigi, Nino, Beppe, Sora Prima or Sora Gaetana. These expeditions to restaurants sometimes ended sadly, following violent discussions and even fights. It should be remembered that the meals shared in restaurants, just like expeditions to the country and general gatherings of artists and intellectuals who meet for the purpose of creating an atmosphere of gaiety and relaxation, are not likely to succeed today. Those taking part in such gatherings are usually too discontented and too dissatisfied with their work and when they want to create a festive atmosphere they only succeed in creating something false, forced and slightly ridiculous. These things used to go well in the old days, in the times of our grandfathers and better still in the times of our great-grandfathers, that is when painters knew how to paint and *did* paint a fine picture and when writers knew how to write a good novel and were able to do so.

On the subject of these meals in restaurants I remember a fantastic meal of lamb, to which Spadini invited us in a *trattoria* which was then very well known, but whose name escapes me now. This meal took place on the evening of a day when Spadini had to appear in court following an altercation which had taken place at the Villa Strohl Fern, between himself and an architect named Rossi. Since I was also present at the scene, along with Bartoli, Melli, Trombatori, Martini and a few others, we were all involved in the business and had to go with Spadini to the court. During the hearing Roberto

Melli was overtaken suddenly with a kind of furious enthusiasm, and shouted at the magistrate, the advocates, the public and all of us: 'Spadini is the greatest painter in Italy!' The magistrate was astonished and looked at Melli, failing to understand the reason for this sudden and unnecessary remark, and Spadini blushed. But afterwards in the trattorio Spadini offered Melli in a low voice two helpings of lamb.

At the Villa Strohl Fern there lived at that time three dancers, sisters who were called Braun. I no longer remember from where the Braun sisters had descended on Rome, where they were introduced by Barilli into the artistic and literary circles of the city. The Braun sisters were disciples of the famous Dalcroze,[5] the mystic of rhythmic dance and rhythmic movements. It is said that the Dalcroze system also has a moral influence on the individual, strengthening his psychic equilibrium, endowing his actions with rhythm and thereby removing, or at least reducing greatly, any symptom not only of hysteria but also of mere nervous tension. If this is the case, I must say that the Braun sisters cannot have been considered three living advertisements of the system, because there was so much hysteria and such reserves of it within them that if it could all have been transmuted into locomotive power it would have kept the state railways running for fifty years and all the trains would have arrived at least half an hour ahead of time.

The Braun sisters sang fairly well; they sang well in tune and all three of them together sang popular Swiss and German songs. But when they sang they seemed to do so out of anger and as though to annoy someone. They had a mania for giving nicknames to people; in this way the writer Ottone Schanzer had become Signor Scanzerio, and they called Lorenzo Montano the Golem. The sisters Braun wore white cloaks like Lohengrin and when they walked through the streets of Rome, with firm Dalcrozian steps, the cloaks flew up behind them and looked like three little horizontal sails. Another of their peculiarities was that there was not the slightest resemblance between any of them; each had a face that looked quite unlike the others'. The youngest was called Leonie. Sometimes she went for a walk dressed as a riding-mistress, with a whip in her hand. Leonie specialised in the art of imitating a cannon firing. In order to do this she sat astride a chair, facing the back, with her arms round it; she would raise her head slightly, make her mouth as round as a chicken's arse and emit two short hoarse sounds, something like 'Uhu, Uhu'. At the same time, moving up and down heavily, as though sitting on air, she would move back along with the chair in order to imitate the kick of the cannon. This imitation of a gun firing was much appreciated by the intellectuals and they often asked Leonie to 'do the cannon'.

The Braun sisters were said to be very intelligent. They belonged to a type that is all of a piece, but the only drawback is that every quarter of a century it deteriorates. For example, in the second half of the nineteenth century, Marie Bashkirtseff[6] was a similar type, but she was much better. She began by being a very beautiful young girl, then she wrote very well and painted moderately well; she knew Greek and Latin, was not affected to the point of hysteria but had a touch of it, sometimes busied herself with boring other people, but not always. Before the First World War, between 1910 and 1914, there lived and reigned in Paris a second edition of Marie Bashkirtseff, but one that had deteriorated greatly: this was the Baronne d'Oettingen, whom I knew personally. She wrote in *Les Soirées de Paris*, the famous review edited by Guillaume Apollinaire, painted badly, was very hysterical and tried to offend and bore everyone somewhat. Later we had a third edition of Marie Bashkirtseff, an edition even worse than the second one: the Braun sisters. Today we have fourth editions, infinitely worse than the third. In about twenty-five years we shall have fifth editions, compared to which the ladies of the fourth edition, those of today, will seem masterpieces of kindness, balance and intelligence. This will go on until the Last Judgment. Let us thank God for not having created us at the same time as the last edition.

The time came when the so-called fascist revolution was brewing. One evening I was in a cinema on the Corso Umberto. When I went in I did not find a seat and remained standing at the back of the auditorium. At a certain moment there appeared four or five young men in black shirts and boots; the oldest might have been eighteen, the youngest fifteen. They were not armed, at least apparently not, and only two of them lashed their boots with little whips. They ordered the show to be stopped, and it was; they ordered the lights to be put on, and they were; they ordered all the war songs to be played, those of the Arditi and the fascists, and all the songs were played; they ordered all the spectators to stand, and everyone stood up like a single man; fortunately I was already standing and so I did not have to get up. Finally, when it suited them, they allowed the show to go on and went out, banging the doors, after glaring at the spectators one last time with glances worthy of Capitaine Fracasse.[7] The hall, as I said, was completely full and as is usual in Italy, more so at that time than now, they were many more men than women; it needed only two men to kick those boys out; but nobody moved, nobody breathed. After that scene I understood that the occupation of Rome, and then of Italy, by the fascists, was only a question of days. In fact about a week later the legions marched along that same Corso Umberto.

During the days following the march on Rome the rhythm of life at the Aragno accelerated rapidly. Certain individuals in black shirts sat at the tables and nobody knew where they had come from. Between their glasses and cups lay weapons of all dates and all types : old carbines from the time of the Risorgimento, antiquated double-barrelled guns, Winchester repeating rifles, woodcutters' axes, revolvers, automatic pistols of all calibres, muskets, hunting knives, old cut-throats' daggers, etc. The intellectuals, feeling uncertain, intimidated, wavering and curious, sat fascinated at their tables and, in order to save their faces, tried to assume the expressions and attitudes of people who are taken up with higher things, are pre-occupied with art and thought and have much more to do than follow the upheavals and tribulations of political life.

One afternoon at this time I too was at the Aragno with a group of acquaintances. Among us was a friend of Mario Broglio's, a certain Mario Girardon, a Venetian, a writer who organised exhibitions of Italian painting abroad. It appears that as a young man he had been with Mussolini at Bologna and had shared a room with the future fascist leader. Girardon was sitting among us and was telling us, in a fairly loud voice, that when he and Mussolini were students in Bologna and shared a room for reasons of economy, Mussolini always got up early and after cleaning his own shoes also gave a good clean to Girardon's shoes, while their owner was still asleep. A few fascists sitting at the next table heard him talking, became excited and began to look at Girardon with grim expressions, but the latter, without noticing anything, went on in his strong Venetian accent and with his air of superiority : 'Every morning he cleaned my shoes as well and gave them a fine polish, really he did !' Excitement at the black-shirts' table grew. At one point, when two or three fascists stood up,

Girardon at last realised the danger, and perhaps some friend had given him a kick or nudged his elbow. He realised the danger and stopped talking; then, with a contrite air, seeing the fascists rising to their feet and moving towards him, he added, with the expression of a child caught in the act, 'But I don't mean that he really polished them for me . . . he just took some of the dust off. . . .' It all ended in loud laughter.

In the meantime official exhibitions were in full swing and in Rome the Biennali took place. At the 1923 show I exhibited a certain number of selected works, in tempera, belonging to that period of painting which the historians of modern art call the romantic period, although they do not dwell too much on this. My personal exhibition, which occupied three walls, was very good from three points of view : the quality of the painting, the novelty of the experimentation and the richness of the media. It was successful from the sales angle and many canvases were bought by foreigners. The French surrealist poet Paul Eluard, who at that time had not yet been 'worked on' by his supreme chief André Breton and told to boycott all painting done by me after 1918, had come with his wife from Paris purposely to meet me and at the Biennale had bought various works of mine, including a large self-portrait with a background of laurel bushes.[8] All this was more than enough to create a good deal of envy in Rome, together with vast displays of hostility and boycotting as far as I was concerned. There was honourable competition between Biancale and Emilio Cecchi as to who could write the most maliciously condemnatory article. The competition was won by Emilio Cecchi with an article that was a real masterpiece; failure to understand, confusion, bad faith and envy, blended together in a symphony of such beauty that if it could have been translated into music it would have figured worthily in the programme of those concerts which in Rome today are called *musica viva*, 'live music', but which ought to be called still-born music. I no longer remember in what review or newspaper this article appeared, I only remember that in referring to some of my finest paintings of fruit Cecchi spoke of corpses, cemeteries and things in an advanced state of putrefaction.

I remained indifferent to all this envy and proceeded tirelessly with my technical research. Rome and the surrounding countryside offered me splendid opportunities for study, observation and meditation which I have rediscovered today with so much delight. But as my painting progressed and developed, hostility and hysteria also developed in certain circles. Two years passed, the 1925 Biennale arrived and I exhibited works, again quite different from those I had exhibited two years earlier. There was a silence as of the grave. The intellectuals and the critics had understood that speaking and writing too much and too often about an artist, even speaking ill of him, resulted in giving him publicity. They had understood that in certain cases, particularly in dangerous ones like mine, the only weapon is silence. The result was that throughout the exhibition not even a couple of lines were written about my painting and my name was not even quoted in the lists that are published in the daily papers whenever there is an official exhibition.

Then, on realising that envy had reached this point, I thought that the moment had come for me to break away. A few friends wrote to me from Paris, saying that my work was selling better and better and there was much talk about me in intellectual circles. Naturally all this meant nothing in reality, but at that time I was still somewhat ingenuous and still had certain foolish ideas. One fine day I packed my bags; I packed colours, canvases and brushes, bought a ticket for Paris in the Via Modane, said good-bye to Rome and the Romans. When it is possible to travel again I think that many people will ardently desire (perhaps they are hoping so already) that just as in 1925 I will once again take a ticket for Paris, or some other place, and move away. I am sorry to have to give these gentlemen the bad news that, with God's permission, I have decided to remain and work in Italy and even in Rome. Yes; it is here that I wish to stay and work, to work harder than ever, to work better than ever, to work for my glory and your damnation.

At that time I had begun to paint in oils again. I had given up oil painting for some time. Once during my many stays in Florence between 1919 and 1924, I was copying Michelangelo's *Holy Family* in the Uffizi when I met the Russian painter Nikolai Locoff. He explained to me that many old pictures, which seem to be oil paintings, are in fact varnished oil tempera. Tempera attracted me; I began to look for ways of using this technique and for a few years I painted in tempera.

During my stays in Florence I often lived and worked in the house

of Dr Giorgio Castelfranco. I had known him in Milan, just after
the First World War, and he had bought one of my self-portraits.
Later, Castelfranco bought many of my pictures. I also painted a
very fine double portrait of him and his wife together.

The painter Nikolai Locoff, whom I visited in his studio, showed
me a few copies he had made of works by Botticelli, Masaccio,
Carpaccio, Titian and Rembrandt. I was amazed by the fidelity and
mastery with which these copies were made, but when I tried to ask
Locoff about his methods, or for some clarification of the procedures
and materials he used, he always replied in a confused way verging
more on literature than on concrete talk about painting. On the
other hand I succeeded in learning something more positive from
the Florentine painter Enrico Betterini, who was very experienced in
tempera painting, and I also had a great deal of help from a book
written by a German named Berger, which dealt with Boecklin's
technique. In fact, the great Basle painter always painted in tempera
and researched with passionate application into all the secrets concerning this method of painting.

When I left for Paris in 1925 I had abandoned tempera for about
a year and had returned to oil painting.

I I

I reached Paris in the autumn of 1925. The great orgy of modern painting was raging in the French capital. The dealers had instituted a real dictatorship. It was they who, with their hired art critics, created or destroyed a painter, and that independently of his value as an artist. In this way a dealer, or a group of dealers, could create extremely high prices for the canvases of a painter completely lacking in even the slightest genius, make his name famous in every continent, while they could also boycott, suppress and reduce to poverty an artist of great value. The dealers did all this by taking advantage of the confusion which reigned and unfortunately reigns more than ever in the art world, and by ignominiously exploiting the snobbery and imbecility of a certain category of people. Their clientèle consisted especially of Anglo-Saxons, who were acutely snobbish, and especially of North Americans; their clients also included a few Scandinavians, a few Germans, several Swiss, a few Belgians and a few Japanese. French clients were fairly limited in number, while Spanish and Italians were even fewer. It must be said in our favour and to our credit that these Italians were taken in less than everyone else.

Between the dealers and those who surrounded them existed a real freemasonry with its rites, rules and procedures, which functioned wonderfully well. One famous trick consisted of false auction sales at the Hôtel Drouot. A dealer would decide, for example, that the works of a certain painter, whom he supported, were extremely expensive. He would put one of these paintings up for auction at the Hôtel Drouot, the painting in question usually belonging to a

115

collector who was in league with the dealer. The dealer would send a
few of his own men to the sale and they would push up the price of
the painting, while the dealer would naturally sacrifice a certain sum
to pay the commissions due to the auctioneers. In this way the
impression was given that the picture had sold for a very high price,
while in fact it had not been sold for any price. Then it would be
left lying for a certain time in the back room of the dealer's shop
or in the collector's cellars.

Luxury magazines were paid in order to support a particular
painting or a particular type of painting, and in all this obscene
manoeuvring the only thing never mentioned was the artistic value
of a painting. Never, since the beginning of the world, since men
have exerted themselves drawing, painting, modelling and sculpting,
never, I say, have the highest values of the spirit and the highest
aspirations of mankind, namely art and works of art, reached such a
state and in this way been prostituted and dragged through the mud.
There are two great scandals of our time : the encouragement given
to what is bad in art and the fact that there is no opposition to this
encouragement by any authority, either civil or ecclesiastical. At the
same time there is speculation based on deceit, even on swindling,
which takes advantage of the ignorance, vanity and stupidity of the
men of today. All this had and still has one sole purpose, one sole
motivation : money—to earn money at all costs, to earn it in any
way, under the aegis of a false artistic ideal. I accuse openly and
courageously all the shameful gang who have helped and are still
helping to make painting decline to the point to which it has declined
today. I accuse them today and tomorrow and assume full respon-
sibility for such an accusation. I am sure that the efforts I am making
and perhaps somebody else is making to restore painting to a level
of nobility and dignity, will not be in vain. I am not a theoretician,
nor someone who makes empty speeches; I am speaking like this
because I have studied and examined the problem deeply. Other
people, too, have spoken and written about the decadence of modern
painting, but these are people who understand only up to a certain
point and have not been able to put their finger on the trouble, as I
have been able to. Also, before one really has the right to speak in
such a way one must in the first place be a painter of great intelligence and one must have been capable of painting the paintings
which only I have succeeded in painting in the first half of our
century. The present method of dealing with art, the method used

by fools, thieves and pimps has since spread throughout the entire world, but the origin and centre of it all were in Paris.

Now that I have written frankly what I think of modern painting and of those who have supported it and spread it abroad and are still doing so, I will return to my memories, observations, reflections and personal adventures.

Soon after reaching Paris I found strong opposition from that group of degenerates, hooligans, childish layabouts, onanists and spineless people who had pompously styled themselves *surrealists* and also talked about the 'surrealist revolution' and the 'surrealist movement'. This group of not very worthy individuals was led by a self-styled poet who answered to the name of André Breton and whose aide-de-camp was another pseudo-poet called Paul Eluard, a colourless and commonplace young man with a crooked nose and a face somewhere between that of an onanist and a mystical cretin. André Breton, therefore, was the classic type of pretentious ass and impotent *arriviste*. After the First World War, M. André Breton, together with a few surrealists, had bought at auction sales, for low prices, a certain number of my paintings that I had left in a little studio in Montparnasse when I had gone to Italy. In order to earn the rent, which I had not succeeded in paying during the war, the owner of the studio had sold my paintings, together with a little furniture which had remained there. M. Breton and his acolytes hoped that I would remain in Italy, that I would die in the war, that in some way I would no longer appear on the banks of the Seine, and in this way they would have been able quietly and gradually to pick up all the paintings of mine in Paris, since later, in addition to those which were sent to the saleroom by the owner of the studio, the surrealists acquired paintings of mine even from private individuals, and especially from Paul Guillaume, the man in love with Derain, who stupidly sold them various paintings of mine which I had sold to him between 1913 and 1915. In this way the surrealists had hoped to monopolise my metaphysical painting, which naturally they called surrealist, and then, by means of publicity, articles and a whole system of skilfully organised bluff, they hoped to do what dealers had done earlier with Cézanne, Van Gogh, Gauguin, Douanier Rousseau and Modigliani, known as Modì, that is to sell my paintings at extremely high prices and pocket stacks of money.

My arrival in Paris with a collection of new paintings, my relationships with local dealers and my exhibitions of painting different in type from what they possessed and whose value they inflated, caused confusion in the Breton camp and made a mess of everything. For this reason the surrealists decided to undertake a large-scale boycott of my new output; when, in 1926, I had an exhibition at the Léonce Rosenberg Gallery, they immediately organised, in a shop they had opened in the Rue Jacques Callot, an exhibition of metaphysical paintings of mine which they owned. The exhibition was arranged in the middle of a collection of Negro sculpture and so-called surrealist objects; then they published a catalogue with an utterly silly preface by that same Aragon who now aspires to sit among the Immortals in the Academy. The preface was a kind of libel and consisted more of criticising the paintings I was showing at the Rosenberg Gallery than of praising those shown by the surrealists. They were so persistent, so hysterical in their envy—which resembled that of eunuchs and old maids—that they were not content with boycotting my work in Paris, but organised, through their representatives and agents abroad, large-scale boycotts of my work also in Belgium, Holland, Switzerland, Britain and the United States. Their silliness then reached the point of doing things of this type. When my exhibition at the Rosenberg Gallery and the exhibition of my metaphysical paintings arranged by the surrealists at their gallery in the Rue Jacques Callot opened more or less at the same time, the surrealists organised a kind of parody of the work I was showing at the Rosenberg Gallery in the window of the other one. For example, in order to represent my pictures showing horses by the sea, they had bought in a bazaar some of those little rubber horses which are given to children to play with and had placed them on a little heap of sand, with a few stones round them and a piece of blue paper, presumably the sea. Then, in order to parody the pictures which I called 'furniture in the open', they had shown some of that dolls' furniture which is sold in toyshops. The result, however, was that this parody in the window of the surrealists' gallery provided great publicity for my show at the Rosenberg and I sold many pictures, which gave the pseudo-poet André Breton a liver attack.

In spite of the hysterical envy of the surrealists and the other agitated failures living in the French capital, my new painting aroused great interest, but I cannot say that the intellectuals put themselves out to support it. The only intellectual who supported me at that time with a certain warmth was Jean Cocteau, but I think he did so more to spite the surrealists than for any other reason;

in fact, I realised later that even he was not worth much more than the surrealists. At first the surrealists had been full of envy because Jean had made something of a name for himself in snobbish Parisian circles, but when Cocteau supported my new painting they became absolutely hydrophobic and resorted to methods which could be called sordid and squalid in the worst possible way. For example, they would make anonymous telephone calls in the middle of the night to Cocteau's elderly mother, who was an extremely fine lady, full of good-hearted kindness, in order to tell her that her son had ended up under a motor-car.

Apart from behaving like hooligans and petty delinquents the surrealists also did things which were incredibly funny and diverting. The meetings in Breton's house reached the heights of comedy. Soon after my arrival in Paris, before the surrealists had realised the danger I represented for their dubious projects, that is before their hydrophobia had been fully released, I twice had occasion to attend their gatherings. The guests would arrive at Breton's place about nine in the evening. His place consisted of a vast studio overlooking the Boulevard de Clichy; there were a few bedrooms and every modern comfort Although the surrealists professed unadultered communist and anti-bourgeois feelings they always tried to live as comfortably as possible, dress very well and eat excellent meals washed down with excellent wines; they never gave so much as a centime to a poor man, never lifted a finger in favour of someone who needed material or moral support and above all they worked as little as possible, or not at all.

The gatherings took place in Breton's studio. Here is a description of one of these gatherings at which I was present. Breton's wife and the friends he had invited sat on huge divans in thoughtful, reflective attitudes. The atmosphere reminded me of that of Guillaume Apollinaire's Saturdays which I had attended about ten years earlier, and it was just as much like Balestrieri's famous *Beethoven* which is on show at the Revoltella Museum in Trieste, except that on the walls at Breton's place, instead of Beethoven's mask or *art nouveaux* paintings, hung cubist paintings by Picasso, some metaphysical paintings of mine, Negro masks and paintings and drawings by some obscure surrealist painter whom the owner of the house was trying to launch; in fact, the scene was more or less the same as that in Apollinaire's house. In this atmosphere of false meditation and ostentatious concentration André Breton walked about the studio reading in a sepulchral voice extracts from Lautréamont. He declaimed the foolish remarks by Isidore Ducasse with a severe and inspired expression. On other occasions a new 'turn', a new genius was presented at these gatherings. The evening when I was there two young men who appeared said they lived in the Latin Quarter and were medical students. One of them, the younger, declared that he could draw the portrait of anyone, even from memory, and even if he had never seen them; but his portraits consisted of one eye only, he drew only one eye. The older of the two, who seemed to be the other's manager, turned to those present and asked them to decide whose portrait it should be. A hysterical woman's voice shrilled out: 'We want a portrait of Proust!' The young student immediately sat down at a table; paper, pencil and eraser were brought to him. The other, his friend, motioned to those present to remain silent and to move some distance away in order not to disturb the artist. They all retired respectfully and you could have heard a pin drop in Breton's studio. The young student became withdrawn for a moment and it looked exactly as though he had fallen into a trance; then, with the gestures of a somnambulist, watched over by his companion, he seized the pencil, looking into space, and began to draw. He drew for a few seconds, then put down the pencil and his companion said loudly, 'The portrait is finished!' Everyone rushed forward and they all yelled together: 'It's Proust! It's Proust's eye!' I also went up and saw a kind of eye, drawn from the side, rather like those attempts at drawing done by children; the eye could have belonged just as easily to the President of Nicaragua as to Proust.

The second time that I went to Breton's studio some spiritualist sessions were organised. There was a young man called Desnos who was considered the medium *par excellence* of the company. He would pretend to fall into a trance and would then begin to recite silly verses, of which this is a sample:

Fertile migrations towards horrible seashores!
I have seen the ants migrating!
Come and remove from the faithless stirrup
The evening's encounter with flesh that is rotting!

And so on, always in the same vein. Breton would give orders and issue instructions; scribes and stenographers would rush up with

paper and shorthand pens so that they would not lose a single word
of all the idiocies which the pseudo-medium rattled off.

I learnt later that in Breton's studio punitive expeditions were
sometimes launched against the St-Sulpice district, which is the
Catholic quarter of Paris, where there were many religious bookshops
and many shops selling sacred images. In Paris there were two forms
of snobbery, especially among certain literati. One consisted of
making Catholics, and so for certain literati the so-called Catholic
crisis was a classic event, and did not happen even on purpose, but
always when the reputation of the writer in question was very low.
The other form of snobbery, which was precisely that of the surrealists, consisted of making atheists and anti-clericals. In those days
in Paris there lived a strange type of priest, probably slightly
unbalanced, who from time to time went down from the St-Sulpice
district to cause scandals on the Grands Boulevards and tear up
magazines such as *La Vie Parisienne*, *Le Rire* and others on sale at
the kiosks, because he considered them dangerous for the morals of
good Christians. Naturally, the owner of the kiosks would protest
and wanted the priest to pay him for the magazines he had torn up,
but instead of money he received only inspired speeches on the
decadence and immorality of our times. In the end a policeman
would come up and take the moralising priest and the owner of the
kiosks to the nearest police station. Whenever one of these scandals
caused by the above-mentioned priest came to the ears of André
Breton he would immediately order the young Desnos, who was
ready to do anything for the triumph of surrealism, to go to the
St-Sulpice district and tear up religious reviews and newspapers in
the kiosks.

Then there was a poet called Benjamin Péret whose complete
works consisted of four lines only with the title 'Asleep'. Here are
the four unique lines by this fertile poet : 'What can you see?'/
'Water.'/'What colour is this water?'/'Water.'

Jean Cocteau supported my painting and wrote a book about it
called *Le mystère laïc* [The Lay Mystery]. I illustrated this book with
a few drawings. I am very grateful to Jean Cocteau for the interest
he has shown in me, but I must say that I do not in fact approve the
kind of praise he accords me and the interpretation he likes to put
on my pictures. Moreover, I have always found myself in the difficult
position of having to side against even my friends, even those few
who have said and still say nice things about my painting, not in a

tendentious way and free of the innuendoes or maliciousness of many
people in Italy and also outside it, especially in the United States
I must unfortunately and most regretfully say this, because even
many people who are favourably disposed towards me do no
understand anything about my painting.

The orgasmic saturnalia in the modern painting market in Pari
reached its climax in the year of grace, 1929. The collectors seemed
insatiable; galleries sprang up like mushrooms. Not a day passed
without some new gallery being inaugurated and they all resembled
each other like Siamese twins. It was always the same thing: a
window draped with grey fabric; a room, or a small room, also
draped with grey fabric; in the window and the rooms were the
usual daubs by modern painters, fixed in stripped wooden frames
with *passe-partout*, also covered with grey fabric, and in the case o
the better paintings, with silk. The dealers paid painters in advance
for pictures they had not yet begun to paint. Every device was utilised
to launch new 'geniuses'. Diaghilev, the balletomane, invited the
better-known painters to execute scenery and costumes. I too was
invited to collaborate in a ballet entitled *Le Bal*, set to music by the
composer Rietti. This ballet was put on in Monte Carlo in the spring
of 1929 and in the summer at the Théâtre Sarah Bernhardt. It was
very successful; at the end of the ballet the audience applauded and
began to shout '*Sciricò! Sciricò!*' I had to come on stage to thank
them, together with Rietti and the principal dancers. While leaving
the theatre I met the industrialist Gualino, who was accompanied,
I believe, by his wife. Professor Lionello Venturi was also with him.
They had been present at the performance and I thought, logically,
that Signor Gualino wished, as would have been natural, to con-
gratulate me and rejoice with me over the success of my scenery and
costumes. Instead, Signor Gualino said nothing whatever about my
work but stood there and began to declaim in an emotional voice a
dithyrambic poem of praise by Felice Casorati. I stood there for a
time listening courteously, but seeing that the dithyrambic praise
continued, and aware that my mother, my brother and my sister-in-
law were waiting for me with a group of friends, I made my excuses,
said good-bye to the Casorati eulogist and left. But in my mind,
through the association of memories, I thought of Paul Guillaume
and his crazy love for Derain.

But all these successes satisfied me only partially and my conscience
as a painter was not very clear. I returned to the study of truth and at

this period painted a whole series of nudes and still lifes. Through their plastic power some of these paintings are among the best of all my work. Many paintings of this period were acquired by the collector Albert Borel, brother-in-law of the Rosenberg brothers. M. Albert Borel, although he lived in Paris and was related to two dealers in modern painting, was totally devoid of any form of snobbery, he understood painting and loved it sincerely; in fact, he was one of the very few normal and interesting men whom I met in Paris.

At that time came the first warnings and first punishment that the Universal Genius sent to stupid men, who had profaned the sacred world of art (I admit here that I am imitating the grand style of Isabella Far). The collapse of the New York Stock Exchange had automatic repercussions in Paris; the dealers put up their shutters. No trickery, no freemasonry, no bluff, no secret society could maintain prices. The Americans, and foreigners in general, came no more and the legendary avarice of the French strongly asserted itself. 'The crisis has come! And this is only a beginning! We shall have to tighten our belts!'

Some painters had not thought of saving, or had not been able tc
save during the years of plenty, and when they heard these word
their teeth began to chatter, as though they had been stricken witl
an attack of malaria, while cold shudders ran down their shoulder
to their ankles. Everywhere there was an atmosphere of alarm
diffidence and discouragement; rumours of catastrophe circulated
the canvases of this or that famous and high-priced painter were o1
sale, with their frames, for ridiculous sums. Naturally, those who ha(
earned a lot and had had time to tuck away a nice little nest-eg{
tried to assume the attitudes of men who had risen above ever
calamity; they pretended to be indifferent, but in fact it was clea
that they too were making the best of a bad job.

During that period of chaos and general consternation, howeve1
I encountered great good fortune and great happiness : that of know
ing Isabella Far, the most profoundly intelligent person I have me
in all my life. Until then the most intelligent people I remembe
were the Greek architect Pikionis, whom I had known in Greece a
a boy and whom I met again in Paris later, and my brother Alber
Savinio, whom I have known as far back as I can remember. I mus
say, however, without giving offence to the two aforementione(
intelligent people, that in the intelligence of Isabella Far I foun(
something more profound and more positive.

The only country in Europe which during this period of crisis stil
kept a certain interest in painting was Italy, since Italy is the onl·
country where there are still a few people who love painting *sincerel)*
I remember that in 1931 I came to Milan to exhibit at the Barbarou
Gallery and sold almost all the paintings I showed. While in othe.

countries the snobbery and dictatorship imposed by the art dealers had raged for nearly half a century, in Italy there are still people who buy a picture not because they have been skilfully talked into it by a dealer, or because the painter is known and they hope to make a good investment, but simply because *they like the picture*. Things have happened to me in Italy which have never happened to me in any other country. In Milan an old servant told me that she had a small sum saved up and that she would give it to me in exchange for what she wanted; I refused the money and made her a present of a drawing. In Florence, during one of my exhibitions, I happened to sell a picture to a gentleman who had never heard my name mentioned; this gentleman also asked me to paint a portrait of his wife. These things reveal the mentality of a nation and show what it is like in comparison with others, since, as I have already said, such things have never happened to me in Paris, London or New York.

From Milan I returned with Isabella to Florence, where I passed a year of intense work. I exhibited at the Palazzo Ferroni, in an art gallery opened at that time by the antique dealer Luigi Bellini who, during the period and also later, showed a great deal of interest in me and was very friendly towards me. Then we returned to Milan; I still continued my research into technique assisted by Isabella Far, whose intuition concerning painting has always been very valuable to me. Nobody is as successful as she is in assessing at first glance both the qualities and defects of a picture. I remember that once, I believe it was in 1933, we had gone to Genoa for a one-man show of mine. During our stay in the Ligurian capital I painted various views of the harbour; one day I wanted to paint a panoramic view of Genoa and the harbour seen from above, from the castle. The weather was cloudy and when we reached the castle it began to rain slightly. I settled down as best I could, with my box of colours between my legs, but I had to work fast. I crouched down in a way that made it difficult for me to stand up and move back to see my work from a distance; but Isabella came to my rescue; she sat behind me holding an umbrella and told me how I should proceed. 'The shadow on the left should be darker,' she told me. 'That sail should be level with the last house on the left; make the grey-purple of the ground a little faded,' and so on. After about three hours of uninterrupted work I was able to stand up, and as I moved aside with stiff legs I saw that this painting was more successful than any I had painted so far on the spot.

This little masterpiece, which I am sorry not to have kept, wa:
bought in Rome at the 1934 Quadriennale by a gentleman from
Padua whose name, however, I do not recall. Now I wonder, dea
reader, what kind of painting would have emerged if Isabella Fa
had not been behind me to guide and advise me, if instead there
had been one of those literary and intellectual women, of whom there
are large numbers both in Italy and other countries?

A few months later I returned to Turin where I had a one-mai
show in a gallery. During my stay in Turin I met Romano Gazzera
one of the few painters of talent whom I have known in my life. The
others, in chronological order are : Kanzikis, Picasso, Derain, de Pisis
Annigoni, Sciltian, Aldo Carfi and the Bueno brothers; there migh
also be the woman painter Felicita Fray, who has been a student o
mine, but I have seen none of her work for a few years and befor
putting her among the good ones I would need to see somethin;
recent. I hope she is still painting well and that she has not take
a wrong turning.*

Romano Gazzera at that time was still a lawyer, but when I sav
some of his paintings and drawings in his house I immediatel
realised that this was a man of genius with a great understanding o
painting. I told him that he must definitely give up his professio
as a lawyer and dedicate himself to painting.

In 1933 I was invited to Florence to design costumes and scener
for Vincenzo Bellini's opera *I Puritani*, which was due to be produce
during the *Maggio musicale*. The première caused a complet
scandal. During this period of the *Maggio musicale* I wanted t
hold an exhibition of my most recent works in Florence. The directo
of the paper *La Nazione* had a room on the premises which he kep
for art exhibitions and suggested that my exhibition should be hel
in his room. However, I wanted to exhibit at the Palazzo Ferron
since this gallery belonged to one of my good friends, the antiqu
dealer Luigi Bellini, who was also my host. In order to have hi
revenge for the fact that I had not exhibited in the newspaper offic
room, the director gave orders that my sets and costumes should b
booed during the show and later ridiculed and attacked in the new:
paper by the official critics; naturally, large troops of volunteer
composed of painters and intellectuals, spontaneously offered th

---

* I have learnt recently that Felicita Fray is painting better than befoi
and *ipso facto* I put her among the good ones.

director some help in his noble vendetta.

In spite of all this organised hostility my work was very successful and caused much interest. Max Reinhardt, the famous German producer, who was present at the première of *I Puritani*, was so enthusiastic about my scenery and costumes that he suggested I should go with him the following month to London to design scenery and costumes for Shakespeare plays which he was due to stage in the British capital. However, I declined the invitation politely, because *entre nous*, all this type of thing did not suit me and suits me now less than ever.

At this period I executed a large mural painting at the Palazzo della Triennale in Milan. I executed it very quickly and in extremely difficult circumstances, using the egg tempera process, and this painting cost me in eggs alone the sum of 150 lire. I had to cover a vast wall with paint. My work was a great success and its effect very beautiful, in spite of the fact that the painter Sironi had put in front of it some gigantic cubist-type chandeliers which looked like colossal geysers, and on top of everything else had placed opposite the middle of my fresco a mosaic by Severini which looked completely out of keeping. This mural painting of mine gave rise to much envy; it was not reproduced in the newspapers or even in the illustrated leaflets which were on sale at the exhibition and included instead the paintings of Campigli, Funi and Sironi. After the exhibition had closed all the paintings in this room were destroyed, probably because they did not dare, owing to possible scandal, to destroy only mine.

I began to realise once again that Italy was becoming intolerable for me. In addition, for personal reasons also, life in Italy became difficult for me; I realised that it would be a good thing to cut the cord once again. I decided to return to Paris. There the situation had become even worse; the dealers who had more or less supported me earlier, when business was flourishing, had ceased all activity. Paul Guillaume, who died a year later, and Léonce Rosenberg were trying to sell off the pictures they still had in stock. Georges Bernheim was no longer in the art world but in the cinema, and Van Lear had emigrated to London. In spite of this disastrous situation I continued to perfect my research into technique. Especially in the field of priming methods I made great progress, assisted by Isabella's brilliant intuition, since she helped me with her exceptional ratiocination to resolve the problems and difficulties presented by rebellious and hostile material. With Isabella I spent whole afternoons at the Bibliothèque Nationale searching in old treatises and writings on painting which had appeared at times when people still knew how to paint, for the secrets and forgotten knowledge of the art of the brush. I also came to know restorers, students of technique, among whom was the painter Maroger, who at that time had given lectures on technique and had put on the market a medium sold in small tubes bearing his name. I sent various canvases, the fruit of those years of intense work and continued research, to the Quadriennale of 1934, where I was invited to exhibit in one room on my own. Then as now my painting caused the usual degree of envy in Rome. There were the usual campaigns in the press, the usual perseverance in attacking me. Two canvases caused more anger than any others: one of my big paintings which showed a few bathers on a beach and a large portrait of myself in my Paris studio with my palette and brushes in my hands, standing at the easel. In order to give the final touch to the wave of hysterical anger caused by the exceptional quality of my paintings among critics, painters and intellectuals, the prize of a hundred thousand lire was given unanimously to Severini, and a few critics extended bad faith and shamelessness to writing in the papers that in Paris the best-known and appreciated Italian painter was Severini.

In spite of the tide of jealous hostility I sold a few pictures at this exhibition and my room was the one which caused the greatest interest among visitors. I was also told by people on the spot that on the opening day Mussolini stopped in front of some of my paintings, praising them and showing great interest; but he was immediately removed, as it were, and taken into another room by the people surrounding him. In Paris, just as in Rome, the surrealists' envy of me *battait son plein*; the art dealers with whom I had been in touch before the economic crisis had, as I said earlier, suspended all activity and as a result the surrealists, suspecting that I was in a difficult situation, rubbed their hands with glee, increased the boycott and defamation of my painting and said to each other with satisfaction, 'Let's finish him off this time!' They were beginning to beat the big drum round the paintings of that dismal pseudo-painter who answers to the name of Salvador Dali and who, after having imitated Picasso, had begun to imitate my metaphysical paintings which he had not understood at all, and a man like him could not possibly have understood them. These paintings have only been understood so far by two or three people in the world and I could not even swear to that. Salvador Dali is the anti-painter *par excellence*; even in appearance, even in name. Those horrible surfaces on which he traces horrible, copiously varnished colours, the mere sight of which causes nausea and painters' colic, have been imitated by others of the same species who, in their turn, imitate him as well as they can and their painting, to say the least, should be referred to the Ministry of Health. Salvador Dali, who is now in the United States, is forced (in order to arouse a little interest in his painting, which basically nobody likes) to create scandals in the most clumsy, grotesque and provincial way imaginable and in this way succeeds more or less in attracting the attention of certain transatlantic imbeciles consumed with boredom and snobbery; but it looks now as though even these imbeciles have begun to have enough of it.

13

I was disgusted by the low level, material and moral, to which painting in Paris had sunk. I therefore followed the advice of a friend and after a short rest in Tuscany I had a certain number of canvases packed up and left for New York.

I embarked one August morning, at Genoa, on the liner *Roma*. It was infernally hot and the liner was like an enormous floating boiler. In addition, the continual motion of the ship made me terribly ill. I was also very depressed in myself. Isabella had not been able to leave with me. On the boat were many parties of young Americans returning home from holidays in Europe and they made an infernal din; these noisy young people caused a good deal of disturbance and all this increased my physical and moral discomfort. The voyage from Genoa to New York has remained in my mind as one of the worst memories of my life. Finally, after nine days of pitching and tossing and the deafening noise made by the young Yankees, we arrived in New York; the sea was soapy and warm, the light that of a greenhouse or aquarium, the temperature equal to that of a Turkish bath, and I was dead tired. I was so impatient to reach the end of this infernal trip that I had not been able to sleep during the night before arrival and spent the entire time on deck. With the first light of morning the skyscrapers of Wall Street appeared on the horizon; I thought of Babylon and of certain archaeological reconstructions modelled in plaster of Paris I had seen in a museum in Germany.

A damp heat, a tropical, mineshaft heat, hung over the oily water in the harbour. The sun could not be seen; men and objects had lost their shadows; a diffused light, as though we were in a photographer's studio at the end of the last century, hung over everything. After the interminable formalities of passports, visas, interrogations, customs and even a medical examination, I succeeded in leaving the floating boiler. On the quay, in an atmosphere saturated with strange odours, Isabella's aunt and uncle, a lady and gentleman whom I had met in Paris, were waiting for me. Meeting these two people, who were so noble, cordial and understanding, consoled and encouraged me greatly. I had barely set foot on American soil when I felt a great nostalgia for Europe, for any European country whatsoever, even for the least beautiful, even for the least interesting. It was strange how in the city of New York I felt I had died and been born again on another planet. Those smooth, monotonous buildings, from which protruded no balcony, no capital or column, no cornice, no ornament, no pole or nail, alarmed me greatly. I thought with nostalgia of the warmth and humanity of the baroque style, the Second Empire style, and even the Umbertino style and *art nouveau*. I consoled myself by remembering that I had come there for my work, for my paintings; I thought that Isabella would soon join me and that I must busy myself in particular with my exhibitions and that afterwards I would be back in that old, harassed, awkward but, all things considered, pleasing Europe.

Later I discovered in New York a certain beauty, a certain metaphysic, but I will speak of this another time.

I came to know a few art dealers and realised that there also, as in Paris, the disgraceful totalitarianism of those who trafficked in painting still persisted. Among those I met was Mr Julian Levy, who was the classic type of good, well-educated American Jew and who, among all the art dealers I met in New York, Americans, Frenchmen, Germans and Poles, seemed to me the most honest and intelligent and, although in his gallery he often exhibited the 'daubs' of the modern painters, he was the least intellectual and the least snobbish of all of them. It was decided that Julian Levy would hold an exhibition of my work at the end of October. In the meantime I met Dr Barnes, whom I had known in Paris and who owned twenty-five of my paintings, including a portrait of him which I had painted during one of his many stays in the French capital. Dr Barnes had a passionate love of painting and near Philadelphia, at a place called Merion, he has founded a type of museum where all the paintings he bought in Paris have been put together. Dr Barnes has a way of treating people which has given rise to the legend that his museum contains extraordinary works, works which have never been seen, paintings which would send into ecstasies even people who were quite accustomed to living among masterpieces. In reality his museum includes merely the paintings that everyone can see in Paris by taking a walk along the Rue de La Boétie and the Rue de Seine. The usual ridiculous Cézannes, the usual badly painted and formless Matisses, the usual Braques, flat and deceptively decorative, etc. : a few good Picassos, a few good Renoirs and a few good Derains. In addition, he possesses twenty-five paintings of mine carried out between 1914 and 1934. Among the old paintings is one attributed to Giorgione and another attributed to Titian; however, the most interesting old painting among the few old ones in the Barnes' museum, and the one which I as a painter found most moving, was a small portrait by Goya. In addition, on the walls of the museum can be seen paintings which look like frescoes by Matisse and seem to be frescoes when you first look at them, but I believe that they are canvases stuck on to the walls, and they are the most insipid, silly, vacuous and grotesque paintings that I have ever seen.

The method used by Dr Barnes to attract the attention of his contemporaries towards his museum consists in being as contrary and misanthropic as humanly possible; it is the same method, with a few variations, as that of Derain. Special permits have to be obtained to visit the Barnes' museum; there are some imbeciles who even make the journey from other American cities, a whole day by rail away from Philadelphia, in order to visit the museum, after interviews, telephone calls and long waits. Many people return home having failed in their purpose, after a categoric refusal from the Doctor. There is no doubt, as Renan says, that the stupidity of mankind is as infinite as the universe, otherwise there is no explanation as to why people apparently of sound mind will go to so much trouble and make so many efforts to see one of those pictures which can be seen in any gallery or at any dealer's in Europe and the States. One need only tell the Americans that at the Metropolitan Museum in New York and at the Frick Gallery in the same city they can see such collections and such quantities of masterpieces that a hundred Barnes' put together, collecting paintings for a whole century, could not have exhibited even half as many.

In the meantime autumn came; Julian Levy's gallery had inaugurated my exhibition which had achieved an outstanding success;
various paintings were sold; dollars poured in; I opened a current
account with the Chemical Bank and Trust Company. After the
pettiness, avarice and meanness of Paris during the crisis period I
confess that although I have never been mercenary, the receipt of
this money did in fact give me a certain pleasure and a certain sense
of security. In the meantime Isabella had arrived from Europe and
I had begun to work again. Life rushed by; for me it was not the
ideal life but in fact I worked and when I work I am always more or
less calm and happy. Some magazines, including *Vogue* and *Harper's
Bazaar*, asked me for illustrations and I did some, but I must confess
that the atmosphere of these magazines, just like other atmospheres
where the snobbery of American elegance flourished, were totally
unpleasing to me, for I have observed in them such stupidity, such
ignorance, such ill-will, such cynicism and such disguised vulgarity
that in comparison the lowest illiterate Neapolitan beggar, thief and
pimp seems a genius, a gentleman and a saint.

Winter passed and spring passed. Summer came, the terrible
American summer. Since I had agreed to hold another exhibition,
again in Julian Levy's gallery, in the following autumn, Isabella and
I decided to remain in the States. The heat, however, was suffocating
and we sought a little coolness by a strange beach called Oyster Bay.
This place was a few miles from New York; we left by train and
arrived at a place where we took a kind of mail coach or bus which
went to our holiday destination. I had rented a bungalow there, a
small villa built of wood and consisting of a ground floor and a first
floor. The beach was very ugly : not a single rock or a single villa.
For ugliness it even surpassed the beach between Poveromo and
Forte dei Marmi, which is saying a lot. Strangely shaped trees, which
I believe no professor of botany would have succeeded in classifying,
were scattered here and there, as though by mistake. We lived a
monotonous life by the sea, in a humid, colonial heat. We passed
most of the day on the beach, lying in the sun and sometimes going
into the water. When I lay on my back I made drawings, in order to
keep my hand in, of the bathers who surrounded me. At night we
were disturbed by the shrill sound of some kind of nocturnal crickets
which made an infernal din from a kind of tree which local people
said were oaks; in fact, the ground beneath the trees was covered
with acorns, but the trees bore no more resemblance to oaks

than does a sewing machine to a lightning conductor.

Autumn came. The atmosphere (in a metaphorical sense) of autumn
in New York has nothing in common with the classic atmosphere of
the good old autumn sung by the poets and writers of our dear old
Europe during the last century. No leaves falling, no melancholy,
memories, yearning and nostalgia for the villas and castles left
behind and the abandoned beaches; nothing; *adieu vive clarté de nos
étés trop courts*![1] No heartbroken accents of the romantic poets. If
Victor Hugo had lived in New York he would never have been able
to write those beautiful lines:

> *Quand novembre de brume inonde le ciel bleu,*
> *Que le vent tourbillonne et qu'il neige des feuilles,*
> *O ma muse en mon âme alors tu te recueilles,*
> *Comme un enfant transi qui s'approche de feu.*[2]

Even less, O reader, will you find in New York, in autumn, that
ineffable melancholy, that strange, distant and profound poetry that
Nietzsche discovered in the clear autumn afternoons, especially when
they lie over certain Italian cities such as Turin.

During autumn in New York you are either oppressed by the
duration of the damp heat, or you are subjected to cyclones with
downpours of torrential rain which are reminiscent of certain old
American films, and galoshes, umbrellas and raincoats with hoods
are powerless against them.

I came back to exhibit at the Julian Levy gallery; I had worked
hard during that year in the States. I had made progress with my
research into technique and I had perfected the preparation of
primings. Many works which I exhibited on this second occasion
were superior as regards quality of painting and plastic power to
those shown at my first exhibition; the critics took an interest and
several articles appeared, not very intelligent but fairly favourable,
together with reproductions of my paintings, in the magazines and
newspapers.

Naturally the critics, as always and as in every country, had
understood nothing of the *quality* of my pictures and spoke only
about the subject-matter. In the meantime I had begun to tire of
the States. During my stay there, in July 1936 to be precise, I received

the very sad news that my dear mother had died. A few months previously my brother had written that our mother's health was declining, and the feeling that I was at that time so far away from her, with that vast ocean between, made me very sad. One night I had a dream; I dreamt that I was in Greece, in the countryside near Athens; I saw those trees and bushes which I had seen during my childhood, and the place where I found myself in my dream was somewhere I once went to paint a landscape with a friend of my own age. In my dream I saw the olives and pine trees just as I had seen them in my distant childhood, and between the trees I saw the back of a little church painted pink, with its small apse jutting out and a door at the side, just as I had painted them so many years before. Suddenly my mother appeared among the olives and walked towards the little church. I wanted to go and meet her, but I could not move; I wanted to call out to her, but my voice failed me; my heart filled with worry and anguish. I saw my mother, who seemed very old, small, bent, weak and unsteady on her feet, just as I remembered her from the last time I had seen her in Paris. I saw my mother pass like a shadow near the apse of the little church, come up to the side door and then disappear. I woke up troubled and weeping and with the terrible thought that my mother had died just at that moment: in fact, when ten days later I read the letter from my brother in which he told me that our mother was alive no longer, I compared the date of the letter with that of my dream and, taking into account the difference in time between the United States and Europe, I realised that *this was really the case.*

14

We decided to return to Italy. The famous liner *Rex* was due to sail for Naples in early January 1937 and we embarked on her. Before I went on board someone, and may God bless him, advised me to guard against seasickness by buying a product called Vasano, which consisted of pills to be taken during the voyage. I was sceptical, but the recollection of what I had suffered during the trip from Genoa to New York induced me to buy the Vasano pills and I immediately took two of them as soon as I had boarded the ship. I can truthfully say that this product is wonderful. During the whole trip the sea was very rough and the liner rolled heavily; at night I had to fasten myself to the mattress with blankets, otherwise I would have been thrown out of my bunk. I was often awakened by the sound of baggage and other objects rolling noisily round the cabin floor. In spite of all this I did not suffer from seasickness; I had an appetite, did a few drawings, made many notes and read a very fine novel by Gerolamo Rovetta titled *Le lacrime degli altri*. This novel is much despised today by the intellectuals and snobs, who prefer to read the boring tirades and the pretentious, empty and long-winded work of a James Joyce or a Paul Valéry.

We crossed the ocean. One night the liner stopped; I went on deck and through the darkness I could see the imposing outline of the rock of Gibraltar, with lights showing all over it. We had reached the entrance to the Mediterranean. This crossing was dear to Nietzsche and the modern intellectuals have produced many silly descriptions of it, but it was even rougher than that of the Atlantic. There was more pitching than tossing, and as everyone knows the former is very dangerous for those who suffer from seasickness. Fortunately I still had some Vasano pills and they were still very effective.

I reached Naples in good shape.

After the usual formalities with papers, customs, etc., had been gone through again we went to Rome. We stayed a few days in the capital, but during this short period I received news about the underground work that the usual eternally jealous people had carried out against me, during my absence, with truly admirable zeal. In Rome they had created the impression that I was anti-Italian and as a result I was never given any prizes at the official exhibitions, while in general I was not able to benefit from even a minute share of all the money that the fascist government distributed so generously to painters and sculptors; the only result was an alarming increase in the already large amount of ugly sculpture and ugly painting. Then the news reached me from Milan that in the Lombardy capital the Milione Gallery, directed by the Ghiringhelli brothers, had started to boycott my painting on a large scale, attempting to distract the attention of the collectors, and of the public in general, from what I was doing then. They emphasised the metaphysical paintings and even the non-metaphysical, whichever I was not doing at that time, and, provided they were not paintings which belonged to me, they tried to cause trouble for me and cut the ground from under my feet. The Ghiringhelli brothers were assisted by many volunteers who gave their services with an ardour worthy of a better cause. The Ghiringhelli brothers took a lot of trouble to persuade the people of Milan that the works they owned were the best I had ever painted. According to them they were the cream of my production, together with the works owned by those collectors who were linked to the Ghiringhelli brothers for reasons of personal interest and therefore helped them in their tendentious activity. They did all this in the same style as the Paris clique, and in particular the surrealist clique.

I realised immediately that I had to take strong action at once. I left for Milan. When I arrived I saw at once that what I had been told was unfortunately true. In Milan I again met Vittorio Barbaroux who straight away offered to hold an exhibition of my recent paintings in his gallery. Vittorio Barbaroux is an energetic and intelligent man whom I have known for a long time. Although he is of Piedmontese origin (a descendant of the noble and historic family of the counts of Barbaroux) he is a pure Milanese and he has all the energy, quickness and clarity of mind, as well as the kind, gentlemanly nature of the pure Milanese. He has no manias, he is not in league with any artistic or intellectual cliques, he does not allow himself to be influenced by snobs and understands painting much better than the people who meditate in the pages of *Verve* and *Minotaure*.

I had brought a few pictures back from the United States, which I left at the Barbaroux Gallery before going to Paris to collect others. These pictures included works from all periods. I immediately noticed that as soon as the paintings were in the Barbaroux Gallery all the people who saw them, before they even looked at any one painting, peered at the canvas to see whether there was a date on it and what the date was. If there was no date they asked with much ado the approximate period in which the painting had been done. These were the immediate effects of the despicable and malicious campaign started by the Milione Gallery. For the people who had been influenced by this campaign the picture had to be as old as possible. Although these were Italians, and Milanese in particular, this snobbery, stupidity and maliciousness, based on boycotting and money, were successful to some extent.

With Isabella I left for Paris, where I hoped to recover some of my pictures which I had left there before going to the States. In Paris I found the commercial situation in the art world slightly improved; not that fortunes were being made there, but in fact after the big international exhibition of 1937 some activity had been developing, due more to the visits of foreigners of all nationalities than to the French themselves, who were still as uncompromisingly mean and took meanness to its furthest limits, except as far as food is concerned, for in that respect the French forget to be mean. When it is a question of the famous rump steak with fried potatoes, which in many Parisian restaurants consists usually of a piece of bloody, limp and rubbery meat which cannot even be cut by a freshly sharpened English razor-blade, the Frenchman reasons no longer and forgets his meanness. And as for the potatoes which garnish the limp rump steak, they consist of a quartered potato, cut into at least fifty pieces and fried in tallow fat. The garnish of this dainty morsel is always completed by a little watercress, which consists of a small bunch of little green leaves, all covered with drops of dirty water. But as I have already said, when it is a question of rump steak with fried potatoes the Frenchman forgets to be mean and willingly loosens his purse-strings.

I returned to Milan with various paintings and began to work again. About two months later I prepared for the Barbaroux Gallery an exhibition of over thirty selected paintings, many of them very recent and embodying the results of that technical research on the value of materials, the quality of pictorial texture, the fluidity and firmness of brushwork, the research that I carried out then and which I still carry out and in which Isabella Far, with her brilliant intuition and exceptional ratiocination, gives me valuable assistance.

The exhibition at the Barbaroux Gallery was very successful; many pictures were sold and most of them belonged, to the fury of the Ghiringhellis and their followers, to the recent period. This was the first blow directed against the Milione Gallery.

After the exhibition we returned to Paris. In spite of the success of my exhibition and the high sales potential I had in Italy, I was slightly disillusioned. When I returned from the United States I had hoped I could start a movement to regenerate painting in our country; I knew that in Italy there were more serious people and much less snobbery than in the other countries; I knew that in Italy there were painters full of talent and good will: Pietro Annigoni and Romano Gazzera. I thought it would be a good thing to have a group of students and teach them what I had learnt during long years of hard work and to let them benefit from those technical and philosophical discoveries concerning painting. On the philosophical side the discoveries were partly mine, but mainly those of Isabella Far. I hoped, as I said, I could achieve all these fine things because I knew that, apart from the few outstanding people, there were young, even very young people, full of talent, but who, owing to lack of will power, had soon allowed themselves to be influenced and led astray by the destructive operations of snobs and intellectuals. For this reason I applied to the minister Bottai to be given a teaching post in an academy, in Milan or in Rome. In order to bring home to the minister that my purpose was entirely idealistic, artistic and patriotic, I told him that if necessary I would teach even without receiving a salary. At that time Bottai did not hesitate to appoint teachers at the Accademia del Regno, most of whom were illiterate bunglers as far as painting was concerned, but he received me coldly; he remained standing, for he was afraid that if he sat down and invited me to sit down I would have stayed too long. He tried to talk without saying anything, and without making me any clear and precise answer he gave me to understand that no appointment was possible and that I should give up all hope of teaching painting in the Italian Academy.

This same Bottai was the protector of all the illiterate people in the art world and a strong supporter of all imbecility and snobbery of the Parisian type. He caused my work to be boycotted in the review *Primato* (which was really outstanding for its stupidity and provincialism) by the usual methods employed by the surrealists, the Ghiringhelli brothers and other individuals of the same type.

At that time I once went in Milan to see a medium called Morosini who, after going into a trance, would read a person's present, past and future. He had barely gone into his trance when he said these very words : 'My son, you are one of the most envied men in the world !' The words of the medium Morosini often come into my mind.

It was early summer, 1938; I had gone to Paris where I held an exhibition of gouaches in a gallery on the Left Bank. This exhibition also was a great success and many gouaches were sold; remarkably enough some of these gouaches were bought on this occasion by French collectors. At the same time the Lefevre Gallery in London, a more serious and less futile place than most of the galleries showing modern painting, gave a one-man show of my recent paintings and I went to London myself, also because I had done sketches of scenery and costumes for a ballet with music by Debussy, which was to be produced at Covent Garden.[1] I reached London on a Sunday; it was near the end of June and the city was bathed in the stagnant heat of a summer's day. London in summer is extraordinarily metaphysical; Jules Verne has expressed magnificently, but perhaps unconsciously, the metaphysical quality of London, when he described Phileas Fogg's return to the capital after his adventurous trip round the world in eighty days. Phileas Fogg, with his faithful servant Passepartout and the beautiful Indian girl, also arrived in London on a Sunday afternoon. During my stay in London I lived through hours of profound metaphysical sensation, especially on Sunday afternoons when I went for walks alone, alongside the Thames, stopping by the offices of shipping companies, and so-called export-import concerns; I stopped also by shops selling canned foods, lines and equipment for deep-sea fishing. As I walked along I thought of my father, my mother, my distant childhood, of so many things which still follow me through life with the silent beating of the wings of memory.

The exhibition at the Lefevre Gallery was in fact a great success and various canvases were sold. Now, dear reader, you will begin to think that perhaps I exaggerate when I say that all my exhibitions in Milan, Paris and London were very successful and that I had sold several pictures at them; but after all, in the life of a man as in that of a nation, there are ups and downs; this was a period when things went well for me.

The good Londoners were beginning to realise that in addition to the usual horrors of modern painting and the stupidity of that still-born painting which is called surrealist, there is also another kind of painting, the fruit of real talent, real intelligence, and of a man's regular and daily work, and which, as Isabella Far says with such profundity, is inspired and assisted by the Universal Genius. There is, as I say, this other kind of painting which is *painting*, and when someone acquires an example of it he can take it home with a light heart, his head high and his conscience clear, for it is something which he sincerely likes and he knows that it will be liked too by his wife, his children, his friends, his parents, his servants, in fact by everyone, and he knows that if one day he, or his children, or his nephews, or even his most remote descendants might want to sell this picture, they will always find someone to buy it, because it is good and the sale will bring them a sumptuous profit.

The ballet at Covent Garden was very successful, and as I had done so many years before at the Théâtre Sarah Bernhardt in Paris, I had to come on stage to acknowledge the applause, holding the prima ballerina's damp fingers in my right hand and the equally damp fingers of the *premier danseur* in my left. That evening I was invited to supper at the Savoy, the smartest hotel in London.

London is a very pleasing city; from various points of view I prefer it to Paris; but I missed Italy; I wanted to return to Milan and Isabella, for when she is not there people and things seem to lose all meaning and interest for me, as the world appeared to D'Annunzio after the death of Wagner, at least so the poet says.

I left for Milan. I crossed the Channel on the usual steamer, but fortunately the sea was calm; then came the train journey to Paris. In Paris I had dinner in a restaurant while reading *L'Intransigeant*. Now, in order not to shed the habit of imitating Paris, we have a paper in Rome called *L'Intransigente*. After dinner I went to sleep

in the room I had booked by telegraph from London at the Victoria
Palace Hôtel which, as I have already said in this book, is one of
the best hotels in Paris, perhaps the best.

The next day, at the Gare de Lyon, I took my seat in a train going
direct to Milan and the same evening I reached the pleasing city
of *risotto*, *pannetone* and collectors of painting.

In Milan too the heat was no joke. The art dealers had closed
their shops, partly because of the heat and partly because their clients
had left with their families for the lakes, the mountains and the sea.
Isabella and I decided for once to do as the others did and we thought
of going to the sea. We bought a Balilla and began to take driving
lessons. I had begun to take these lessons a few months earlier in
Paris, but I failed my test and had to begin again in Milan. Then
we decided to take the driving test at our holiday place. My brother
had offered us hospitality at his villa at Poveromo, a strange and not
very cheerful name for a locality near Forte dei Marmi. We left in
the direction of La Versilia in the Balilla, driven by one of our
friends. I did not like Poveromo and all that district very much.
These places were frequented during the summer by a great number
of intellectuals and painters and they are places where nature is not
only not picturesque but definitely ugly; it is strange that such places
are chosen for holidays by so many painters, many of whom have
bought or had built houses and villas. It is true that these are modern
painters, and modern painters, where the beauty of a landscape is
concerned, have curious ideas which are not exactly those of a
Giorgione, a Poussin or a Titian, and not even those of a Corot or
a Fontanesi.

The Forte dei Marmi district is in fact ugly; the sea and the
beach are the most boring and the least picturesque imaginable; not
a rock, not a boat, not a sail, not even a mast stand out of the water,
not even an old basket floating on the water. Nothing that makes
you want to pick up your pencil or brush. About 11 or 12 o'clock
when the sun starts to be really hot, large numbers of intellectuals
are seen arriving on the beach, coming from all parts of Italy, but
mainly from Rome and Florence; they stretch out on the sand with
their wives, children, parents, friends and acquaintances. They stay
there gossiping, running people down, or remaining tensely silent,
expressing in various ways their inexhaustible anger and eternal
discontent. Behind them shapeless pine trees with unpleasant colours,
looking like so many useless pens, as Delacroix rightly says, form

pineta which are like gigantic refuse heaps; they are real *cloacas* full of filth of all kinds, but especially of human and animal excrement, and over this excrement fly myriads of mosquitoes, with iridescent wings and voracious probosci, buzzing and then alighting, then buzzing again and then, coming back and through the doors and open windows, they go into the houses of the painters and intellectuals and like so many minute harpies they soil and contaminate the bread, provisions, fruit, water and wine destined for the tables of the intellectuals, painters and their families. And to think that in Italy, especially in the Lazio and the Veneto, but also in Piedmont and Lombardy, there are so many enchanting sites, so many dream-like sites, so much fresh, fertile countryside, where the beauty of nature unites with the beautiful buildings of the past, and seems to form paintings by Old Masters. During the afternoon the intellectuals, after a couple of hours' rest, ride their bicycles along the road following the coast. It needed all my unlimited love of work and painting before I could decide to paint a few landscapes and seascapes in that extremely ugly and utterly tedious place.

At Poveromo and between Poveromo and Forte dei Marmi Isabella and I studied the art of car-driving and happily passed the test at Massa Carrara. However, we still did not have our licences and could only receive them in Milan. Therefore, around September 1938, we returned with our equipment and baggage to Milan, taking the Balilla which was driven part of the way by a mechanic and afterwards by my brother.

15

In the meantime black clouds were growing denser in the sky over
Europe. The destructive wing of the Spirit of Evil extended also,
with inexorable gloom, over Italy. Mussolini had gone to Germany
and had come back full of evil plans, perverse desires, intolerance,
cruelty and sadism. The notorious racial laws were passed. In Italy,
a Mediterranean and Semitic country, where at least five out of
every ten people show physical characteristics which might easily
indicate that they belong to the people of Israel, these laws appeared
not only senseless and inhuman but also somewhat ridiculous. A
Russian grand duke, whose name I do not remember, returning home
after a trip to Italy and a long stay in Naples, was asked by his
friends for his impressions of the Parthenopaean city; not for nothing
did he reply that he felt he was in the Cracow ghetto.

These so-called 'decrees for the defence of the race' brought to
the surface many obscure feelings, much wretched pettiness and
much servility which, although cultivated during long years of
dictatorship, still lingered deep down in the hearts of so many
inhabitants of the peninsula. I remember one such woman, an
elementary-school teacher who, immediately after the anti-Semitic
laws had been promulgated, began to speak ill of a few unfortunate
Jewish children who were in her class, saying that they never washed
and that they stank. People began to use the word Jew instead of
Hebrew, for they thought that such a word would remind people of
the not very sympathetic figure of Judas Iscariot, the prototype of
the traitor, and thus create in Italy a current of hostility against the
Jews. On the other hand, those uneducated people did not know

what Jewish means: belonging to the tribe of Judaea and implying no reference at all to the apostle who betrayed Jesus Christ. The tribe of Judaea was the most noble Hebrew tribe, belonging to King David, and from it came the Redeemer. In spite of so much zeal the government never succeeded in creating hostility, neither then nor later. I remember that my father, who was a perfect gentleman of the last century, intolerant of everything that was inhuman and unjust, had taught me and my brother to say *Israelite*.

In Milan we settled down once more in our apartment in the Corso Porta Nuova. I began to work again and to pursue my technical research with my customary energy. But the atmosphere in Italy was more unbearable than ever. The thing that disgusted me most was the pettiness, servility and low moral state to which many people had sunk. In all circles they used the pretext of anti-Semitism to annoy any man near to them, especially if he had got himself talked about and reached a position of some importance.

I remember how in artistic and literary circles people tried at all costs to find Jews everywhere; the sculptor Messina was said to be a Jew because his surname was the name of a town; in fact he came from Sicily and like many Sicilians his surname was that of a town but did not make him into an 'Israelite'. Campigli was said to be Jewish, although he certainly was not. In Rome some dear, witty friends, including the producer Anton Giulio Bragaglia, started the rumour that I and my brother Savinio were Jewish and they would say with a hypocritical air of concern, 'What will the poor de Chiricos do now?'

In order to stop living in a country from where all humanity, dignity, civility, conscience and shame had been completely banished, we decided to go back to Paris. We packed our bags; I rolled up my new canvases and after everything had been stowed in the Balilla, under the aegis of a picture of St Christopher which we had fastened up inside the car, we left for the French capital.

It was a remarkably adventurous journey. When we went through Turin the painter Romano Gazzera and his wife came to meet us in their car and accompanied us to the French frontier at the Alps. Both Isabella and I, but I in particular, were not very experienced drivers; also it was late autumn, November already, and thick fog hung over the Piedmontese plains and especially over the Alps. Romano Gazzera went in front to show us the way through the mist, but when we reached the French frontier he had to leave us and so we went on alone over those alpine roads. To complete our misfortunes Isabella did not feel well and had to stop driving; it thus fell to me, who was less experienced, to drive the car. Since it was already late and I was afraid we would have to spend the night right up in the mountains, I increased speed and drove on as fast as my brief experience and the highly dangerous locality allowed me. It was truly miraculous that there was no accident and we did not end up in a ravine, something which, moreover, would have been welcomed by many people with delight and a great sigh of relief. But St Christopher protected us; we went down the other side without any trouble and as the mist thinned and on the horizon there flared a magnificent sunset, worthy of Claude or Turner, we came in sight of the French valleys. By this time we had reached the plain; we decided not to stop at Modane and to go on, although night had fallen. We went on until we reached a small town whose name I have forgotten, and there we stopped. The next day we resumed our journey in good conditions. The roads were excellent, the weather calm, the countryside smiling and picturesque. We travelled on all day. Evening came, then night. We were not sensible enough to stop in some inhabited place before it was dark; we hoped to reach Paris, but instead we mistook the way twice and towards midnight, while we were going through a forest, the car suddenly stopped. It was the classic breakdown. Outside it was pitch dark and we did not know where we were; I looked for some signpost, but in vain. It was also very cold. Since we were afraid of some sinister encounter we decided to push the car off the road, hide it behind a clump of trees and switch off the lights. This is what we did: Isabella sat at the wheel while I got out and pushed the Balilla along a narrow path and then into a thick clump of ancient oaks right in the forest. We got back into the car, wrapped ourselves in long woollen scarves and covered ourselves up with coats, closed all the windows and in this way, smoking and dozing, we waited for the dawn.

As soon as the first rays of morning light appeared I went out to explore and was amazed: I had hardly walked a few steps away from the dense-growing trees when I found myself surrounded by memories of Napoleon: eagles with outspread wings and ceremonial N's rose up everywhere, carved in stone. We were at Fontainebleau. I ran back to tell Isabella the good news; then, when it was lighter, I went to find a garage and asked them to send out two mechanics with a car to tow back the Balilla and repair it. The garage proprietor promised us he would send the car back, repaired, in the early afternoon. We spent the morning visiting the historic city, so evocative and melancholy on that grey autumn day, as the withered yellow leaves floated down over those buildings and damp stones which all round us recalled the epic of the great Corsican.

About noon we had an excellent luncheon in a restaurant where a group of elegant travellers, including a lady who was a great-niece of Victor Hugo, recognised me and gave me a little improvised demonstration of sympathy, calling me 'Sciricò'. We left for Paris, where we arrived in the evening and immediately went to stay at the best, the most comfortable, the most sympathetic, the most welcoming, the most distinctive, the most restful and the cleanest hotel in the capital, which is situated near the Boulevard Raspail, close to the Gare Montparnasse, in a street named after Blaise Desgoffe. This is the Victoria Palace Hôtel. Now, as for the name of the street, if you were to ask me, dear reader, who was Blaise Desgoffe, I would tell you that I do not know. I have looked up this name in the second part of the *Petit Larousse illustré* but did not find it; instead I found an Alexandre Desgoffe, a French painter who was born in Paris in 1802 and died there in 1885.

16

I began to work again in the hotel room and returned to my former technical research, constantly helped by Isabella whose advice I valued greatly.

One afternoon at the Louvre we were standing in front of a portrait by Velasquez and talking about the mysterious materials used by the Old Masters and which have no connection with the crude, dull materials of modern painting. Isabella had been looking at the picture by the great Spaniard for a long time. 'This is not processed colouring,' she said suddenly, 'but fine material that has been dyed.' Isabella's words were a revelation to me; I realised at once that a new horizon had opened for me now with new and vast possibilities. At the same time I met a restorer called Vandenberg who specialised in the restoration of Flemish pictures and who worked at the Louvre. He showed me in his studio a kind of whitish oily substance, a kind of pomade with which he diluted his colours, but it was a question of using a lot of pomade and a little colour. I thought again of Isabella's words : 'Not processed colouring but fine material that has been dyed.' The restorer Vandenberg, however, did not want to give me the recipe for his oily substance, which he called 'painters' butter'. I understood all the same that it was an emulsion of oily resinous substances, with gums, or with glue and water, an emulsion produced by means of an alkaloid. In fact, this oily substance gave off a strong smell of ammonia.

I began to make emulsions of my own, but without using alkaloids, and I discovered that tree gum, and also gum diluted in large quantities of water added drop by drop into a mixture of fat oil and varnish, stirred continuously with a stick, forms an emulsion which, used together with colours, produces fine, precious and transparent material, makes work much easier and gives that delicacy of modelling and depth of execution which have been completely forgotten for about a century.

This was the first step towards the conquest of great painting; it brought release from the ugliness and boredom of bad modern painting. Some of my pictures which I had painted with this new technique were noticed and praised by various particularly competent people, including the well-known painter and restorer Maroger, who, as I said earlier, also invented a medium which is sold in small metal tubes by artists' colourmen in Paris.

In the meantime the winter had ended and the fatal year 1939 had begun; spring came, then summer; the atmosphere became red-hot, charged with electricity; war was in the air, imminent. Those months reminded me of the months which preceded the outbreak of the conflict in 1914 : the same wildly alarming news in the papers, the same nervousness among people. In the streets of Paris you could see men who had been called up going to barracks with cases and bundles. Frightening rumours began to circulate; people said that the Germans would attack Paris with a fantastic number of aeroplanes and destroy it completely. Many people left the capital; cars of all types, full of people and luggage, went through the streets towards the Porte d'Orléans. We also left in the Balilla which was piled up with cases and packages. We went to Cannes; but people said it was dangerous to stay because the Italian fleet would bomb the entire coast. I was also afraid that if Italy entered the war I would be sent to a concentration camp and I realised the situation in which Isabella would find herself. We left Cannes for a little place in Provence called Uzès. There, while we were staying in a dismal hotel full of flies, we heard the news that the Germans had invaded Poland; notices of general mobilisation appeared on the walls; all the horses and mules in the district were requisitioned; the squares and streets were full of animals and the immediate result was an enormous increase in the already large number of flies and horse-flies. The heat was unbearable. We left for Vichy in the hope of staying in a place less dirty and more civil. Meanwhile war had been declared. Italy had not moved and I felt calmer. But the prospect of awaiting developments in the midst of a war, in a foreign country, without being able to work or earn any money, did not seem very pleasant to me, and I thought it would be much wiser to return to Milan.

Once more we stowed the luggage into the faithful Balilla and left for Nice. During the entire journey we met endless strings of soldiers, lorries, vehicles of all types which were going up north. The villages were full of soldiers and long railway convoys also passed, carrying troops, guns, horses and arms. On seeing all this avalanche of arms and armed men converging on the Eastern Front nobody would ever have thought that after a few days and little fighting the Germans would take and occupy Paris.

All the newspapers praised the genius, intelligence and skill of General Gamelin. It became clear, however, that General Gamelin understood nothing whatever about the art of war and especially of modern war; probably he understood nothing about anything, for he was an intellectual and, as everyone knows, intellectuals are destined never to understand anything about anything.

When we reached the entrance to Nice we found the street barred by Friesian horses and Senegalese troops with fixed bayonets and faces blacker than the devil's behind. We slowed down, thinking that we had to stop, get out of the car, show papers, be questioned and have our baggage searched, but none of this occurred; the horses were reined in, the Senegalese drawn up practically at attention and we passed through without trouble. Later we succeeded in learning why; our car had a Milan registration number, so that at the back, next to the number plate, were the letters MI. These letters were interpreted by the good Senegalese as standing for the French word 'military' and this made them think that I was a senior officer in the Republican army who, wearing civilian clothes and accompanied by his wife, was going to Nice on some important and secret mission.

In Nice, however, difficulties arose. We needed special passes in order to leave France. Before the local authorities could give them they first asked approval from the Prefect of Police in Paris. This business was likely to take a long time and we ran the risk of having to spend the winter in Nice, which in other circumstances would have been pleasant, but at that time, and in our case, was not so at all. By good luck, one afternoon when we were sitting in a café on the Promenade des Anglais, we met a French gentleman, the Comte Gautier Vignal, whom we had known in Paris and who was a fervent admirer of my painting. I talked to him about my problems and said that we were anxious to return to Nice and also knew the military commandant of the city very well. He very kindly went at once to see these two men and the next day Isabella and I received permission to cross the frontier. We lost no time, the following morning the Balilla was started early and that same night we stayed in a hotel on the Italian Riviera. Next we went through Turin, stopped a day there to see our friends the Gazzeras and then started again for Milan.

In Milan the Ghiringhelli brothers, taking advantage once more of my absence, had again undertaken with admirable obstinacy the campaign to boycott my works and were trying to confuse people by organising exhibitions of metaphysical painting with catalogues, the prefaces to which were written by certain hermetic cretins who contributed to the review *Primato*. Once again I arrived with my stock of new paintings carried out in emulsion. I immediately took an apartment in the centre of the city, in the Via Gesù, close to the Via Montenapoleone. I set to work eagerly. With the help of my friend Barbaroux I began to sell my new paintings which, in spite of the perfidious manoeuvres by the Ghiringhelli brothers, assisted with great zeal by all the pseudo-painters and failed writers of the Lombardy capital, were very popular in Milan. The people there are always looking for good and true painting, and although the perfidious and destructive influence of the intellectuals and their dishonesty can sometimes lead them astray, the process does not go very far.

Three years passed in which I worked intensively and made much progress, perfecting my technique. I painted many portraits; some of men in costume were very successful and were a novelty in the field of portrait painting. I held various exhibitions in Milan, Florence and Turin. Naturaly the envy of the intellectuals and jealous, petty-minded people did not slacken and I often remembered the words of the medium Morosini: 'My son, you are one of the most envied men in the world!'

Then Italy declared war. We watched, with utter disgust, those despicable, insincere demonstrations during which young boys shouted and wrote on the walls: 'France is a sow and Churchill a pig.' Ridiculous manifestoes appeared everywhere; caricatures which showed John Bull, symbolising the people who were supposed to eat five meals a day, receiving an almighty and devastating kick on the behind from an Italian soldier and dropping a huge tray laden with ham, roast chicken, tarts, puddings, bottles of alcohol, etc. Passers-by looked with indifference at all these political drawings which were intended to make them enthusiastic about the war and embitter them against perfidious Albion.

In this way, amidst shameful behaviour and lies of all kinds, we reached 1942. That year, during which I had worked hard, I had accepted an invitation to send thirty or so paintings to the Biennale in Venice. During the same year I at last succeeded, after many attempts, in persuading Isabella to put her ideas and thoughts on paper. She had always astonished me with her exceptional intelligence and philosophical acumen, especially in relation to everything concerned with art and thought. Isabella's first publication was the famous *Considerations on Modern Painting*, which was published in entirety by the Milan review *Stile* and serialised by the *Corriere Padano* in Ferrara; it aroused many complaints, outbreaks of fury and envy of all kinds. The article appeared over my signature and was reviewed in neutral but predominantly hostile terms, on the radio. I received many letters, including some of praise, but the majority of them consisted of vulgar insults, inspired by the envy which was the most striking proof that the article had struck home and that the modernists had felt the blow.

At that time the official critic of *L'Illustrazione Italiana* was Signor Leonida Repaci, whom I had known in Milan. He had always shown me considerable friendliness and had spoken and written about my painting in terms of praise, while I on my side had returned his kindness. But there came a fateful day; Leonida Repaci asked me to publish articles in *L'Illustrazione Italiana*. There were in fact some very fine articles, very recent ones, which Isabella Far had barely finished writing: I signed them, and one after the other they were published in *L'Illustrazione Italiana*. These writings aroused great interest, but also a vast amount of envy. One fine day Repaci, who shortly before had seemed somewhat irritable and nervous on the telephone, began to be more distant and could not be seen; he had probably learnt that those fine articles which I had signed had been written by Isabella. It was just before the opening of the Biennale in Venice. One afternoon I was working in my studio when the director of *L'Illustrazione Italiana* informed me that he wanted to see me very urgently and asked me to go to his office so that he could tell me something very important. I went to *L'Illustrazione Italiana* and the director told me that the day before, Leonida

Repaci, beside himself with rage, had resigned. The director asked me if I wanted to take on Repaci's job or if I would at least write an article about the Venice Biennale. I declined the invitation, saying that it was impossible for me to act as critic, for all my criticism of modern painting could be reduced to one single word : *filth*.

Meantime Repaci had become incredibly hostile towards me. He began to criticise my painting in the most despicable and stupid manner imaginable, even trying to alienate possible buyers by writing that my canvases were liable to crack. At the same time he stepped up his praise of other painters, especially Romano Gazzera, whose talent deserves more intelligent and sincere acclaim. Not satisfied with all this, and probably in order to justify his behaviour, he tried to foist on me a reputation of being a dishonest, perverse and treacherous man, telling people that I had intrigued surreptitiously with the intention of taking his place at *L'Illustrazione Italiana*. This is the truth and I defy anyone to prove me wrong.

A few more months passed. Late one October afternoon, while the sun was setting, I was on my way home to my apartment in Milan after making various calls. While I was in the Piazza della Scala I heard the dismal wailing of sirens; I looked up and saw big aeroplanes glistening in the light, coming down slowly to the east of the city. The first shots rang out and there was a rumble of distant explosions. I rushed back home remembering that when I had left Isabella had not been too well and was in bed. I met her on the stairs on her way down to the cellar with our dog and cat. She was being hustled along by the other people in the house who were frightened by the increasing noise of the explosions. These were coming nearer and everyone was rushing to the shelter. It was the first large-scale bombardment of Milan and it lasted a long time. When we came out of the shelter it was almost dark and fires could be seen glowing red all round the city; this spectacle reminded me of Boito's opera *Nerone*. A few houses close to ours were destroyed and others damaged. We thought it would be wise to leave Milan and so a few days later we set out for Florence.

Meanwhile autumn came and with it bad weather. Isabella was not at all well and felt very weak. In Florence we stayed as guests for the whole of the winter with our friend Luigi Bellini the antique dealer. I started to work again and in Florence I held a one-man show with various new paintings. At that period in Florence I came to know two young Spanish painters, the Bueno brothers, young men full of talent. The painter Pietro Annigoni, a gifted and highly serious artist, still lives in Florence. Unlike nearly all painters today, and I am not speaking only of Italians, but also of foreigners, he understands and studies the technique of painting and realises the importance of it.

There is no doubt that as far as painting is concerned Florence provides a much more serious and moral atmosphere than Rome. Let us hope that things will not change for the city of the Red Lily.[1]

The degree of amorality that exists today in the field of art, especially in Rome, is incredible. These men who want to be artists and are aware of their impotence are full of subdued anger. All this frenzied race towards all that is bad, worse and worst is like an upsurge of anger because, such is the impotence that dominates them. I will not say they cannot achieve the fine and the good, they cannot even achieve mediocrity.

I have already said it, but I will repeat it again: the Italy of Pascoli, Carducci, D'Annunzio, the Italy of Tito and Michetti, the Italy of Boito and Mascagni, although it was far from the Italy of the great periods, was still an Italy a hundred times more respectable and respected, a hundred times more worthy of esteem and sympathy than the Italy of today, where the loftiest things of the mind, the plastic arts, literature, poetry and music are dragged down into the mud by a band of castrated, illiterate men, real bootblacks, real arse-lickers of everything foreign and who, in a cowardly and criminal manner have reduced all forms of art and thought to an obscene aping of the most decadent, empty and frivolous things that are done outside Italy and especially in Paris.

The envy of this horrible tribe then leads them to attack those in whom they see danger and to attempt in the vilest and most amoral fashion, capitalising on the confusion, anarchy, ignorance, indifference and laziness which reign today in people's heads, to do harm to those who work seriously, to those who have the temperaments of men and not of pederasts, eunuchs, onanists and old maids, to those who are *real* artists and refuse with disdain to join the ranks of the blackguards, the impotent and the imbeciles.

I repeat once more that in Italy, in the academies, where the young should be educated in the difficult, exhausting and mysterious work of painting, the teachers should be serious artists, men who know how to hold a crayon and a brush in their hands, and not illiterates and individuals who do not even know how to sharpen a pencil.

I write these things and will continue to write them, remaining indifferent to reactions, since I know that in addition to being a great painter and a great man, I *also have a mission to fulfil.*

I write these things and will go on writing them and in this way men of good will, of whom I hope there are still some in Italy, will be able to judge today and tomorrow. I would even like some man of good will to be able to judge certain perfidious manoeuvres, certain acts which, so far as art is concerned, are acts more deserving of condemnation than when a lunatic slashes a masterpiece in a museum. I am referring to the arrangement of the rooms at the Gallery of Modern Art at Valle Giulia. The selection of the works on show there today has been made in a particularly tendentious manner. In order to protect, defend and justify the stupidity, impotence and ignorance of the modern painters, the entire art of the last century has been represented in this gallery by some ridiculous portrait by Mancini, in which the picture-postcard quality of the faces contrasts in a comic way with the home-made modernism of a hundredweight of ivory-black wasted on painting clothes. There are also a couple of portraits by Boldini, wooden and falsely elegant in style, and a few paintings by Spadini, chosen from his most mediocre works and of an inferior imitative quality. Where are the works of Giacinto Gigante, Palizzi, Giovanni Carnovali, Fontanesi, Segantini, Previati, Vincenzo Gemito? It did not suit the treacherous organiser of this exhibition, Signora Palma Bucarelli, to hang the works of these artists, because she knew that the comparison of such works with the horrors of the modernists could be dangerous. In the same room, and for the same reasons, the entire sculpture of the nineteenth century is represented by a few ectoplasmic wax figures by Medardo Rosso, funereally protected by bell-shaped glass covers.

All this has been done in treacherous fashion, in order to confuse people's ideas and make ingenuous people believe that the asinine productions of the modernist painters are in the pure Italian tradition. It is a fact that the person responsible for the nineteenth-century room in this museum of horrors, Signora Palma Bucarelli, very cunningly chose works by painters at the end of that century and also from the beginning of this one, such as Spadini, because she realised that if, in order to justify the ugly painting that is being done today, she had sought works from the first half of the last century, she would have burnt her fingers and performed the worst possible service towards the people she was protecting.

In Florence I continued to work. The new technique I was using achieved better results than those produced with emulsion. It was with emplastic oil that I painted my famous self-portrait in the nude, which is perhaps the most finished painting that I have carried out so far.

In Florence we were installed in a villa situated some way outside the city, at the start of the Via San Domenico which leads up to the Florentine hills. They are all covered with beautiful villas, prominent among which is one surrounded with cypresses where Boecklin, the great painter from Basle, lived and worked in peace for so many years.

I too hoped to live and work in peace in my villa near Florence, if not for many years, at least for a little time. But destiny, that destiny which until now has always forced me to flee from one lot of people to another, had arranged things otherwise. One evening, it was July 25th, 1943, Isabella and I were in the drawing-room listening to the radio, waiting until it was time for supper. At a certain moment came the announcement that fascism had been overthrown, Mussolini had resigned, Badoglio was head of the government. We thought it was a joke. I immediately telephoned some friend or other; it was true, the Swiss and the British radios were giving the same news. At that moment I regarded this news as good and I was very pleased about it, but Isabella, who has truly exceptional perception and understanding not only about matters of art and thought, but about all other matters, tempered my enthusiasm. She made me see that an event of this kind, at that moment, with the Allies still far away and with the major part of Italy full of Germans who were well armed and in angry mood, could, from one minute to the next, turn into a situation which for the Italians could be exceedingly tragic.

The tragedy, however, did not come immediately. In the meantime came the 9 o'clock curfew; the streets of Florence were absolutely invaded by soldiers armed with guns and model 91 Pattuglie rifles, while lorries full of soldiers passed by with an infernal din. Troops from all branches of the army camped in the courtyards of the old Florentine palaces. The Germans had disappeared. But there was no point in relaxing, for the sickness was still there, the black beast of evil was still alive and silent in the darkness, awaiting its moment.

The announcement of the armistice came. Two days of uncertainty, confusion and contradictory news, and then one morning the German armoured cars and motorcyclists came down from the Trespiano heights : a few men with dark skins and hyena-like eyes, a few soldiers, but strongly armed. Their cars, white with dust, were crammed with hand-grenades, machine-guns, automatic rifles and automatic pistols. The people of Florence were anxious and kept out of the way. The central police station was occupied by the Gestapo. The first SS guards appeared. They were like phantoms of ectoplasmic creatures with nothing human about them; they were not soldiers, not warriors with a harsh, determined look, but frightening apparitions who, according to a perceptive definition by the writer Kessel, had the colouring of minerals and glaucous, impenetrable eyes.

Preoccupied by personal matters, I decided to leave the place where we were living.

During this troubled period which lasted for nine months and which we spent partly in Florence, partly in the surrounding countryside and partly in Rome, I was able to observe several things, among which only a few can sometimes be recounted. Some people were totally indifferent to us. Others laughed and sniggered when they talked about our situation; I know who they are and as long as I live I will pay them back in their own coin. There were others, mere delinquents, who took advantage of the circumstances to steal things from us and blackmail us.

During these nine months I worked very little, but Isabella, who was much more courageous and calm than I was, worked a great deal, writing various philosophical essays, each one finer than the last, and almost finished a very fine novel which she had begun in Milan and which is an intellectual, political and moral critique of our time.

But June 4th, 1944, came. The last ectoplasmic creatures with the glaucous, impenetrable eyes had vanished towards the west and north. We could go out and live like human beings.

When the first American lorries and armoured cars appeared at the gates of Rome late on June 4th, 1944, the people were overwhelmed with hysterical, delirious joy. Everyone felt that a horrifying nightmare, a reign of terror, injustice and sadistic cruelty which had been more horrible than the worst infamies of previous centuries, had come to an end. The streets were full of jubilant people; many of them embraced each other, even strangers. The American soldiers waved and smiled to all these men, women and children who crowded round the military vehicles, offering flowers and wine. In return the Americans gave out handfuls of sweets, chocolate and cigarettes. This enthusiasm reminded me of the announcement of the armistice at the end of the previous war, in the autumn of 1918, but multiplied by ten and even by twenty. This enthusiasm, this joy shown by so many people who felt they were coming back to life, was really moving because it was spontaneous and it was certainly not like certain organised demonstrations of enthusiasm which took place in the Piazza Venezia during the famous assemblies.

I began to work again. After that long interval I really needed to do so. I had a small exhibition of small pictures in the Margherita Gallery. I realised immediately that in Rome the *furor histericus* over my painting was becoming as overwhelming as it was exhilarating.

Of all the Italian cities Rome is the one which includes the greatest number of intellectuals—that is, irritable and discontented people. These people have been and always will be my worst enemies, because in me they see what they would like to be, in my paintings they see what they would like to have : that is talent, power, knowledge. As a result they express their anger in the most underhanded and cowardly ways. The method they prefer, the one which they probably regard as the most efficacious, is to try by every means to distract the attention of the public and at the same time that of buyers from what I am doing today and direct it towards the painting I did earlier and which in fact I am still doing. This was the practice of the surrealists and also of the Milione Gallery in Milan. In Rome too, as I see it, there are galleries whose policies are like those of the Milione Gallery but slightly less obvious.

All these attitudes and suppressed feelings of envy which I have noticed for so many years, more or less everywhere, and which now apply also to the writings of Isabella Far, are in fact much less mysterious than might be believed. In these recollections of mine I have explained the situation on various occasions, but before I come to the end I would like to explain it once more. Above all it must be remembered that during the last thirty years or so Italy has probably been the country with the greatest number of failed writers and impotent intellectuals, and the Italian city where this genus is particularly prevalent is Rome. It can be appreciated that the kind of painting I do, reaching such a level of plastic power and mastery, and writings like those of Isabella Far, whose philosophical acumen, descriptive strength, logic, clarity, efficacy, in fact *talent*, can only find an equivalent in the times of Arthur Schopenhauer. It can be appreciated, I say, that such painting and such writings, whenever they appear, are like a burst of grape-shot in the aviary at a zoo. The wretched victims must therefore express themselves as best they can.

In fact even Mussolini was above all an impotent intellectual and a failed writer. He threw himself into politics, he created fascism and did all those terrible things in order to express himself. Fortunately cases like that of Mussolini are more than rare, for it is certainly going too far to subject an entire country to twenty years' dictatorship, to reach the point no less of declaring war on Britain, Russia and the United States, to reduce one's own country to the state in which Italy is today, all because one feels and knows that one will never become a Flaubert or a Dostoevsky, or even a gossip-writer for the *Tribuna Illustrata*. Let us be grateful, therefore, to all those inhibited people of today who, instead of creating similar catastrophes, restrict themselves, in order to express their envy, to exalting metaphysical painting, running down my present painting for this reason, and, so far as Isabella Far's writings are concerned, maintaining a hysterical and highly diverting silence.

Thus, dear reader, recounting my memoirs, observing, judging and examining so many events and people, I come to July 1945; a torrid July, a discouraging season, not so much because of the exceptional heat, but because of the confused, immoral, wicked and ridiculous spectacle that humanity continues to offer.

I console myself by painting as much as I can and as well as I can, and by reading the writings of Isabella Far. These are the two things which first and foremost interest me in life today. And so be it.

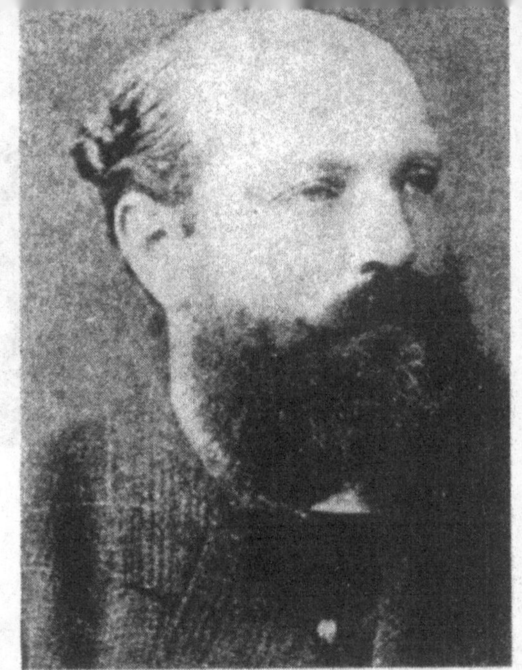

1 Evaristo de Chirico, the author's father

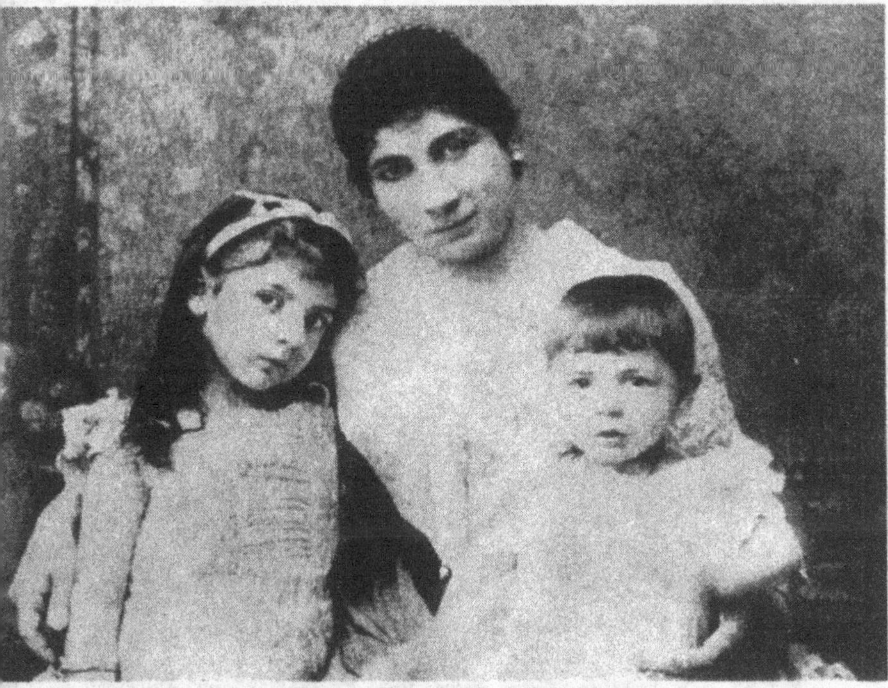

Gemma de Chirico with her children Adele and Giorgio, Athens 1890

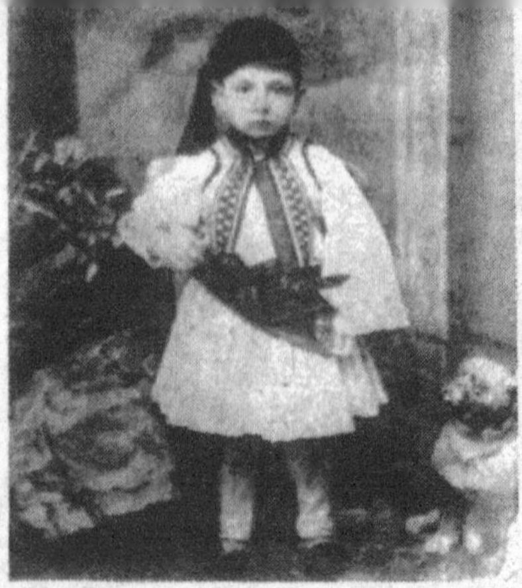

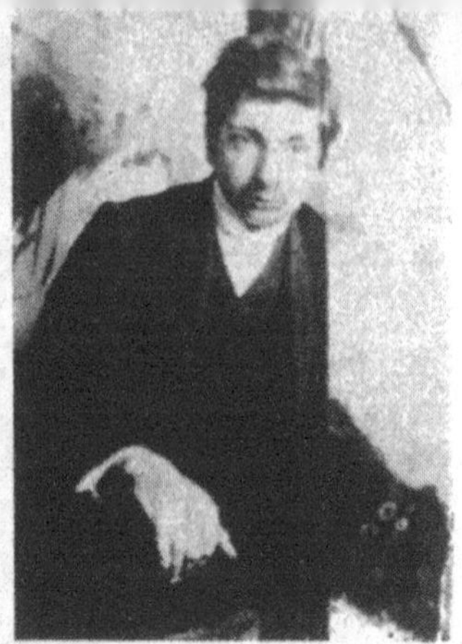

3 Giorgio de Chirico aged four years, in evzone costume

4 Giorgio de Chirico at the Munich Academy, 1908

5 The author in Paris, 1930

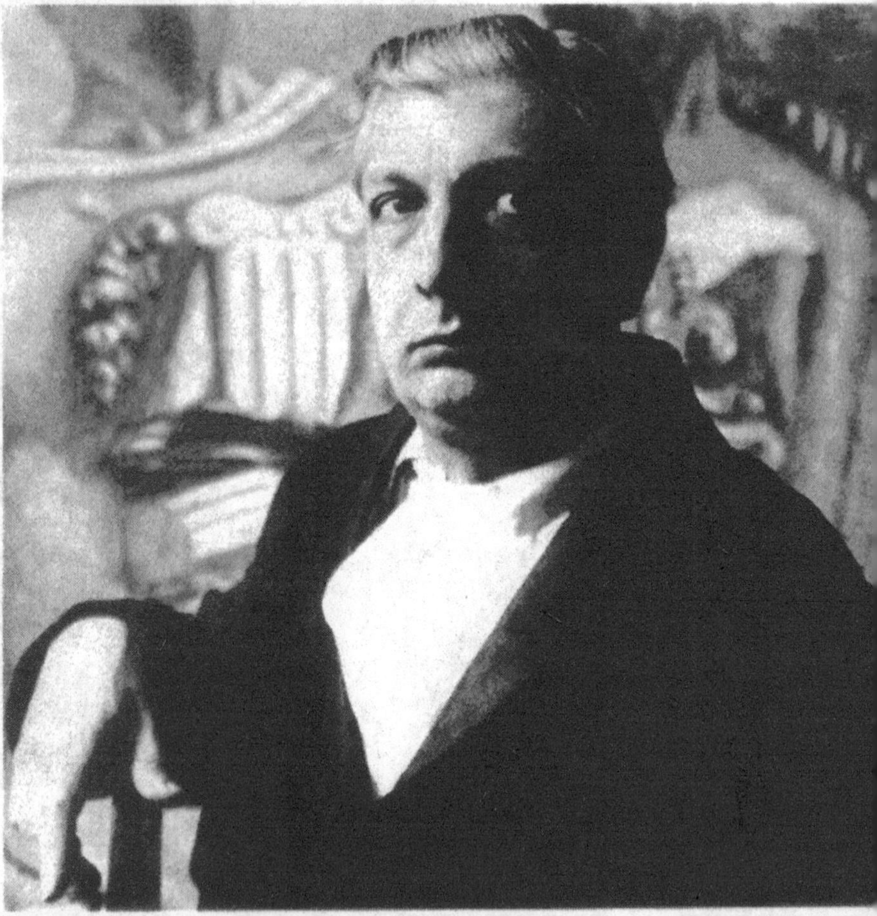

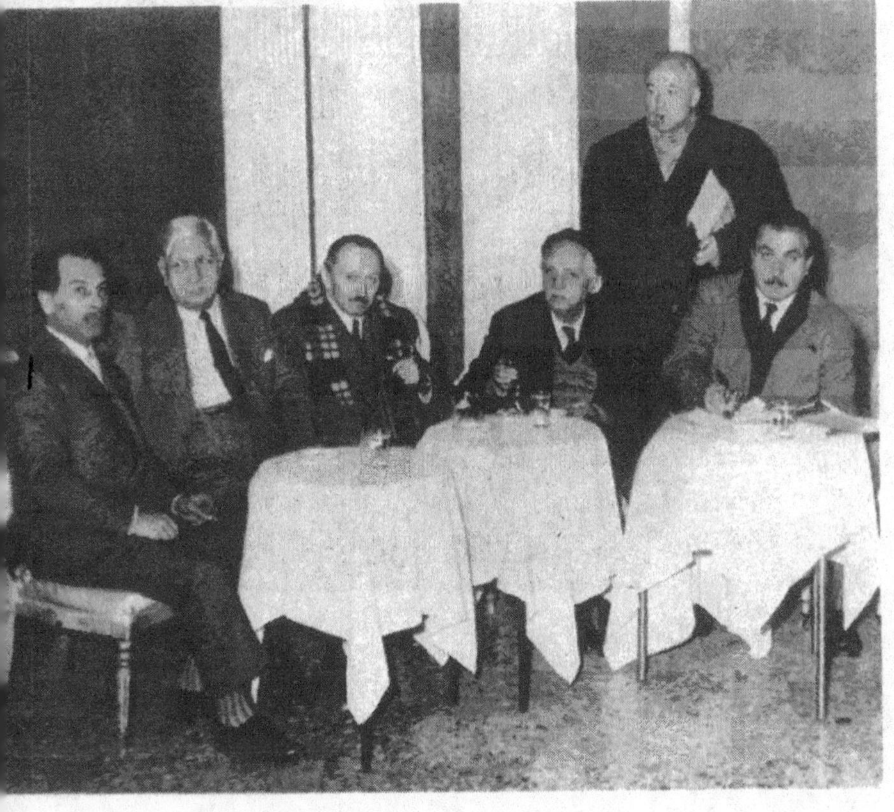

De Chirico with fellow-artists at the exhibition held by the Association of Italian Artists,
Milan 1955

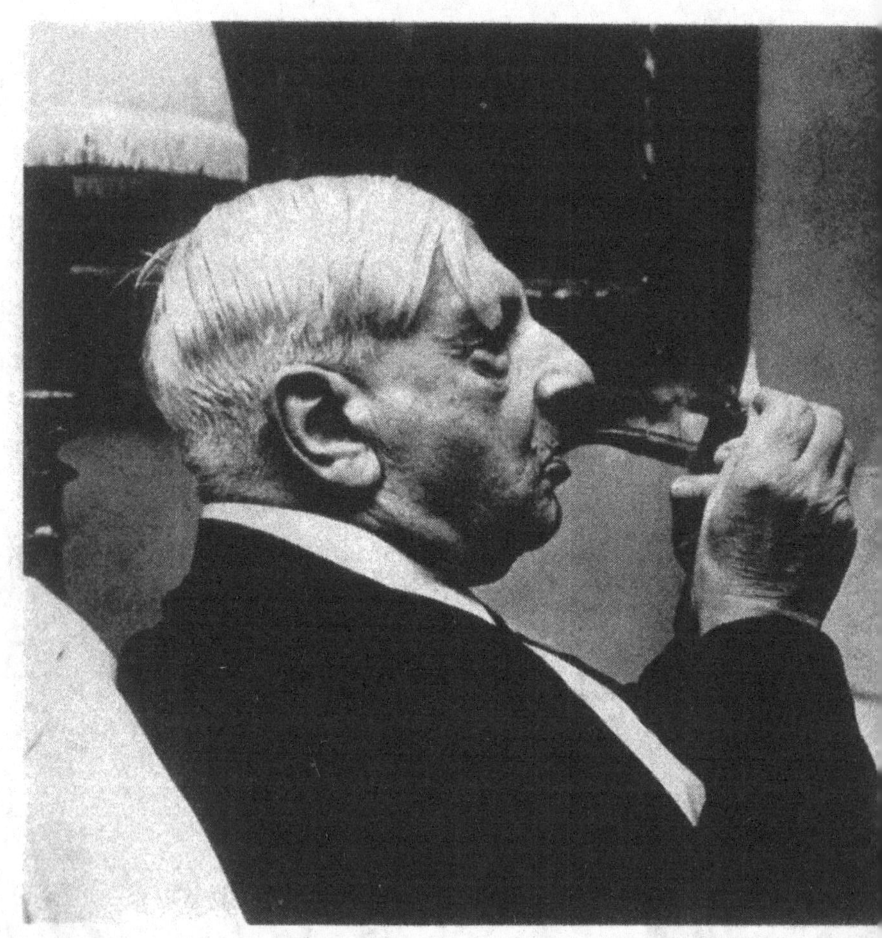

7　A recent photograph of the author

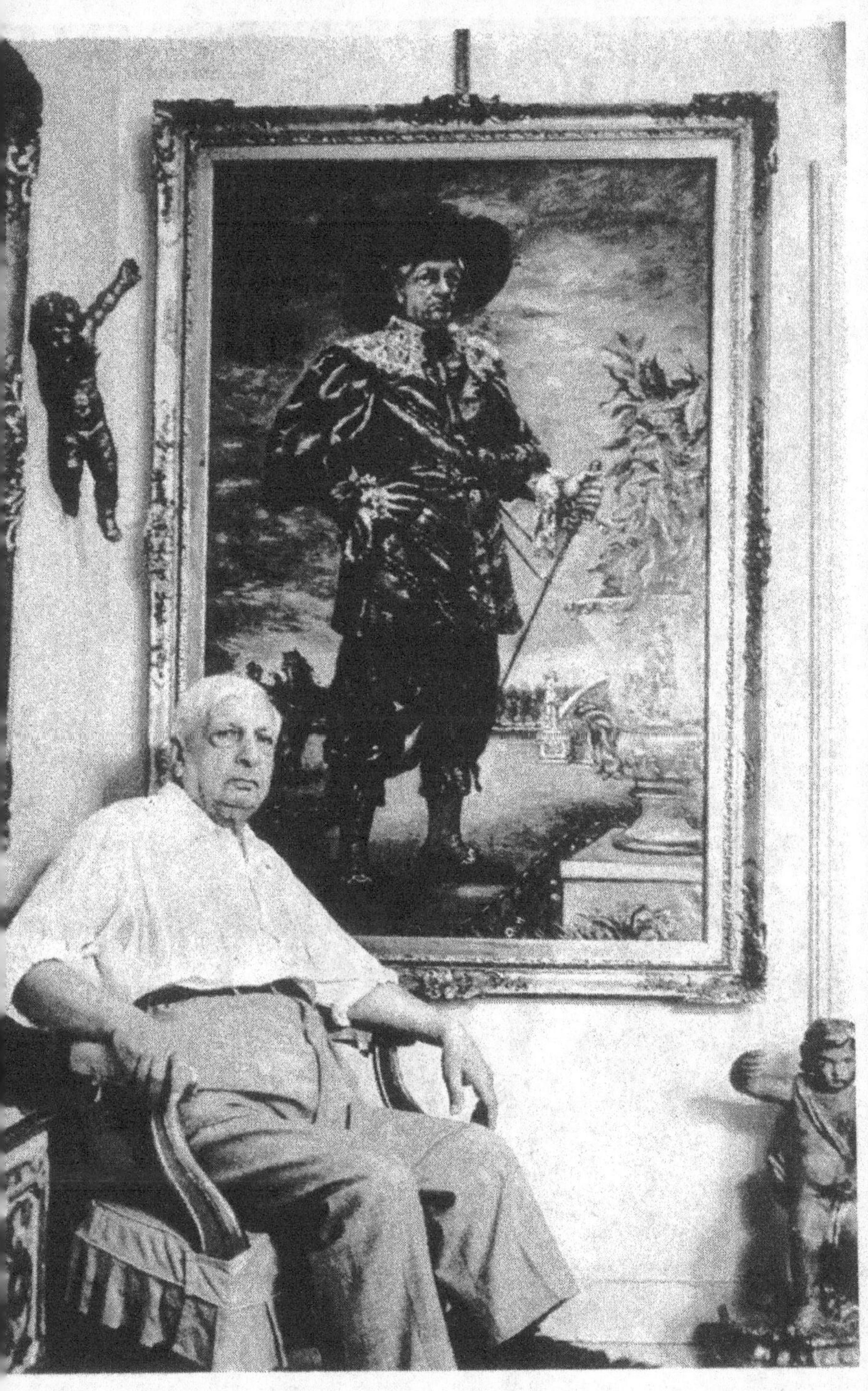

De Chirico in his apartment, Rome 1968

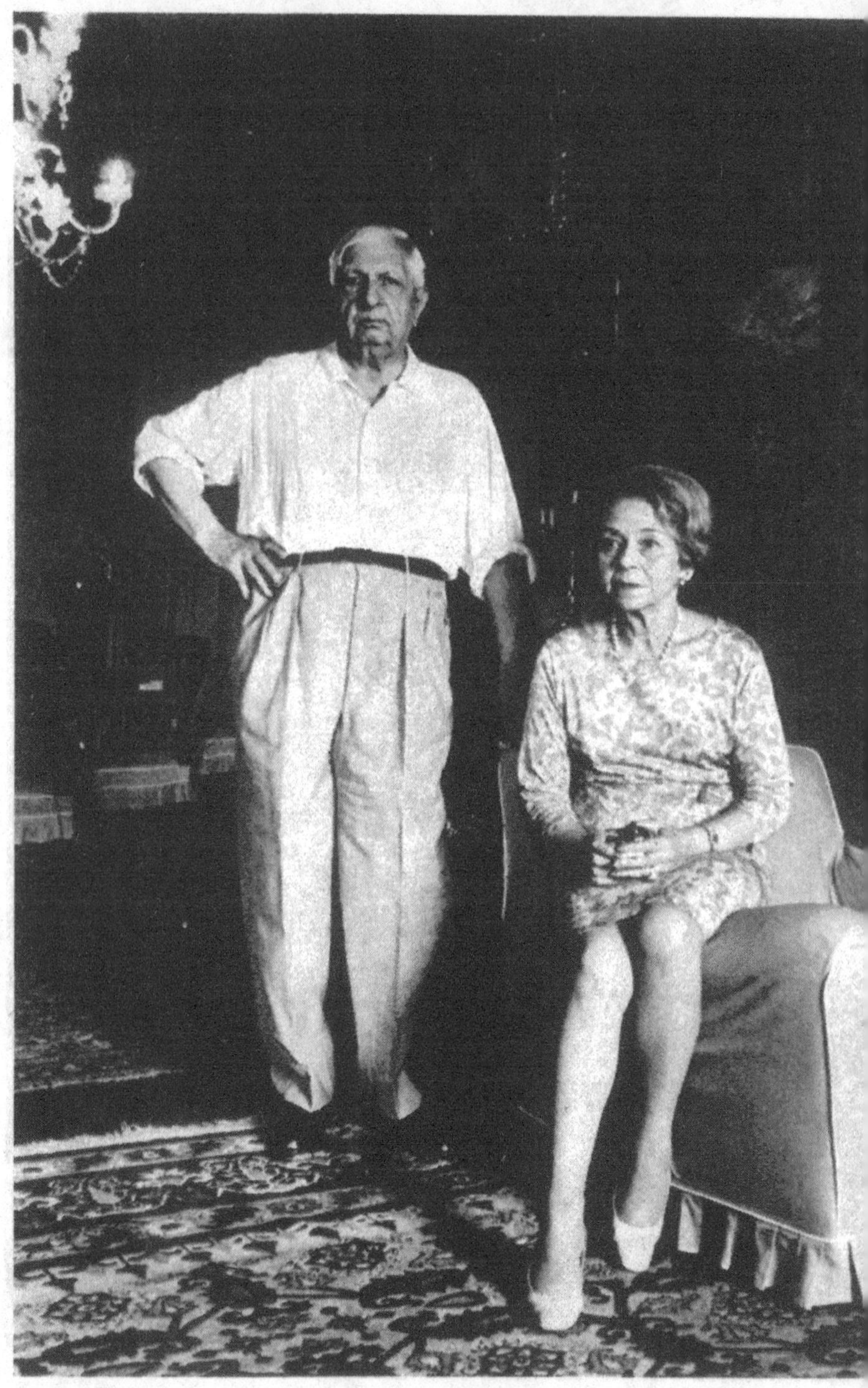

9   Giorgio de Chirico with his wife Isabella in the dining-room of their apartment in
Rome, 1968

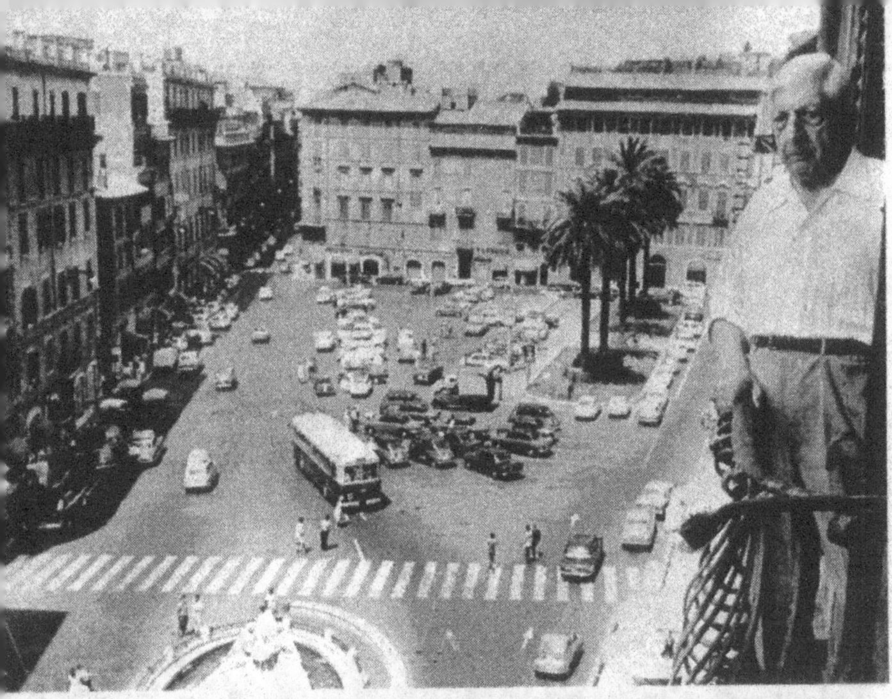

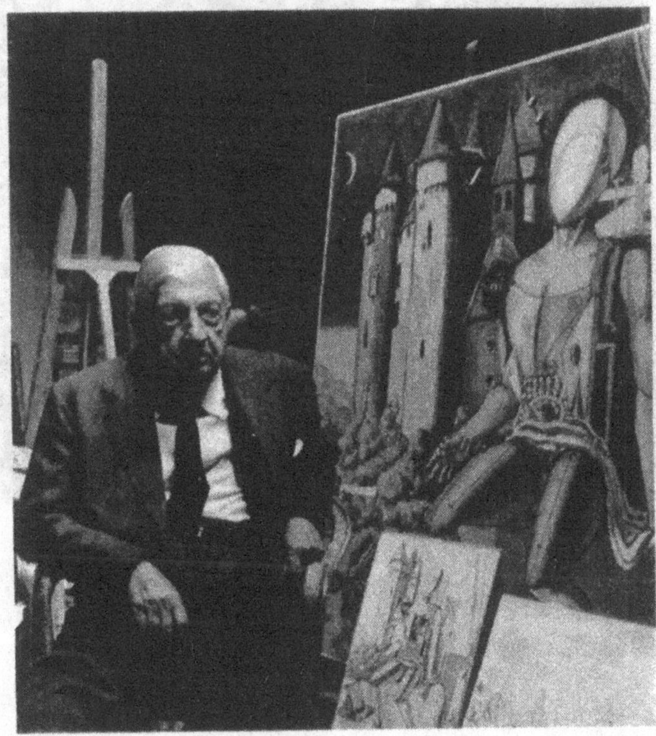

De Chirico on his
balcony, over-
looking the Piazza
di Spagna

1   De Chirico in his
    studio

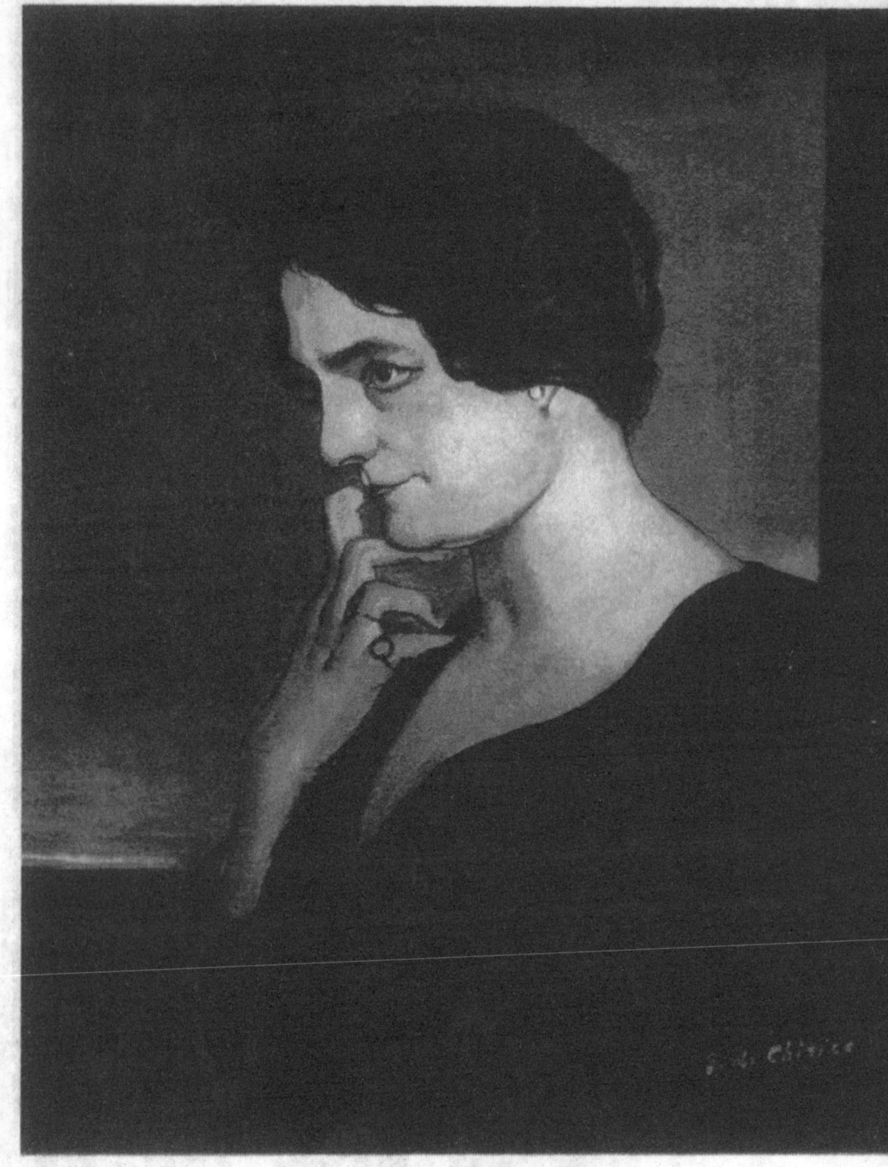

12 *Portrait of a Woman*, metaphysical period, 1912

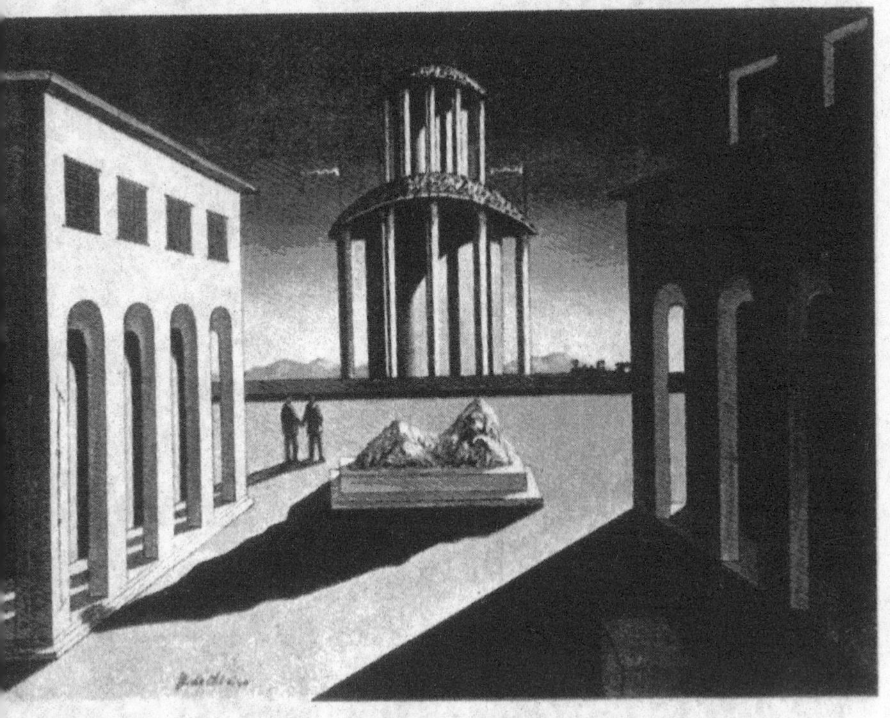

Piazza d'Italia, 1954 (metaphysical style)

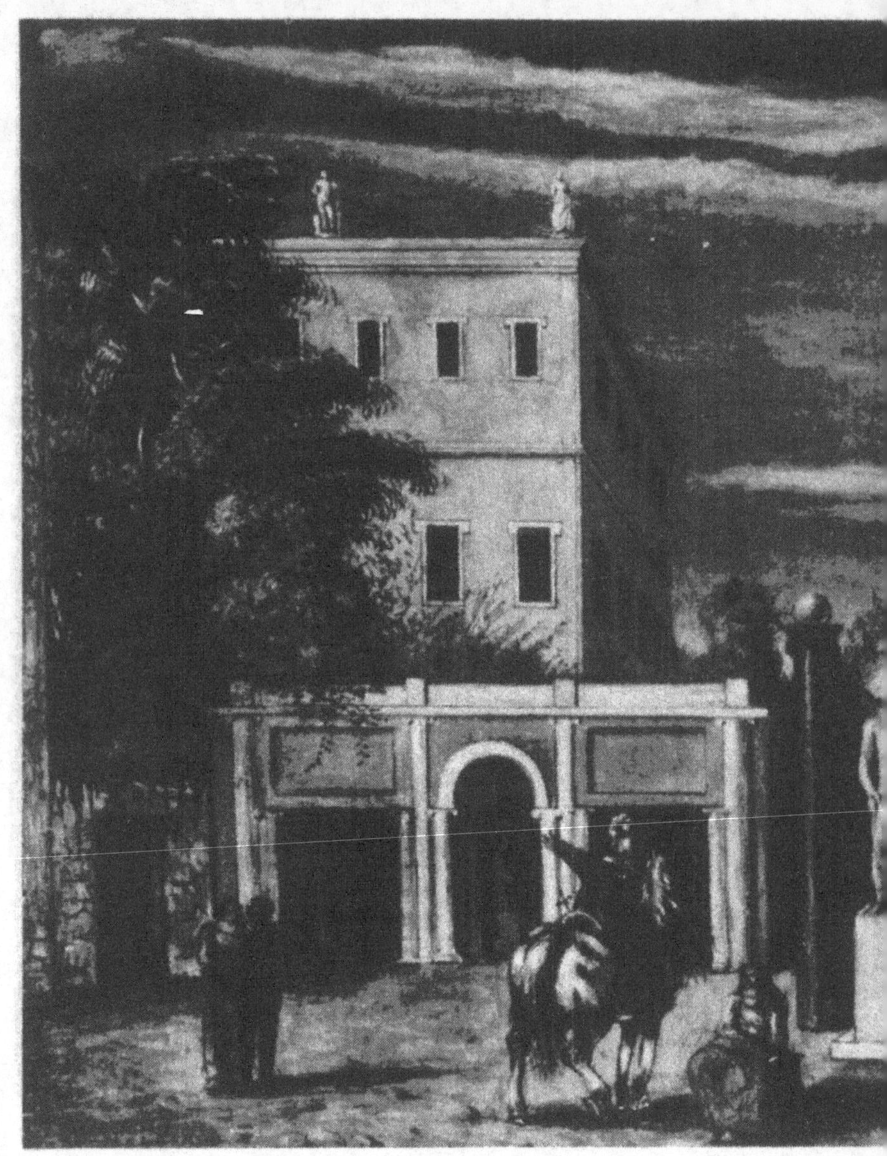

14 *Farewells*, 1924

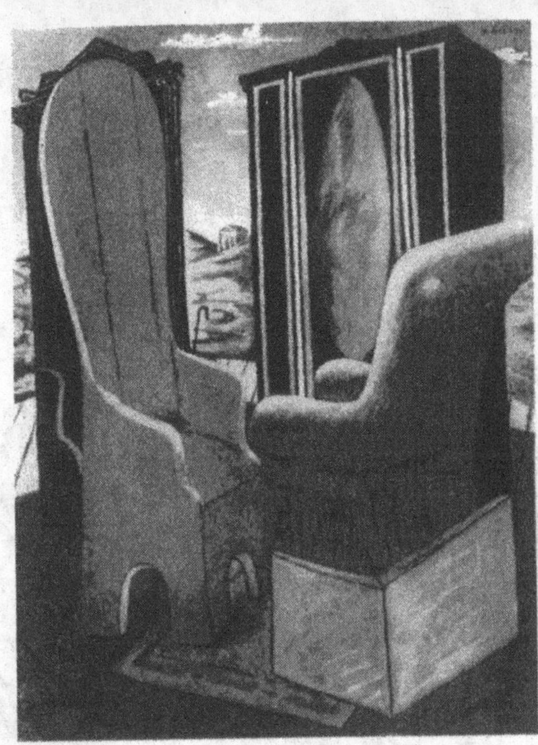

15 *Furniture in the Valley, 1926*

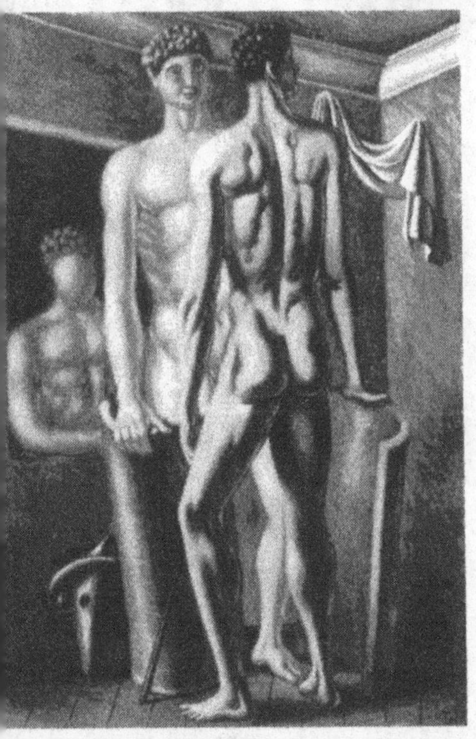

16 *Two Gladiators in a Room, 1927*

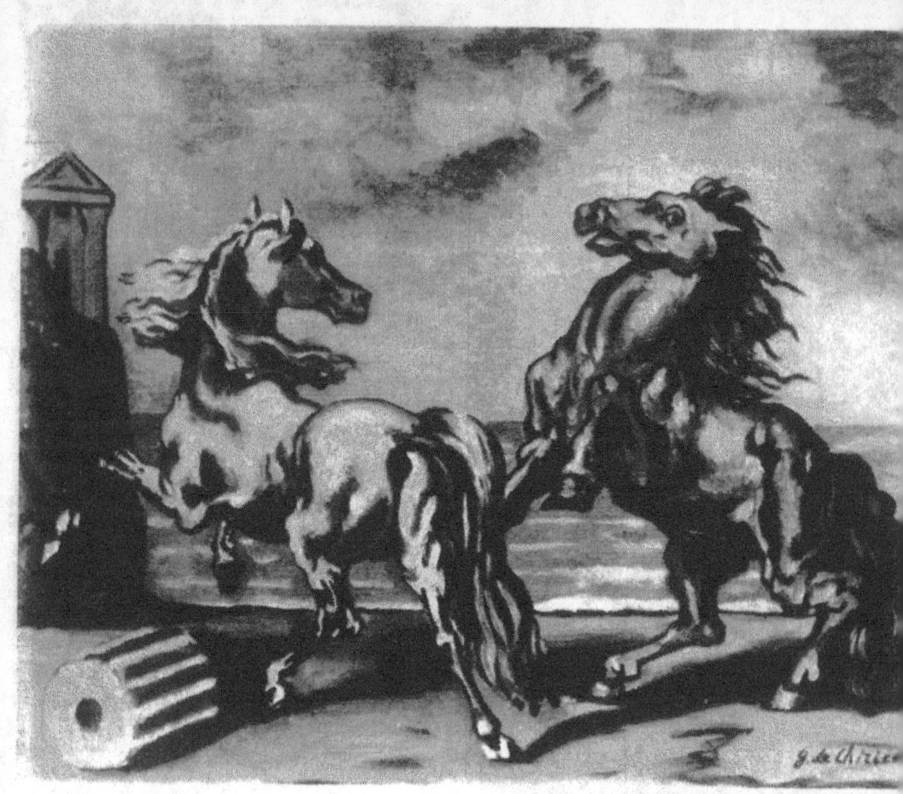

17   *Two Horses on the Seashore*, 1930

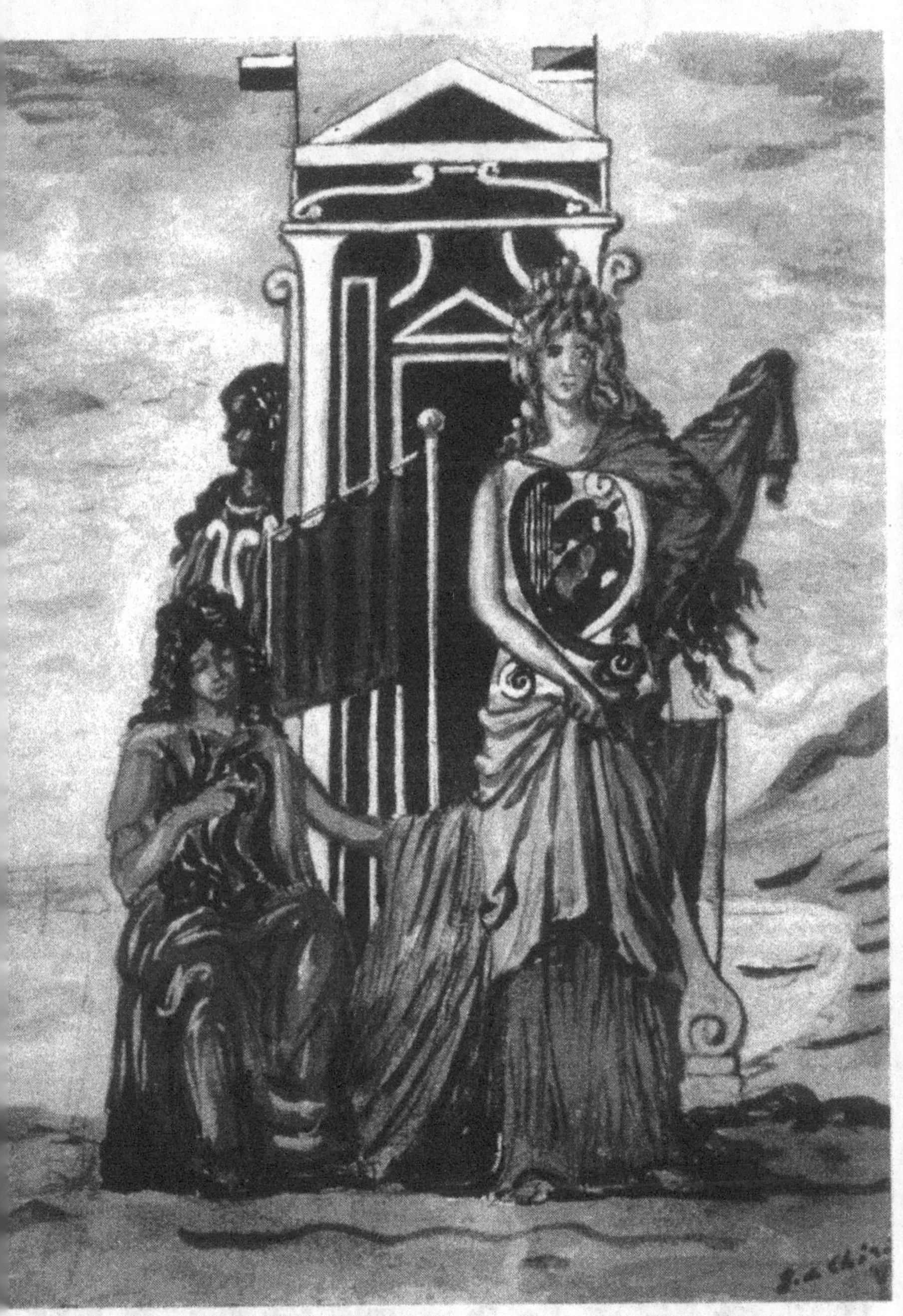

Muses on the Beach, gouache on paper, 1937

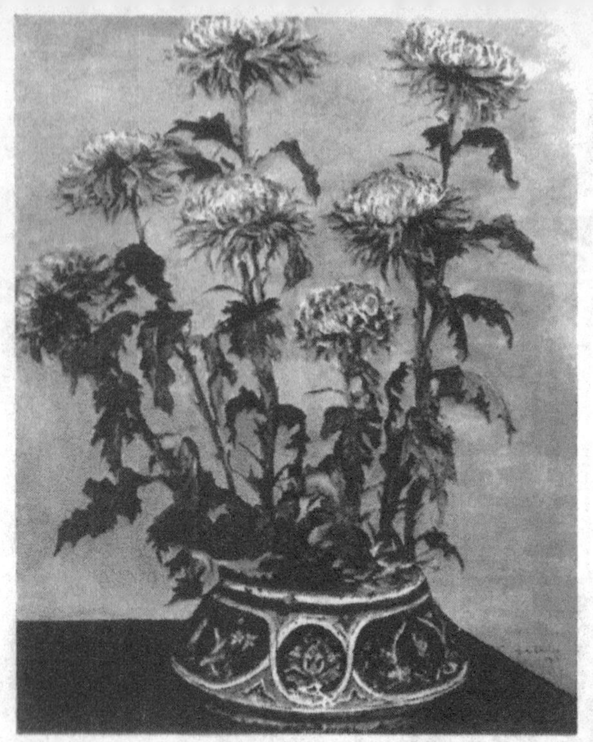

19   *Vase of Chrysanthemums, 19...*

20   (*below*) *Fruit*, 1966

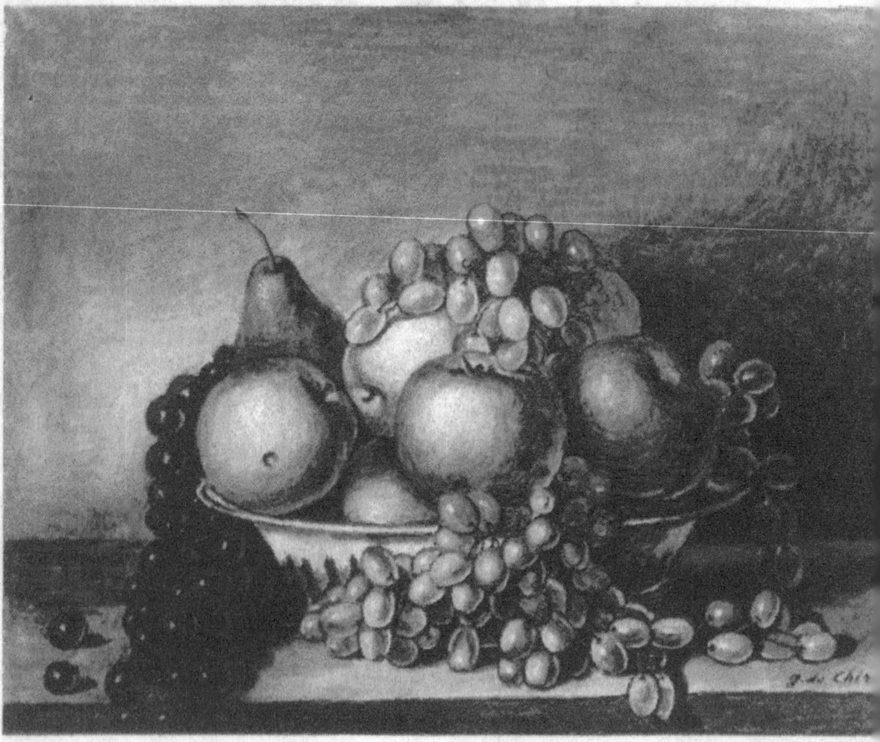

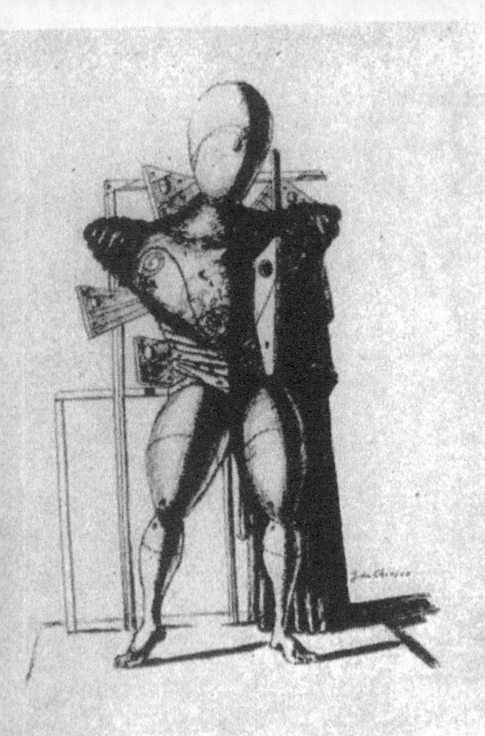

21 *Mannequin*, black and
white lithograph, 1966

22 (*below*) *Hut of the Mysterious
Bathers*, lithograph in
colour, 1968

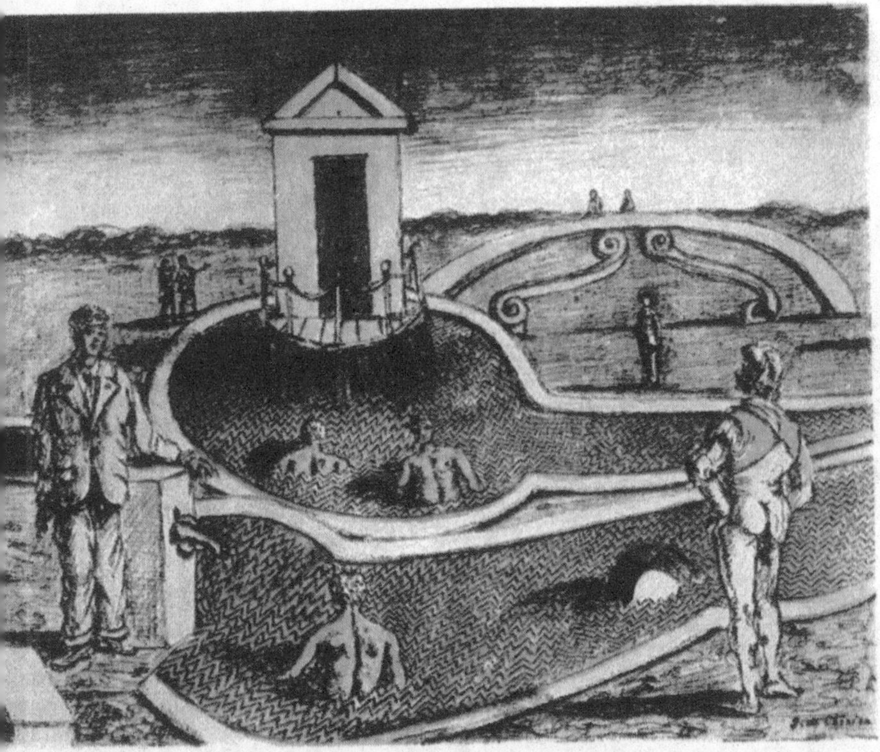

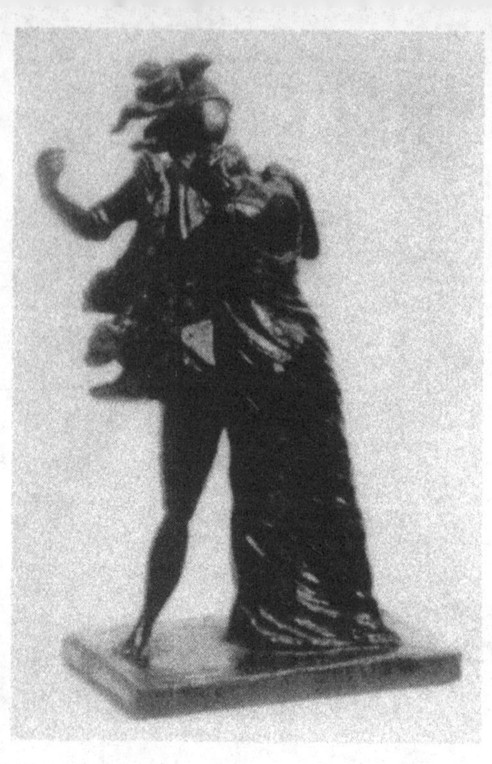

23 *Hector and Andromache*, bronze, 19[...]

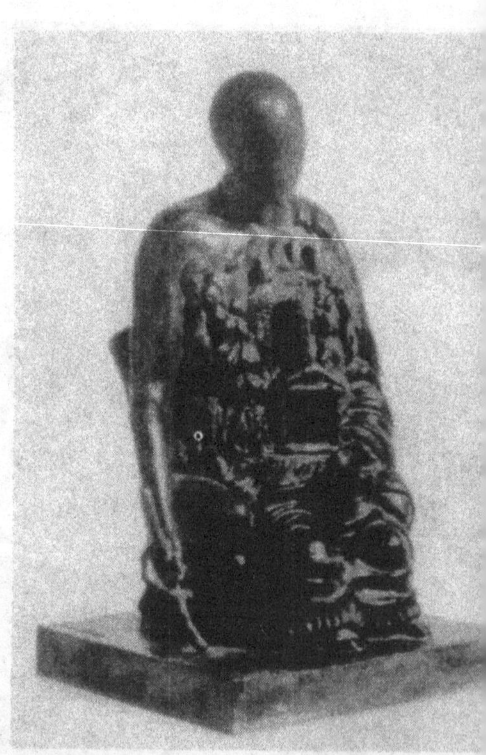

24 *The Painter*, bronze, 1968

Part Two

17

On August 8th, 1960, after more than thirteen years, I am starting to write my memoirs again, that is to recount things seen, heard and read during almost three lustra, and to express my opinion with clarity, sincerity and courage about people and facts I have been able to know and observe at my leisure.

As in that distant July of 1945, today, as I start my memoirs again, I am in Rome and there is a sultry, damp and oppressive heat. Sometimes there is not even any refreshing breeze from the famous *ponentino* or north wind which usually blows over the city in summer, after sunset. Three or four times during the day I go on to the terrace outside my studio, and like the captain of a ship with its sails shortened in calm weather, I watch and scrutinise the sky before me and above me. I look to the right, towards the north, where stands the beautiful Villa Medici with its impressive gardens. At one time this villa harboured painters such as Fragonard, David and Ingres; today it harbours the winners of the Prix de Rome who come to the city to paint certain modernistic things which could very well be painted by the banks of the Seine. Then I look towards the west, towards Monte Mario and the dome of St Peter's, then to the south-west where can be seen the outline of the chariot which supports the roof cornice on top of the Palace of Justice, the so-called 'ugly' palace. I look farther south where I can see the upper part of the monument to Vittorio Emanuele II, a monument which has always been very much criticised and spoken of ironically, like the Palace of Justice, but in comparison with the wretched things put up by certain modernist architects who proceed with their eyes fixed on the line of the horizon, such as Le Corbusier, Wright, Gropius and others, these two buildings, unlike the aberrations of certain modern architecture, are authentic masterpieces, worthy of a Bramante or a Brunelleschi.

But nothing can be seen towards any of the four cardinal points, not even the smallest cloud. Then I imagine typhoons and cyclones, sudden frightening clouds which descend on the city, gusts of wind and torrential rain, and afterwards, when the washed sky becomes clear again, a delightful coolness, the fragrance of washed soil which hovers lightly in the air, allowing all nature to breathe. Instead, I see in the west a fiery disc going down slowly and disappearing behind the mist on the horizon. *Mist on the horizon*—these words make me think of Otto Weininger and his book *Concerning Supreme Things* in which he says that the sun setting on the horizon is like a severed neck. I say that it is also like one of the two halves of a melon cut in two. Weininger also says in the same book that when a volcano erupts the defecation of the earth is coming out of the crater. But all these definitions, based on comparisons between images, have no great value. A few years ago, when I read *Sex and Character*, and *Concerning Supreme Things*, I was interested in Weininger's work; later my interest diminished and now I confess that he no longer interests me. On the other hand I have always kept an interest in the works of Arthur Schopenhauer.

Let us return to my memories.

In July 1945, then, it was oppressively hot in Rome. The Americans had dropped the atomic bomb on Hiroshima and the war was drawing to an end. Some people were saying at that time that the oppressive heat was due to the so-called thermonuclear explosion. There are still many people today who attribute meteorological anomalies to the atomic explosions carried out in Russia and the United States. But I do not believe much of what they say and it seems to me that the meteorological situation is more or less the same as it has always been.

At that time I lived with my wife in an apartment at the corner of the Via Mario de'Fiori and the Via delle Carrozze. It was an apartment which we had had to rent in a great hurry, because it was no longer possible for us to stay in the rooms we had rented in a small palazzo situated in the Via Gregoriana and almost entirely

occupied by Signor Gualtieri di San Lazzaro and his wife. The reason
was that he was making life impossible for us, although he himself
had offered us these rooms when we met him in Rome after the
arrival of the Allies in June 1944.

One day, while in fact we lived in the Via Gregoriana, San Lazzaro
showed me a photograph of a picture attributed to me, which he
said he had bought in Paris before the war. I realised at once that
this was one of those crude fakes with imitations of my signature
which were being mass-produced in Paris as in other places. I told
him so and I suddenly realised that he had been in a very bad mood
even before I had seen the photograph, for he had told me that the
painting had cost him a fortune; in addition to a large sum in cash
he had also given—I do not quite remember—one or two paintings
by de Pisis.

From that day Gualtieri di San Lazzaro began to behave towards
us in a way that was really unspeakable; he no longer said good
morning to us; during meals, which we ate together, he growled in
our direction, then one fine day he came up to me with a determined
air and a severe frown, saying that he was giving me a few days to
find another place to live, since he needed the rooms I occupied.

Knowing how difficult it was at that time to find somewhere to
live in Rome I replied that I too did not want to live under the
same roof with him, but I could not guarantee that I would be able
to leave before finding another place. Then Gualtieri di San Lazzaro
was seized with a kind of hysterical fury. In a voice suffocated with
anger he began to scream, 'Blackguard! Rascal! The surrealists were
right, Breton was right!' and then, seizing a clothes-brush which
happened to be nearby and holding its handle in hands apparently
shaken with convulsions, as though he had been stricken with an
attack of epilepsy, stamping more frantically on the floor, he went
on screaming, 'Blackguard! Rascal! The surrealists were right,
Breton was right!'

In the meantime his wife appeared, attracted by her husband's
screaming, and, realising the grotesque nature of the scene, she
pushed her spouse firmly into their bedroom and immediately locked
the door. I went back upstairs, where our rooms were, and from there
I heard the hysterical imprecations which reached me from below
as though from some subterranean place, stifled and faint, and the
voice more strangled than ever, still yelling as though obsessed:
'Blackguard! Rascal! The surrealists were right, Breton was right!'

Through the association of memories this scene made me think of Gabriele D'Annunzio's *Francesca da Rimini*, when Francesca finds herself in her room with Malatestino whom she reproaches for his bloodthirsty cruelty, while from the vault where Montagna is held prisoner come the cries and lamentations of the condemned man. The scene provoked by Gualtieri di San Lazzaro did not evoke the horror of the scene from D'Annunzio, but there was something comic and also slightly painful about it.

Fortunately we soon found an apartment in the Via Mario de'Fiori. In the Via Gregoriana, apart from the rooms where we lived, we had the use of an attic lit by a skylight. This gave me a magnificent light, in which the contours of people and objects were intensified, as in the paintings of Rembrandt and Caravaggio. In that attic I painted some extremely fine silent lifes[1] with objects, copies of ancient sculpture, old books and game. I later took these highly successful paintings down to the first floor where there was a drawing-room. My paintings were still on show there one day when I had invited a few friends and acquaintances to take tea. Among the people invited there was Dr Palma Bucarelli, director of the Gallery of Modern Art in Rome, a gallery which, through antonomasia, many people call the Museum of Horrors. I can still see, even after so many years, Dr Palma Bucarelli looking at those extremely fine paintings of mine with a cold, remote and disgusted expression, rather like one that would be registered by a high-grade cook, those whom the French call *cordons bleu*, who had gone to do the shopping for a highly important meal and was standing in front of a barrow looking at half-rotten and wormeaten turnips. The famous doctor's attitude was one of so many irrefutable proofs that she is totally lacking in any understanding of painting. In fact Dr Bucarelli, like Professor Lionello Venturi, is an ardent supporter of all the most ugly, trite, tedious and shameful manifestations of so-called modern art. In the United States this modern art is also called art in progress and in New York the Museum of Modern Art, which for horrors even beats our Museum of Horrors in Valle Giulia, has published a volume dedicated to the works in this museum. The volume is entitled *Art in Progress* and a few years ago the director of that museum had the exquisite kindness to send me the volume. But I, who have a profound horror of everything that does not correspond to the truth, stuck over the title *Art in Progress* a fine strip of white paper and wrote on it with a brush, *Art in Progressive*

Putrefaction, having seen that the results of such pseudo-painting, so far as putrefaction is concerned, clearly progresses every day.

In this way, as I said earlier, I moved house early in 1945 to flee from the implacable anger of Signor Gualtieri di San Lazzaro. We went to live in a furnished apartment in an old house in the Via Mario de'Fiori. This street is a very well-known street in Rome, near the Piazza di Spagna. It is well known especially for the great number of *maisons de tolérance*, or tea-houses, or brothels or what you will. I do not know which is the least antipathetic of all these words; perhaps tea-house, which makes one think of Japan and the music of *Madame Butterfly*, music which everyone likes, although I would say that it is especially the leading conductors who like it, although they do not say so: Puccini's music, however, gives me goose-flesh. Now, after the passing of the Merlin law, all these so-called *maisons closes* have really been closed, but the fact of their closing and its consequences have filled the papers with such fine words as meretricious, sensuality, procuration, carnal, lasciviousness, etc. It is strange that for me, when I read or hear these words here and there, they evoke pictures which have actually nothing to do with the true and proper meaning of the words in question. For example, 'sensuality' and 'sensual' suggest to my mind a Rubens-like vision of great salons in the seventeenth-century style, the walls hung with very fine pictures, their magnificent frames gilded with real gold, and valuable tapestries, stuccoes, splendid furniture and gentlemen and ladies, clad in silk and satin with stylish, ostentatious jewellery, walking about in these surroundings conversing together with gestures and expressions of quiet euphoria. The Italian word *lenocinio*, however, which means procuring, makes me see the image of a little lion with enormous claws and an exceedingly nice face, born in a zoo and fed from a feeding-bottle by a beautiful blonde young woman wearing a kind of uniform somewhere between that of an air hostess and a nurse. The word *meretricious* makes me think of a crowd of mothers of all kinds, all races and all ages, from all countries, during a kind of congress, like those which are organised today by communist women in support of peace, with many displays of Picasso-like doves and speeches against the manufacture of atomic bombs. At those congresses, however, it is not stated, but I think it is upheld, that atomic bombs should be manufactured in Russia and *only* in Russia, then things would go well, even very well, and the more that are made the better things would be. The word *carnal*, as in carnal sin, carnal violence, etc., arouses in me the image of a corpulent, red-faced gentleman sitting at a table with his napkin tied at the back of his neck, armed with a knife and fork, about to attack a huge beefsteak, Florentine style, on a plate in front of him. As far as the word *lascivious* is concerned, it makes me think of some sturdy washerwomen with their arms plunged in a great rectangular basin of water, washing and rinsing clothes. Lastly I must say that the word *adultery*, although it does not arise through the closing of the *maisons closes*, makes me think of a kind of club or circle, where men of about thirty, looking like Charlie Chaplin as a young man, with little straw hats and little bowlers meet, men in fact who are prototypes of those who have reached *the age of adultery*.

A mass of legends, each one more false and absurd than the last, have arisen in Italy and beyond about the *maisons closes*. In particular it is said that in these places the women are like prisoners in a prison, like galley-slaves, who were condemned to remain where they were until they died and when, overcome with faintness and fatigue, they abandoned their oar and collapsed at the bottom of the boat, they were simply thrown into the sea and replaced by another slave. In addition to this untrue story it was also said that the women in these houses were terrorised by the *padrona*, the boss or someone else; that they were continually watched, that they could never go out and so on. All this is completely untrue. The women in the *maisons de tolérance* were free citizens, almost like the employees in an office or servants in a private house. Naturally they entered into an agreement with the owner of the 'house' just as the owner did with them. But they were completely free to leave when they wished, to change their way of life, as people usually call it, when they wanted to. Many of them, after a certain time, when they had put some money aside, married and became excellent wives and mothers.

Nor is it true that these places were places of unbridled luxuriousness and eroticism taken to the nth degree. In fact for the sake of truth it must be said that in the *maisons de tolérance* everything concerning sexuality, sensuality, luxuriousness, which is solemnly defined as carnal sin, was reduced to a minimum, to strict necessity. In the bedrooms of couples on honeymoon, in fashionable gatherings, in de luxe places, at balls, parties and receptions with a background of riches and luxury, there is a hundred thousand times more eroticism and luxuriousness, while 'carnal sin' is extolled there in a more or less hypocritical and discreet manner, a hundred thousand times more than in all the brothels which, before the Merlin law, existed all over Italy.

What is more, the women living in these *maisons de tolérance* were not in fact cynical, shameless and impudent, as some people naïvely and stupidly believe, and here I would like to repeat what a great English philosopher, writer and poet, Thomas De Quincey, who lived at the beginning of last century, said in his *Confessions of an Opium-Eater* about an extremely pure love he felt for a London girl named Ann, who was, as he said with exquisite euphemism, a *peripatetic*. Often, late at night, the young Thomas De Quincey would walk with Ann along the banks of the Thames, as Socrates walked with Aspasia along the banks of the Ilissus, talking of many lofty things concerning the mind and human sentiments. But one day he could no longer find Ann, nor did he succeed afterwards in learning anything about her. But he remembered her always even when he grew up and when he was old, and always saw her in his dreams, while in his *Confessions* he described this poetic and profound vision :

> And at a vast distance were visible, as a stain upon the horizon, the domes and cupolas of a great city—an image or faint abstraction, caught perhaps in childhood from some pictures of Jerusalem. And not a bow-shot from me, upon a stone, shaded by Judean palms, there sat a woman; and I looked, and it was —Ann !

In the Via Mario de'Fiori I worked hard, as usual. At that time various paintings of mine were bought by South American diplomats and I also painted the portraits of the wives of some of them. One very successful portrait was that of a Brazilian lady, whose surname was Fonseca, who was the wife of a secretary to the Brazilian Ambassador to the Holy See. I also knew a Brazilian ambassador who was called Nabucco. He was an elderly, tall, plump gentleman who was very kind to us and invited us on several occasions to the Embassy for lunch and dinner. But his kindness was perhaps not entirely disinterested, since one fine day he asked me to do a few drawings for him to illustrate a book he had written about the art of preparing cocktails. He did not mention a fee and I realised that it was a question of working *gratis*. I did three or four drawings for him which he admired very much and he even invited a few of his friends and acquaintances to look at them during a dinner party at the Embassy. My drawings were greatly admired and I was warmly complimented by the Ambassador and everyone present. Only one lady, the classic type of modernistic snob, turned up her nose. Then, after telling me that she was a friend of Breton, Dali, Cocteau and various other dismal phenomena of our dismal times, she asked me point-blank why I had *repudiated metaphysical painting*.

I replied that I had not in fact repudiated it, and that from time to time I painted a metaphysical painting, and that actually I had just sold a *Troudadour* to a Swiss collector, and what was more I told her that if she wished I would wager ten million lire to ten that she could not prove to me beyond all doubt that I had *repudiated metaphysical painting*.

The modernistic snob looked at me in surprise and perplexity; she did not understand if I was speaking seriously or joking; then in anger and agitation, she went on: 'But everyone says you have rejected your early manner!'

'I don't know,' I replied, 'who *everyone* consists of, but they are usually four troublemakers who try everywhere to confuse the ideas of people as naïve as you, in order to fish in the turbid waters of so-called modern art and so-called new culture. I have never had either a first or a second or a third or a fourth manner; I have always done what I wanted to do, standing loftily apart from the gossip and legends created about me by envious and interested people. And then, dear lady, why don't you ask Picasso if he has repudiated or rejected the harlequins, acrobats and beggars he painted more than half a century ago?'

When I had finished speaking the modernistic snob was no longer to be seen; she had disappeared as though by magic.

At the same period I met again one of my old friends whom I had known from the time after the First World War, the sculptor Alfredo Biagini and his good wife Wanda. Biagini and his wife both died a few years ago. He was an able sculptor and an honest, serious and studious man. He had a sacred horror of the modernists and of the shallow attitudes which prevail today in the field of the plastic arts. He was also an excellent draftsman and knew the anatomy of the human body well, something that few sculptors and painters know today. He often came to see me in my apartment in the Via Mario de'Fiori and there we would talk at length about drawing, looking through monographs on the work of Michelangelo and

Dürer. And in order to put our principles into practice Biagini and I would draw from memory faces and parts of human faces, trying to imitate the manner of this or that master. Sometimes, as we worked, we would talk about the decadence of our era and about the fact that today artists, or those who call themselves such, unlike the situation earlier and until almost the whole of the nineteenth century, never talk about art when they are together, and the themes of their conversation are always gossip and malignity and this happens when they are somewhat in form and are not yawning from boredom as they usually do.

Every summer Biagini went to Fiuggi to take the cure and in July 1945 he also advised me to do the same. I joined him at Fiuggi a few days after he had gone there and I too wanted to drink the water. But I did so rashly and without first consulting a doctor. At Fiuggi you drink the water in the morning, on an empty stomach, and you drink it very cold. At Fiuggi it was very hot and I was thirsty, so that swallowing a few glasses of this near-iced water every morning was a real pleasure for me. But a few days later I was stricken with extremely violent stomach pains and a high temperature. I hastily packed my bags and rushed away from Fiuggi like a scalded cat. I took refuge in the bosom of my family in my apartment in the Via Mario de'Fiori. It is true that my family consists only of my wife Isabella, but when you are ill only your own house and your own wife can console you and give you a sense of security.

I stayed in bed for a few days, but the illness lasted for more than two weeks. On that occasion I met Professor Carlo Barbarossa, the doctor, who looked after me with great care and later became one of our friends. Dr Barbarossa is an intelligent young scientist who is studious and capable, but he too, like so many young and not so young doctors today, never prescribes the old remedies which are regarded as outmoded, just as the modernist painters consider the old painters to be outmoded. But some of the old remedies are often more effective than many drugs with complicated names of Greek origin, which the international pharmaceutical industry puts on the market today in ever-increasing numbers. For example, stomach cramps are very effectively treated by drops of laudanum drunk with a little water and the application of warm poultices to the stomach. Taken by mouth myrrh is also highly effective against intestinal upsets; apparently in certain areas of Libya the natives cure dysentery and even cholera by taking large doses of myrrh. But if you mention these remedies to a doctor today he smiles with benevolent irony.

On this occasion I said nothing to the doctor but sent my servant to buy a little laudanum from the chemist's and I drank a few drops of it in water; the pains subsided and after a few applications of poultices I felt better. All this, however, in no way diminishes the merits of Dr Carlo Barbarossa and I must say for the sake of truth that some of the remedies he prescribed for me, such as, for example, the Squibb methianone, for the prevention of possible liver disorders, and the Heptas B-12 syrup, have been so effective for me that I recommend them to anyone who suffers from liver trouble.

At that time Pietro Mascagni died in a room in the Plaza Hotel, opposite the church of San Carlo. When the cortège left the hotel a band, either military or municipal, played the intermezzo from *Cavalleria Rusticana*. The crowd present seemed to be moved; many people stood to attention. Mascagni was, after all, an Italian artist, known in all countries and popular in his own; an Italian artist had gone into the kingdom of darkness and although efforts had been made to keep the fact quiet, because Mascagni had been made an Italian academician under the fascist government, the people present felt a certain emotion and I felt it too, even though I have never liked Mascagni's music.

Then one afternoon we heard the sirens. Many people immediately thought that German aircraft were carrying out a raid, but instead this dismal sound announced to the people of Rome that the war was over. But there was no outburst of joy as when in the distant autumn of 1918 the announcement came that the Austro-German armies had asked for an armistice. This lack of enthusiasm was due to the fact that the Romans regarded the war as over when, at the end of June 1944 one Sunday evening, at the Porta Sangiovanni, the first American armoured cars arrived, sincerely acclaimed by the population who felt that the nightmare of Nazi oppression was over.

Towards the end of that year, 1945, I had to go to Florence to retrieve some paintings as well as clothes and other things that I had left with people whom I knew when I left in Florence in 1943 after the announcement of the armistice and the occupation of the city by the Germans. The railways were not yet functioning, but there were some private individuals who for a certain sum of money took passengers from Rome to Florence and vice versa. I remember that at the period when I decided to return to the Tuscan capital

I occasionally felt some minor twinges of rheumatic fever, but I decided to leave all the same. Very early one morning I got into a car with other people and we left. I had taken the precaution of bringing a few sulphonamide tablets with me. When we reached Florence, in the afternoon, I went to stay at the Albergo Fenice, in the Via dei Martelli, but during the journey I had already realised that the attacks of rheumatic fever had returned and when we reached the city of the Red Lily I felt very ill. I was preoccupied with the thought that perhaps in these circumstances I should have to remain ill in bed at a hotel. I then decided to take some sulphonamides. I knew that when you take sulphonamides you should eat something but avoid eggs. I then went round the streets of Florence looking for a delicatessen where I could buy a little roast chicken.

In the Via Calzaioli I suddenly found myself face to face with Roberto Longhi, looking like some devil who had sprung from a trapdoor. The first part of my memoirs had recently appeared in book form and when Longhi saw me he probably remembered what I had written about the time when I saw him in Florence coming through the doors of the Central Post Office and then saw him all at once raise his arms and disappear into the pavement. When I turned round a moment later and saw his form disappearing down the Via Strozzi I deduced that he had dived into the pavement and that like St Anthony he had the gift of ubiquity. When Roberto Longhi saw me he stopped and, coming up close to me, began to jump up and down and grin horribly like some Mephistopheles laughing coarsely in Dr Faustus's laboratory. 'I shan't disappear into the pavement now,' he hissed at me loudly, 'I shan't disappear into the pavement now!' I felt that I had a high temperature and could hardly stand on my feet. 'Listen, dear professor,' I replied, 'I have a high temperature and have to go back to the hotel and go to bed.' Longhi remained there looking slightly puzzled, not knowing whether I was serious or joking; he raised his hand to say good-bye and moved away while I went on looking for a delicatessen.

In the end I found one, bought a little roast chicken and went back to the hotel. As soon as I was in bed I swallowed a few sulphonamide tablets and then immediately ate the roast chicken. The first part of my night was disturbed; I had nightmares, I saw in my dreams one of my uncles who had died in Florence eighteen years earlier and in my dream I reopened a discussion that I and

my brother Alberto Savinio often had with my uncle about the Old
and the New Testaments. Our uncle was very religious, even bigoted,
going to church twice a day. As a young man he had suffered greatly
from intestinal upsets and the doctor had advised him to eat grilled
meat every day. Since he fasted every Friday he had obtained from
the Vatican a kind of dispensation granting *nulla osta*, written in
Latin on a kind of parchment and bearing all the signatures of the
Ecclesiastical Authority. This special permission to eat grilled steak
even on Friday began, I remember, with the words: *morbi intestinalis
causa licet Gustavo de Chirico carnem in die veneris edere*, etc., to
eat meat even on the day of Venus. The discussions with our uncle
often centred on the problem of whether King David was a saint or
not. Our uncle hesitated for a moment and then said in a solemn
voice, 'Not a saint, since the fact of having placed his concubine's
husband in the front line during a battle was an act deserving of some
reproof, but later he repented and now he is in heaven with the
others.'

I slept badly for the first part of the night, then I fell fast asleep
and when I awoke, late in the morning, my temperature was quite
normal. It is true that my legs were shaky and very limp but in fact
I could go out into Florence and the surrounding district to look for
the furniture and pictures I had left behind three years earlier. Some
things had been lost and some stolen, especially sketches and drawings
of mine, but I succeeded in regaining possession of nearly all my
belongings. I took a few paintings with me and together with my
suitcase I put them on top of a car which made the journey from
Florence to Rome and vice versa, taking passengers. The paintings
were badly secured on top of the car and while we were going out
of the city, passing through the San Frediano district, two paintings
fell off into the road without my realising it. These paintings consisted of one of my self-portraits and another work, one of my best
paintings, a double portrait of my wife together with my sister-in-law
Maria. When I reached Rome and realised that these two pictures
were no longer there I was very upset and wrote at once to the
antique dealer Luigi Bellini asking him to put an advertisement in
the Florence newspapers to see if we could trace the paintings. A
few days later Bellini wrote to me that two men from San Frediano
had come to see him, because they knew that he knew me. They
said that they had found the pictures and kept them, but before they
would hand them over they demanded a certain sum of money

which was not exactly small, in fact it was blackmail. However, I was so glad to have found my paintings, to which I was very attached, that I immediately sent Bellini the sum demanded so that the pictures would be restored to me.

During my journey from Florence to Rome I talked to the man driving the car and learnt that his name was Venturoli. I then asked him if by chance he was related to a writer and journalist called Venturoli, who had come to me a few years earlier declaring sympathy, admiration and support and making me give my opinions on art and artists today. Naïvely, I told him everything, thinking he was sincere, but Venturoli published a book titled *Interviste di frodo* and maliciously included what I had told him, adding also opinions and thoughts that I had never expressed. Venturoli thought he would create a scandal with this book, stirring up a lot of controversy and becoming famous as a result. The book, however, was a complete flop; nobody mentioned it, nobody sued Venturoli and everything ended in complete calm. The driver heard what I had to say and told me that in fact Venturoli was his brother, adding honestly that he had behaved very badly in doing this.

I returned to Rome and began to work again. At that period I painted various important works, among which was a self-portrait in which I wore a grey-blue seventeenth-century costume and hat, the latter being lent to me by the Opera. I have kept the self-portrait in my private collection because I consider it to be one of the best works I have ever painted. At that time the Rome Opera was directed by the Allies, and its administration was in the hands of a British non-commissioned officer named Aronson, a cultured and intelligent man whom I knew and with whom I became friendly. He is passionately fond of Italy and comes to spend a little time there every year. Now he has come to the Isola del Giglio where he has bought a villa overlooking the sea. The director of the ballet was Aurel Miloss and I designed the décor for a ballet titled *Don Juan*, with music by Richard Strauss.

At that time too the first part of my memoirs came out, published by a gentleman named Meschini-Ubaldini; the publishing firm was called Astrolabio. The appearance of that first part of my memoirs was like a bolt from the blue, especially among the modernistic intellectuals. There was a moment of perplexity; but then people realised that the most effective tactic was one of silence and boycott. In fact I noticed that my book, after making a timid appearance in the windows of a few bookshops, disappeared completely. One day when I was in the Bocca bookshop in the Piazza di Spagna I heard an employee mention my name over the telephone; I then asked him what it was about and he replied that several people had asked for my book but that the shop, in spite of several telephone calls to the publisher, could not manage to get even one copy. In fact, it was clear that the director of the publishing firm, Signor Meschini-Ubaldini, had been attacked by the modernist intellectuals and bombarded with complaints for having had such an irritating book printed. He had, therefore, decided to relegate it to obscurity by not sending it to the bookshops, perhaps even recalling the copies he had already sent out. I understand Signor Ubaldini very well. I certainly understand him! . . . I understand him and I forgive him.

Since I spoke favourably in my memoirs about Pietro Annigoni and the Bueno brothers I received letters of cordial thanks from them; but I must say that later the Bueno brothers disappointed me both from the personal and artistic point of view. From the personal point of view, their negative attitude towards me almost made them go over to the other camp, hoping in this way that the modernists would forgive their positive sides and all the mastery they had achieved so far. From the artistic point of view the elder one disappointed me by behaving somewhat like Picasso, the Picasso of the big feet and hands, while wavering somewhat towards the left —that is, in order to follow a fashion that was already rather out of date, he began to play the communist and even went to hold an exhibition in Mexico. The other, the younger one, began to be a leucophile, that is a lover of white, and also imitated Piero della Francesca, with undertones of Morandi. This was a pity, for if they had gone on painting as they were painting in 1942 and had continued trying to improve, I believe that by now their situation would be much better from every point of view.

It is strange how the few, and there are very few, painters today who know more or less how to hold a brush in their hands, believe that they are forced to carry out a little surrealism, to sacrifice something to the Moloch of modernism. Apart from the Bueno brothers this has also happened in the case of the painter Guariente and the Prince of Hesse. Annigoni proceeds in a more or less straightforward way, although even he imitates the surrealists a little; just a little, a very little, but something shows through his paintings also; for example, in the background to the portrait of Queen Elizabeth there is a man who is, I think, sitting by a canal or a lake fishing, I don't remember which, but this is vaguely reminiscent of Brueghel the Elder, who has nothing to do with the style of the portrait. At the British Embassy in Rome I have seen a copy of this portrait, done, I am told, by a pupil of Annigoni; it has been very well painted.

The only man who resists, one hundred per cent, these morbid tendencies of modernism is the painter Gregorio Calvi di Bergolo. He possesses solid mastery and an intelligent understanding of the art of painting. He has resisted so far; but will he always do so, or at least, until when? *That is the question.* . . .

We were in the year of grace, 1947. The house where we lived in the Via Mario de'Fiori, the one I had to take in a hurry in order to escape the persecutions and strange moods of Signor di San Lazzaro, was rather dismal and dark. By good luck someone came to tell me one day that in the Piazza di Spagna there was a place to let on two floors with big balconies from which you could see the whole of Rome. I went to look at it straight away, and although the rooms in this place were in the worst possible state—in some the rain even came through the roof—I told the owner that I wanted to rent it and with his consent I hastily occupied the place by having my bed brought into one of the rooms. However, before my wife and I could finally live there I had to repair the rooms, and for about three months there was a continual coming and going of builders, plasterers, painters, varnishers, etc. In addition, we had to carry out a complete disinfection of the rooms and bedrooms, because they were full of beetles of all sizes and colours.

The place in the Piazza di Spagna was worth renting in every way, especially because of its central position. In the Piazza di Spagna we are close to all those places and shops which we more or less need to frequent. In the Piazza di Spagna there are first-class chemists, banks, international bookshops, travel agencies, high-quality hairdressers, art galleries, shops selling things for men and women, etc. Then you only have to go up the Trinità dei Monti steps to reach the Pincio; you have only to go down the Via del Babuino to reach the Piazza del Popolo, originally the Piazza del Pioppo, since in Latin *populus*, which in this case was feminine, as were all the names of trees and plants in that language, also meant poplar and through this confusion it was later called Piazza del Popolo, as well as the

Piazza del Pioppo, as it should have been called, and was probably called originally, perhaps because there was a poplar tree there. And then there is the Via Condotti, with the Caffè Greco, which they tried to remove a few years ago, probably in order to put an American bar in its place, with abstract bas-reliefs and cubist fittings. Fortunately there was a movement in its defence, a movement in which I took part with enthusiasm, and at least for the time being the Caffè Greco is safe. Let us hope that it is safe for a long time, for the day will certainly come when the black wing of modernist lust will sweep away this place where there is a collection of so many old photographs, letters, drawings and documents which bear witness to a time when painters knew how to paint, sculptors knew how to model and sculpt, and even knew how to work marble, unlike people today who give their work to the marble specialists; documents which bear witness to a time when writers knew how to write and had something to say; when poets were inspired and knew at least the principal rules of prosody and musicians knew nothing of the twelve-tone scale which I, for increased clarity call dodecacophonous, and knew nothing either of electronic music, but in compensation composed music which was very beautiful.

In the Piazza di Spagna there are important art galleries such as the Galleria Russo, organised and directed in a businesslike, intelligent way by the pleasant Russo brothers, Ettore and Antonio. It is said that Rome is the centre of the world and that the Piazza di Spagna is the centre of Rome, therefore my wife and I, if we live in the centre of the centre of the world, have in fact achieved the extreme of 'centrability' and the extreme of 'anti-eccentricity'.

In fact, I have always tried to live more or less in the centre of cities and have always had a downright horror of the outskirts. Thus in Paris I lived for a time in the Rue Meissonier, in Milan I lived in the Via Gesù, almost at the corner with Via Montenapoleone, in Florence I lived for a time in the Piazza della Repubblica, formerly the Piazza Vittorio Emanuele II, and so on. In the same way I always choose the most central hotels, the Continental in Milan, the Danieli in Venice, the Savoia in Florence, the Bristol in Genoa. The Bristol in Genoa is also an unusually metaphysical and evocative hotel and you feel you can see Alexandre Dumas and Garibaldi or Giuseppe Verdi and Jules Verne walking close together arm in arm through its rooms. In Rome one hotel which is evocative in this way is the Plaza, facing the church of San Carlo in the Corso. There perhaps one can imagine not the ghosts of Verdi and Garibaldi but perhaps those of De Amicis and Marie Bashkirtseff.

In my house in the Piazza di Spagna I have a magnificent studio which is on the fifth floor. From my studio balcony I often see splendid celestial sights, grim skies and misty skies, fiery sunsets, moonlit nights and nocturnal effects with clouds edged in pale yellow, as in certain marine landscapes by Dutch and Flemish masters. I am always ready with pencil and colours to note down rapidly these spectacles of nature, and notes of this sort are of use to me later when I paint my pictures. Corot used to say, 'Nature is the best teacher.' Nature is the best teacher, but the famous French landscape painter was wrong, or at least exaggerating, and when Delacroix said that nature 'cannot teach us how to achieve a masterpiece' he was much nearer the truth. In fact, the things which can teach us to paint well, draw well and continually make progress are the works of the Old Masters. It is normal and useful to work from reality and study nature, but this study should be accompanied by an even more constant and systematic study of the works of the great masters. Only after copying for tens and hundreds of times drawings and studies of trees by authentic masters such as Titian, Rembrandt, Poussin, Claude Lorrain, Fragonard, etc., can one afterwards copy a tree from life, and then you will be able to do it with mastery and confidence and not, as happens with many painters today when they paint from life, thinking only of Cézanne or Van Gogh, after which they succeed only in creating remarkable horrors.

At that time two memorable things happened to me, and the Italian press took a wide interest in them, but almost always adopted a malignant and poisonous tone towards me. One thing was the case brought against me by the Milione Gallery in Milan, because I had not only refused to authenticate a forged de Chirico but had taken it to the office of a notary to deposit it there in order to prevent it from remaining in circulation. At that time I used to take fakes to the office of a notary, but later I adopted a more expeditious method : I simply had them taken away with the authority of the police.

To return to the fake which emerged from the Milione Gallery, this is what happened. One afternoon, while I was working, a lady came to see me and showed me a painting of the metaphysical type, an Italian square in fact, on which my signature had been forged. As soon as I saw the picture I immediately realised that it was a fake and I told the lady that it was a fake and that I could not give it back to her; the least I could do was to put it somewhere where it could no longer circulate. I should never have said this : the lady began to shriek and say that what I wanted to do was a very serious thing, that the picture was extremely valuable, etc., etc. But as usual I did not allow myself to be either intimidated or impressed and I suggested to her that we should go together to deposit the fake picture in a notary's office. The lady rushed to the telephone and called a lawyer, an acquaintance of hers, asking him to come at once to my house where this terrible thing was being perpetrated. The lawyer arrived shortly afterwards, and so all three of us, with the fake de Chirico, went to a notary to deposit the object of the crime.

That same evening a certain Signor Dario Sabatello telephoned me. I think that Signor Sabatello, whom I had had occasion to know several years earlier, is the son of a well-known antique dealer. Sabatello told me in an excited tone of voice that what I had done was very grave, that the picture was authentic, that he and the Milione Gallery had proofs and superproofs and abundant evidence to prove its authenticity, that Signor Ghiringhelli of the Milione Gallery, who had sold the picture to him, Sabatello, would sue me for four or five million lire of material and moral damages and that on top of everything, he, Sabatello, had already bought his air ticket for the plane leaving that same day from Ciampino direct for New York. Because of me he, Sabatello, had been forced to postpone his departure, and this caused him a tremendous loss, since not only had the picture which I had withdrawn, declaring it to be a fake, already been sold by him to an American millionaire for an astronomical sum, but the millionaire was waiting for him at the New York airport in order to receive the picture and give him the money. Apart from all this Signor Sabatello, because he could not leave that day, due to me, was losing other highly important business for which he was going to the United States, business clearly important enough to rock the Bank of Italy together with the Bank of France and the Bank of England. In fact, it was clear from what he said that judgement would be given against me and I would also have to pay him an astronomical sum in compensation, and in order to do all this I would have to sell all my furniture and my house, all my pictures and take my last pair of shoes to the pawnbroker's and go about in slippers.

However, believing still *meo pristino more*, I stood firm. I replied that the picture in question was a fake, and that it was also a fake

of the worst kind and that I, especially in order to keep my conscience clear, felt it my sacred duty to stop it from circulating further.

The day of the hearing came. I was defended by two able lawyers,
Senator Giovanni Persico and Michele Grimaldi. I appeared in court
several times. Once, while the judge was questioning various witnesses, the painter Corrado Cagli, a friend of Sabatello's, appeared,
and said that he had been present in the United States at the sale
of an extremely small metaphysical painting of mine and, according
to what Cagli said, it was sold for several thousand dollars. The
engineer Della Ragione of Geneva then came and stated that in this
picture, which I had declared to be a fake, he recognised perfectly
the same picture that he had bought from me in Milan many years
earlier. Other witnesses, including a frame-maker from Milan and
a certain Signorina Bernasconi, also came to give evidence on behalf
of the Milione Gallery. Then a lady, whose name I no longer
remember, but who had been appointed as a witness by the court,
made a statement against me. In this way, in the face of this phalanx
of accusation and 'conclusive evidence', beneath this defence of the
Milione Gallery, judgement was given against me. In the press the
modernists were exultant; one who was particularly exultant was
the critic Marco Valsecchi, the mystic of modern stupidity.

I took the case to the Appeal Court. This time some witnesses
solemnly told lies and I was astonished that the magistrates did not
even reprove them, for I have always heard it said that false evidence
is punishable by law. New experts were appointed and here I was
able to consider the mentality of two gentlemen, whom until then
I had regarded as my friends. One of these gentlemen was Dr
Giorgio Castelfranco, whom I had known for about forty years and
who in the past bought various pictures of mine which were very
useful to him. He was Jewish and the pictures enabled him to send
his sons to the United States during the period of the notorious 'racial
laws'. The second of these two gentlemen was the minister Rodolfo
Siviero, who is now occupied with the recovery of Italian works of
art removed by the Germans during the last war. Signor Castelfranco
was nominated as an expert by the court and the minister Siviero
was the expert acting for me.

Shortly before the case was heard by the Appeal Court Signor
Siviero came to see me and showed me two or three, I cannot
remember exactly how many paintings, which were attributed to me
and were sketches rather than finished works. He told me that he

had bought these paintings in Florence and that among them was a small self-portrait which I immediately recognised as a fake and told Siviero so. The latter flew into a rage, fuming and protesting and swearing that it was an authentic work, that he had bought it from someone whose name he did not remember, but it was a woman who had been in the service of Dr Castelfranco, with whom he had stayed several times between 1920 and 1925. I replied that if this servant really existed and had said what the minister had told me, this meant that she was either insane, in the clinical sense of the word, or that she had lied. I also stood firm on this occasion.

A few days later both the minister Siviero and Dr Castelfranco refused to act as experts on my behalf. In spite of their absence, however, I won the case on appeal. This time the modernist critics abandoned the struggle and it was exceedingly comical to observe the difference in their tone on this occasion and the outburst of joy when it was announced after the first hearing of the case that I had lost. As I have already said, the most jubilant, the most highly delighted, was Signor Marco Valsecchi who, together with the renowned Professor Lionello Venturi, is an ardent supporter of all the daubs, small and large, and all the stupidities of the modernists in Italy and beyond and, in order to defend this collection of ugly things, fought with an ardour worthy of a more noble cause. When I lost the case at the first hearing Signor Sabatello had taken euphoria to the point of being photographed with the fake picture under his arm and smiling with cheerful satisfaction. This photograph was published in an illustrated American magazine which took his side, one of those many American reviews which are always ready to stand up for snobbery and support the decline of art. But it should be noted that Signor Sabatello, perhaps because of his prolonged stays in the United States, has forgotten an old Italian, in fact a European proverb which says: *He laughs best that laughs last.*

After my victory the Milione Gallery and Signor Sabatello had one last hope: the Court of Cassation.[2] The result of the appeal was announced in the newspapers and magazines through clenched teeth and the news caused great fright among the modernists, the envious people and all those petty-minded people who are always angered by my powerful personality, my courage in acting as the implacable enemy of every lie and deceit in the sacred field of art and most of all by my outstanding painting which makes continual progress. As a result all these ridiculous, dismal and negative people still hoped

for success at the Court of Cassation. The Milione Gallery and
perhaps Signor Sabatello also turned to the well-known lawyer
Calamandrei of Florence. He died a few years ago, but on this
occasion he immediately agreed to defend my opponents and to
prove to the magistrates that I was in the wrong. I learnt later that
during the hearing at the Court of Cassation he conducted himself
like a lion, yelling and raving to such an extent that someone, I don't
remember if it was one of the magistrates or one of the lawyers
present, reminded him that they were dealing with a civil action,
that they were not at the Court of Assize and that therefore all that
yelling was quite unnecessary.

In spite of the lawyer Calamandrei's screaming I also won the
case at the Court of Cassation. This time the modernist critics were
forced to bow before the inevitable. The modernists' death-knell was
sounded and I, who at heart am very human and am even moved by
the suffering and misfortunes of my enemies, thought of the sufferings
of Signor Marco Valsecchi and Professor Lionello Venturi; I thought
of the sufferings of Signor Ghiringhelli, the director of the Milione
Gallery; I thought of the sufferings of Signor Sabatello, and of
Signor Carlo Ragghianti and of so many others, including Dr
Castelfranco and the minister Siviero who would so much have
enjoyed seeing me lose this case; I thought of their sufferings and
I maintained an attitude of dignified respect. Suffering is always to
be respected even if, as in this case, its causes are far from edifying.

I must say, however, that I was astonished that in the judgement
pronounced by the court it was decided—I do not know whether this
was for the sake of Sabatello or the Milione Gallery—to remove the
fake signature on the fake picture. I thought that the court would
at least have ordered the destruction of the fake. In fact, when the
State discovers a fake banknote they have it destroyed. In fact, this
case was as though a cheque had been taken out of someone's cheque-
book and someone else, unknown to the rightful owner, had written
a cheque out to himself and forged the signature of the rightful
owner; and then, when the crime of forgery was discovered the man
possessing the forged cheque had merely been ordered to cancel the
signature. There are often strange and inexplicable things in the
judgements of the courts. However, the important thing was that
the judges had declared the picture to be fake and that as a result
I had been proved right. If, on the other hand, they had proved me
wrong, declaring that the picture was authentic, this would have

given a great deal of encouragement to the manufacture and ready sale of faked pictures; in fact, in defence of the fakers, and those who sold their products, various legends have been created about me, the principal ones being that I *have denied or repudiated the metaphysical paintings* and that, whenever I am shown a metaphysical painting, I automatically declare it to be false.

Let us come now to another fact that proves the mentality and morality of some people today. This is the notorious Exhibition of Metaphysical Painting conceived and carried out at the Venice Biennale in 1948. It was the first Biennale after the interruption due to the war. Six years earlier, in 1942, there had been a Biennale in which I had a room to myself. In 1948 the intention was to show the world what the Italian painters had done during those years of silence or semi-silence. Efforts were made too to spread the legend that fascism, like Nazism, had forced our artists to paint for a long time in a conventional manner and forbidden them to go along with 'liberty in art', linking them to the 'glorious' Paris school, directed and organised by the dealers in the Rue de La Boétie. But for the sake of truth it must be said that the fascists never forbade people to paint as they wished. The majority of the fascist hierarchy were in fact modernists enamoured of Paris, just as the democratic and republican Italians are today, including the same minister Bottai who was, as I have already said, a great modernist and Francophile and published a magazine which imitated the French reviews such as *Minotaure*, *Art Vivant* and others which were born, and which lived and died by the banks of the Seine.

The 1948 Biennale, therefore, was to be presented as the art exhibition *par excellence*, where the poor painters and sculptors were freed from the chains which had kept them enslaved and forced them to produce endless works in conventional academic style portraying fascist subjects which tended to exalt the achievements and events of the Mussolini period. Under the aegis of 'liberty in art' people were finally allowed to produce as much rubbish as they wished. However, as I have already said, there had been no law or regulation preventing painters from painting as they wished. As for the portraits of the leaders and the pictures and frescoes on fascist subjects which the painters were commissioned to carry out at that period, these could also have been consummate masterpieces like the paintings which, from the sixteenth century until the mid-nineteenth century, were commissioned from the painters of the time by governors, popes, princes and benefactors. If the official works carried out during the fascist period have left no trace, it is only because they were painted during a period when mastery and quality had completely disappeared from painting, as is the case with all modern painting, which will also pass without leaving the slightest trace; but it was not the fault of fascism.

The Exhibition of Metaphysical Painting arranged at the 1948 Biennale had one sole purpose: Giorgio de Chirico. But it was a totally negative purpose from my point of view. More than ever it was a question of attracting the attention of the Italian and also the foreign public to one type only of my painting in such a way that people could not take too much interest in another part of my production, the one I have been creating and perfecting for more than forty years. The many works of this type, precisely because of their unmistakable appearance of quality and mastery, are liked a great deal, a very great deal; basically everyone likes them, unlike the modernist types of painting which *nobody likes*. Furthermore, the organisers of the 1948 Biennale who had written idealistically about the glorious standards of their 'liberty in art' legions, knew that exhibiting those works of mine full of plastic qualities and mastery would constitute a highly dangerous contrast with the silliness, ugliness and stupidity which the members of the Biennale committee, re-emerging in 1948, sustained, defended and publicised with truly admirable zeal and ardour. The trick they played on me consisted in blowing with hysterical vigour down the long trumpets of publicity to announce and proclaim metaphysical painting, that is to limit to the maximum extent the creative power of a painter of my calibre, to limit it to a few dozen paintings carried out, according to them, in a moment of mad inspiration. The surrealists even talked about hallucinations, and as a result I would suddenly have been turned into a living corpse. I would have become an individual who, according to one gallery in Milan, 'had lost his nerve'. But the most incredible fact about the arranging of the Metaphysical Exhibition at the 1948 Biennale was that of calling two other painters, Carrà and Morandi, metaphysical, and putting their paintings together with mine. The special committee member appointed for this strange exhibition of metaphysical works was Professor Roberto Longhi: Professor Longhi, who for about forty years has specialised in the art of always being ready when it is a question of something negative so far as I am concerned. In fact, more than forty years ago, when

I had an exhibition of metaphysical paintings, as I have already said, he wrote a sneering and destructive article titled *To the Orthopaedic God*, yet more than forty years later he was quite ready in Venice to arrange an exhibition of metaphysical painting, because even there he smelt the smell of anti-dechiricoism. Another noteworthy fact about this obscene manifestation was that the worthy Biennale committee, after having consecrated Carrà and Morandi as metaphysical painters, established a prize of a few hundred lire for the best metaphysical painting.

Now everyone knows that Carrà plagiarised in an unpleasant way some of my metaphysical paintings which he saw me paint in a military hospital at Ferrara during the First World War. As for Morandi, he has never been a metaphysical painter. The limit was reached when the prize for metaphysical painting was given unanimously, but probably through the insistence of the modernistologist Professors Roberto Longhi and Lionello Venturi, to their beloved Morandi. Now you, dear reader, if you want to realise the mentality and morality prevailing today in certain circles of modern art and modern culture, think on this fact: an official exhibition, organised in Italy with money from Italian taxpayers, includes the paintings of a very well-known Italian painter without even inviting him and without even informing him, going against all rules of good behaviour and all usual morality. This very well-known Italian painter, who has created a style or a genre, if you wish, of painting, a style or genre which belongs to him and *only to him*, is exhibited along with works of other painters described arbitrarily and tendentiously as metaphysical, one of whom, as I have said, did no more than plagiarise, while the other has nothing whatever to do with metaphysical painting. Then to cap everything a money prize was even instituted, this prize being given to the man whose paintings had nothing whatever to do with the metaphysical style. Think about it hard, dear reader, and you will find it impossible to imagine anything more improper and shameless.

The furthest limit was then reached, because in the group of metaphysical paintings attributed to me there was a fantastic fake; it was such an obvious fake that, in order not to see it was a fake, you had to have your eyes covered not with slices of ham but with slabs of reinforced concrete. Not even Professor Longhi or the illustrious modernistologist, abstraction-lover and idolater of things French, I mean the illustrious Professor Lionello Venturi, the implacable supporter of 'liberty in art' and energetic defender of all daubs and stupidities bearing the sign of the decrepit and disorderly Paris school, neither Professor Longhi nor Professor Venturi realised throughout the five months of the exhibition that in the midst of the works by the hated de Chirico, *Shirico,* as the French call him, they had exhibited a fantastic fake on which his signature had been forged. This fake came from a collection in Milan and had been brought from Paris, where apparently it belonged to the surrealist poet Eluard, that man with the crooked nose and mystic look that I prefer not to define. During the five months of the 1948 Biennale *none* of these luminaries of modern painting, who included the worthy committee, realised that among the authentic de Chiricos there was also a shocking fake. Not bad as a display of incompetence! The members of the committee knew very well, however, that not only in Italy but all over the world large quantities of paintings falsely attributed to me and bearing my forged signature were circulating; therefore, the most elementary sense of propriety, and above all common sense, should have suggested to them that, before the exhibition, they showed me at least the photographs of those pictures which they had decided arbitrarily, tendentiously, against all rules and all sense of civil behaviour, propriety and morality, to exhibit.

Probably the members of the worthy committee felt themselves protected by the hostile attitudes shown towards me by all the modernists of Italy and beyond, and also felt they were defended by those false and malicious legends created about me, like the legend that I have 'repudiated metaphysical painting' and declare false all the metaphysical paintings shown to me. I once published in the Italian and foreign papers an offer that I would wager ten million lire against ten with anyone who thought he could provide me with irrefutable proof that I had rejected metaphysical painting. No takers; nobody dared accept the challenge; even though the risk consisted only of losing 10 lire! All this proves that today in certain circles there is bad faith and a lack of the slightest propriety and even the slightest courage.

I took legal action against the Biennale, but partly because the lawyer who was defending my interests did not act with much zeal and partly because the rules in such cases are not very clear and it is always possible to find loopholes, the court gave judgement in favour of the Biennale.

I decided to go to the Appeal Court and meanwhile, in articles and lectures, I systematically unmasked the bad faith and bad behaviour of the Venice Biennale. At the Appeal Court the lawyers on both sides agreed to a compromise, probably because the Biennale realised that in the last analysis I was right. But when the result of the hearing at the lower court was made known the Italian press was nobly exultant.

In 1949 the Royal Society of British Artists elected me as an honorary associate and invited me to exhibit a hundred paintings in the rooms at its headquarters. I accepted and a few months later I sent a hundred of my works to London. The exhibition lasted for a month and was very successful from every point of view.

At the opening the president of the Royal Society, the painter John Copley, gave a banquet in my honour in the Society's concert hall. During the exhibition various of my works were sold and one was bought by the well-known critic Eric Newton who wrote art criticism for the *Sunday Times*. It was the first time that a critic had bought one of my paintings. On this occasion, while my paintings were being triumphantly received in London, an Italian weekly magazine in Rome—I don't remember its name very well, but I think it was called *L'Elefante*—published a spiteful article saying that the English did not like my 'slimy' painting. On top of everything, together with the poisonous article, *L'Elefante* published a photograph where I was seen from the back, all alone in a corner of the exhibition. Now you should know, dear reader, that at my exhibition there was a continuous stream of visitors, although there was a charge for admission. Yet the writer of the spiteful article published this malicious and tendentious photograph, probably taken a few minutes before closing time, after the last visitor had gone, to make Italian readers think that nobody came to my exhibition. This is another typical example of the envy produced in Italy by the high quality of my work and my outstanding personality; this is another example of how in Italy there is a lack of all dignity and all national *amour propre*, especially among the scribblers and pseudo-intellectuals, who are always ready to play down the work and success of an Italian and equally ready to clean the shoes of any foreigner, however much of a bungler he is, especially in the case of a Frenchman. The mentality of old maids and ruffians. Furthermore, on this occasion there was a solemn silence throughout the Italian press concerning my successes in London.

At this period one of my friends, an antique dealer named Giorgio

Zamberlan, was in Venice. He also dealt in modern painting. He liked me very much, a feeling I reciprocated, and he had great admiration for my painting. He had the idea of organising in Venice, during the summer season, some major exhibitions of my work. The first of these shows was to be arranged in a room on the ground floor of the Ca' Giustinian, but the permission of the city council had to be obtained before this room could be used. At that time the mayor of Venice was a communist gentleman named Gianquinto. As a rule the communists, like the Christian democrats, show maximum hostility towards me, since they are nearly all modernists and they cannot tolerate that I, with my words and my brush, and above all with the exceptional quality of my painting, should destroy their idols with their feet of clay. In Russia modernistic things are soft-pedalled by the Moscow leaders, but countries outside Russia, the democratic countries, do nothing to prevent the continual debase-ment and the continual disintegration of all forms of art. They think, and probably with reason, that the huge mystification of which modern art consists, together with the increase of homosexuality, the use of drugs, the spread of juvenile and non-juvenile delinquency, the excessive liberty of the press and so many other splendid things of our time, contributes towards the increasing weakness and decreasing seriousness of the Western countries. But I do not believe that among the people concerned with art and culture in Russia today this *rejection of modernism in art* is a very sincere sentiment. I also believe that many of them think with great affection of Paris, Picasso, Matisse and other so-called leaders of the school of Paris, and of the cafés of Montparnasse. In fact, during the Stalinist period the so-called 'Paris school' was put in the cellars of the Russian museums; then, after the death of Stalin, spreading the notion that 'something had changed in Russia', that the rigorous oppression was over, those in charge of the art world had taken advantage of this and had rushed, *corde micante*, to take out of the cellars the 'masterpieces' of Matisse, Cézanne and so many others, and it appears that now, in the same Hermitage Museum, there are whole rooms dedicated to the pseudo-painters of Paris. All this is done naturally on the pretext of 'historical and educational reasons', but also very much, I think, because in the country of the hammer and sickle there are several people today who feel nostalgia for *la ville lumière*, as happened with us during the days of fascism. This is bad, just as the Stalinist system of putting the modernist paintings in the cellar was bad, a system similar to that of Hitler, who had them destroyed. In order to cure the plague of modern painting it is necessary first of all *to have a deep understanding of painting* which, however, is not the case either with those who support modern painting today and pretend to like it, and do this out of snobbery or commercial interest, or with those who, during periods of dictatorship, through conformism, or rather through fear, pretend not to like it.

To return to my exhibition that was held at the Ca' Giustinian, the kindness towards me of the honourable Gianquinto, who at that time was mayor of Venice, was very useful to me because he over-rode the strong opposition exercised by the Biennale. It appears also, from what I was told, that Senator Ponti fought like a lion to stop the municipality from giving me the room, and also another room in the same palazzo which I had chosen in order to give a lecture on the scandal of modern painting. In this way, through fighting and surmounting the difficulties, my exhibition was arranged in the room on the ground floor of the Ca' Giustinian. I think that if Matisse, or Braque, or another 'genius' from France had expressed a desire to exhibit in Venice, the entire ducal palace would have been placed at their disposal.

A few days after the opening of my exhibition I gave the lecture which received much applause and was a great success, as in fact all my lectures are. There were, it is true, the usual 'objections' on the part of a group of modernists who seemed to be led by the abstractionist Vedova, who resembles Segantini and makes one think of a Segantini who, by some miracle, has been restored to life and come down from the snowy mountains of the Engadine and settled in the city of the Doges to dedicate himself with ardour to super-modernism. When I had finished speaking and the roar of applause had died down, I braced myself to go down to the room where my exhibition was being held, but I had barely left the platform from which I had been speaking when suddenly there appeared at my side the faithful Zamberlan, who as a young man in Treviso had been a champion wrestler, and the Sicilian painter Privitera. They told me they were ready to accompany me and protect me, in case the modernists had decided to attack me, and so, with solemn steps and our heads high, we all three went out, flanked on both sides by the reverent audience. Between my two bodyguards I was like the apostle Peter between two gladiators converted to the Christian faith and determined to defend him to the death against anyone who dared to touch him.

My friend Zamberlan later arranged other exhibitions of my works in Venice, but this one was in the hall owned by Bucintoro, the company which controls the Venice boatmen. During the second exhibition I published a single issue of a paper titled *Biennale under Fire*, and by *Biennale under Fire* I meant that the Biennale was under examination, in this case from an *objective point of view*. But when this paper went on sale at noon and the newsboys rushed into the Piazza San Marco in front of the Caffè Florian yelling 'Biennale under Fire', many of the people who were sitting at the tables, painters, journalists and others, rushed at high speed towards the Riva degli Schiavoni and looked anxiously towards the gardens to see if columns of smoke and tongues of fire were rising from them. I went on with my articles and emphasised all the negative aspects of these manifestations or reviews or whatever one likes to call them, such as the Biennale, which cost many millions, all coming from the pockets of our poor taxpayers, and which merely help to damage and disgrace the reputation of art. Since the last war the Biennale has become a kind of market-place for French dealers and their kind from other countries. This exhibition, which should above all place on display what is being produced in Italy, and attract the attention of foreigners to it, has become instead a great outlet for dealers from beyond the Alps and allows them to open a market here among us for selling off merchandise which is becoming harder to sell each year on the old markets. It is an incredible fact that in a country like Italy, which has the reputation of being a poor country, there are gatherings like the Biennale, official gatherings, supported by the Government, where important money prizes are awarded. Prizes have been given to sculptors like Zadkine, painters like Max Ernst and so on. And to think that there are painters in Italy who work seriously, but they, like me in fact, have never even received a prize of a thousand lire.

This, dear reader, is the situation then of the arts in Italy. The people mainly responsible for the collapse of art today are protected, supported and encouraged, especially by leading officials of the Ministry of Public Education, who act in total accord with the men and women directing the museums, professors of art history, critics and other people more or less well-known, who for one reason or another find enjoyment or interest in fishing in the turbid waters of modern art and the so-called 'new culture'!

During the period of my exhibition in the Bucintoro company's hall I had occasion to prove that during my exhibition in London in 1949, which cost the Italian Government only three or four thousand lire, the British magazines and newspapers published many more articles than the British press, and in general the entire foreign press, had published about the Biennale exhibitions. In fact Count Zorzi, who at that time directed the Biennale press office, published in our papers a number of articles written abroad about the Biennale of 1950 or some other year. I on my side wrote in our papers that the number of articles written about me on the occasion of my London exhibition, which, as I said, cost our government only three or four thousand lire, was somewhat larger than the number written about the Biennale, which on the other hand costs our government many millions every other year.

I have kept all the articles about me written in the British capital, and in order to prove that I was not lying and not exaggerating I invited Count Zorzi to come and see me so that he could see *de visu*, in reading those articles, the truth of what I said. Count Zorzi did not come, but perhaps he could not come; in any case it was up to him to come or not, but I should add that Count Zorzi, whom I knew personally in Venice, was a perfect gentleman and not at all like most of the people who have their fingers in the pie, so far as modernist art is concerned.

As for the subsidy granted to me a few years earlier by the Ministry of Public Education for my exhibition in London, this is what happened. A few months before sending the paintings to England I went to the Ministry of Public Education to tell the minister, who at that time was the Honourable Gonella, and to ask for moral and possibly material support for this highly important exhibition of mine outside the country. I feel that I had a right to this, since whether one likes it or not, when a well-known, even a very well-known artist has an important exhibition abroad, it would seem fair that the Government helps him. The minister Gonella was very kind and affable towards me; he immediately called Professor De Angelis d'Ossat to his office and spoke to him about my exhibition, telling him that I ought to be helped and subsidised and that everything possible should be done to make certain that my exhibition had the success it deserved. However, when I returned to Italy after the exhibition I found, I will not say to my astonishment, for I am used to this sort of thing, but to my dismay, that the help from the Ministry consisted of three or four thousand lire, which represented a very small sum set against the cost of transporting the pictures from Rome to the Swiss border, while as for the Italian press moral support was reduced to a stupid and misleading article accompanied by an equally stupid and misleading photograph published in the magazine *L'Elefante*, which I have already mentioned. The other papers did not write a line, misleading or otherwise, about the fact. And this is how outstanding Italians are treated in Italy today by their government and by our press; as a result it is not surprising if their reputation abroad is low or nil. And to think that newspapers compete with each other to publish endless photographs of French people. Even yesterday, in a Rome daily paper, there was a large photograph showing Picasso with Cocteau and other people somewhere on the French Riviera. If one day someone institutes a Nobel Prize for provincialism, silliness, xenophilia and masochistic lust for *La France Immortelle*, I am convinced that this prize would be awarded to the Italy of today.

At that period I was invited by La Scala in Milan to design scenery and costumes for operas and ballets. I designed for the ballet *The Legend of Joseph*, with music by Richard Strauss, and for Boito's *Mefistofele*. All these designs were a great success and were very well received. I noticed, however, at La Scala that there was a persistent and subtle hostility towards me that emanated even from the more active sides of the theatre. The reason was always the same: envy; envy on account of my artistic strength and my personality as a man. Some people who are prone to vanity and intrigue do not care very much for an individual of my calibre. People of this type prefer to create an atmosphere, a level of mediocrity, and avoid anything that could lead to dangerous comparisons. In fact, I was only invited to collaborate in a production at La Scala on one other occasion, and this was probably due to the insistence of the dancer Lifar who had come to Milan for the staging of a ballet, a short one in fact, which was entitled *Apollon Musagète*, with music by Stravinsky, and produced at the Piccola Scala. The staging of the ballet was, however, totally neglected by Lifar and the production was very poor, with the result that my scenery and costumes could only make a limited impression. As for the costumes, on the pretext that there was not enough time to make them in accordance with my designs, they were made out of old rags in commonplace colours, which certainly did not contribute to the success of the ballet.

On the subject of scenery and costumes I must now relate a fact, and I do so not out of a desire for revenge but from a desire for justice. This is what it is about. One day in 1946, when I was still living in the Via Mario de'Fiori, a young Argentinian from Buenos Aires came to see me, accompanied by his mother. He told me his name was Martin Alzaga and that he was a secretary at the Argentinian Embassy to the Holy See. He also told me that a cousin of his, named Anchorena, who lived in Paris, wanted me to paint three panels symbolising three seasons, spring, summer and autumn; the gentleman wanted to fix these panels on the doors of the drawing-rooms in his Paris apartment which was in the Avenue Foch, leading out of the Avenue du Bois de Boulogne. I accepted the fee that was offered and undertook to carry out the work; then I asked the young diplomat if he was interested in painting. He replied that he was not only interested in painting but was passionately devoted to it, adding that he painted himself and in particular made many drawings, devoting all his free time to drawing and the study of drawing. I asked him to show me some of his drawings, although at heart I was sceptical. I was sure that he was one of the usual dilettantes who amused themselves with drawing, producing things of no value and no serious achievement, thinking of Picasso, Matisse or some other representative of the Paris school. This supposition, in fact this certainty of mine, was also strengthened by the fact that Alzaga told me he had come from Paris, where he had been living for a few years, and mentioned to me the names of a few people he knew in the French capital, people whom I knew too and who belonged to the world of international snobbery. I was very much surprised, therefore, when the following day the Argentinian diplomat brought me a parcel of the most beautiful drawings, executed with a mastery somewhat rare in our era. I realised at once that he had studied with intelligence and consistency the drawings of the Old Masters. In fact he told me that he often worked till late at night copying the drawings of masters from the past, without restricting himself to any one genre, century or school. He copied Rubens and Titian, Fragonard, Boucher and Leonardo, Rembrandt and Canaletto and also nineteenth-century French drawings, by Ingres, Géricault and Delacroix.

194

I was really amazed, because in the art world of today it is rare, I would say almost impossible, to meet a person of this type. I immediately respected and liked this young Argentinian and we met very often. On the average he came to supper with us three times a week, and after supper he often stayed late talking about drawing and painting and consulting volumes reproducing the Old Masters. Both he and I had a good library of these books. I was really happy to think that at last I had found someone with whom I could talk sincerely and seriously about painting. In fact Alzaga understood painting just as he understood drawing, and in painting too he showed that he possessed both intelligence and knowledge. I often gave him descriptions of the things I had done and the experiments I had made or was making in the vast field of technique, a field in which few, very few artists are working here and there, and it is they, only they who are still carrying the torch of art. The others, however, the hateful and destructive modernists, not content with dragging art through the mud, work with shameful zeal to cloud and obscure the minds of their contemporaries to an even greater extent; their perfidious intention is to turn them into easier prey and make them accept with ever-increasing readiness, and in exchange for good money, the indecent filth of their pseudo-artistic production. For this reason the friendship between me and the Argentine diplomat who drew and painted continued for a good seven years.

Meanwhile I had carried out the three panels for his cousin in Paris and a little later I painted a large painting on canvas for the same gentleman, and this was fastened to the ceiling in the main drawing-room of the Anchorena apartment in Paris. Alzaga did not want me to give him a percentage of the fee for either the first or the second painting that I had done for his cousin. However, I gave him two of my paintings which represented something more than the percentage that was due to him. Furthermore, I always spoke enthusiastically about him to all my friends and acquaintances and also mentioned him to dealers and owners of galleries; but they were all very sceptical, especially the dealers in modern painting, about the qualities of Alzaga's drawings and painting and certain gallery owners, such as Signor Del Corso, of the Obelisco Gallery, never wanted to have anything to do with Alzaga. I spoke to Signor Del Corso many times and insistently advised him to exhibit some of Alzaga's drawings in his gallery, even if he did not wish to buy them, but he always replied just in the same way as the others had done, saying that these drawings 'smacked too much of the museum', that they were 'outmoded' and with other such commonplace remarks.

Here we come to the volte-face on the part of a man to whom I showed esteem and friendship for a good seven years. I had often told Alzaga to resign from the diplomatic service and dedicate himself entirely to art. I told him that he was endowed with exceptional talent, that he was sufficiently well off, that he was free and would certainly succeed as an artist. In the end he decided to take my advice. I should add in the first place that during the seven years when we used to see each other he offered on two occasions to enlarge any sketches and scenery that I was due to carry out for La Scala, because in this way they would be easier to execute. When Alzaga had decided to leave diplomacy for art, he again offered to enlarge some sketches that I had in fact just made for a film, which a film company was in the process of preparing, the title of which was *The Bridge of Sighs*. I accepted the offer on this occasion also and sent the sketches, enlarged by Alzaga and signed by me, to the film company.

After this I noticed that Alzaga, who, as I said earlier, used to come very often to our house and very often stayed to supper, no longer gave any sign of life. I thought he must be ill and tried to telephone him, but his servant replied in a vague way that her master was away from Rome. Shortly afterwards I received a notice from the Rome court, ordering me to appear before the Public Prosecutor. I went to the Palace of Justice on the date arranged and the Prosecutor showed me a denunciation for alleged plagiarism presented by Signor Martin Alzaga, who accused me of having taken some drawings of his and signed them with my name. I explained to the Public Prosecutor that in fact I had not taken drawings by Alzaga and signed them with my name, but that Alzaga had simply enlarged some drawings of mine and that he had done this work on other occasions and, as on the other occasions, he himself had suggested that he should do this work. I added that, according to the criteria of Signor Alzaga, if I gave the sketch for a curtain in a theatre to a scene-painter and had written my name at the foot of the curtain, the scene-painter could have sued me for plagiarism. It was clear to me that Alzaga, at the moment when he decided to dedicate himself to painting, thought, perhaps on the advice of some treacherous individual, that if he made his début with a scandal, accusing a painter of my reputation and importance of plagiarism, this would be an excellent means of getting known quickly and seeing his name in all the newspapers and magazines. Furthermore, he knew very well how many people were hostile towards me and thought that in his case he would be supported by my enemies. But his approach was so blatant that it offended even my most obdurate adversaries.

I was defended at the hearing by the skilful lawyer Bucciante, and Alzaga lost the case in the lower court; he did not take it to the Appeal Court. But suddenly he began to do surrealist paintings, hoping in this way to have the modernists on his side; but not even the modernists wanted him. The only man who welcomed him with open arms was Signor Del Corso, the owner of the Obelisco Gallery, who, as soon as it was known that Alzaga had accused me of plagiarism, hastened to offer him the gallery for a one-man show, while before, when I had recommended Alzaga to him, he did not even want to hear his name mentioned. Together with Signor Del Corso, Dr Giorgio Castelfranco, who during the case brought against me by the Milione Gallery had refused to act as expert after having agreed to do so, also hastened with loving zeal to write a preface to the catalogue for Alzaga's exhibition, a preface which aimed to be a hymn of praise to the Argentinian's surrealism, but ended as a piece of tedious and incomprehensible prose. He had exhibited a few silly things in the Arcimboldi style[3] and, in order to increase the silliness of the exhibition, over each painting that showed figures composed of turnips, cabbages, carrots, onions and other things, there was a ledge on which had been placed real turnips, real onions and other vegetables and herbs.

I am a perfect gentleman and I have an innate sense of justice and truth. In spite of Alzaga's disgusting attempt to punch me in the back in order to obtain publicity for himself, in spite of his unfortunate incursions into the camp of modernism and surrealism, I still state that he was a man of exceptional talent and exceptional intelligence, so far as drawing and painting are concerned. His volte-face filled me not so much with rancour as with sadness and disappointment. I said this in the past tense, was, because I hope he is still alive, that he has repented of what he did to me and that now, after trying to paint in the manner of Arcimboldi and having made sacrifices on the altar of modernism, he has returned with his former courage to his good drawing and good painting.

In the meantime the problem of the fake de Chiricos was becoming continually more serious. From Milan, Florence, Turin, Alessandria and other cities I constantly received photographs of fake pictures with my signature forged on them, accompanied by letters asking me to write an authentication on the back of the photographs. I would put the photograph in a drawer and then reply to the sender saying that the picture was a fake and asking him to send me the name and address of the person from whom he had bought it. I hardly ever received a reply. I also had other fakes deposited at the police headquarters in Milan and Rome; after depositing them there, however, and in spite of all the reports supplied, no results were ever achieved. What is more, the laws in Italy concerning faked pictures are very elastic, not very clear and not very logical. This gives the lie to the saying that justice is equal for all. In fact, so far as works of art are concerned, justice does not seem to be that woman who is always represented with a pair of scales in one hand, a sword in the other and a bandage over her eyes. For how can it be explained that a beggar half-dead with hunger is arrested, tried and punished for stealing a small loaf or a little fruit, while so many nimble-fingered people cheat others out of tens and hundreds of millions through the sale of fake pictures and do all this without punishment? Explain it to me, dear reader, if you can. Are the two sides of Justice's scales not always on the same level then? As for the bandage that this noble lady wears over her eyes, I would remove it and give her instead a large and powerful pair of opera-glasses so that she could see, especially what is happening in the distance and what escapes normal vision.

At that period there were various scandals concerning fake de Chiricos. The biggest were those of the fake exhibited in the Musée National d'Art Moderne in Paris and that of the two fakes reproduced in a catalogue published by no less an organisation than UNESCO. As for the scandal at the museum in Paris, this is what happened. One day I was in a bookshop in Rome, looking through an encyclopedia of contemporary painting, published by a French publisher named Hazan. I realised that opposite the critical-biographical piece about me, which was, moreover, shamefully misleading, there was a reproduction of a fake metaphysical painting with my signature forged on it. I bought the encyclopedia, took it to a photographer's and had the reproduction of the fake photographed. I sent an enlargement of the photograph to the director of the Musée National d'Art Moderne in Paris, who was called X——. In the letter which was attached to the photograph I informed him that the picture in the museum was a crude fake; I told him that I was astonished to find that a national museum, in Paris, exhibited fakes and requested him to remove the picture from the museum. I should never have done so! M. X—— became a kind of wild and hydrophobic hyena. He did not reply to my letter, but in Paris called journalists together for a press conference and there, in terms extremely injurious towards me, let loose his envy which was typical of a modernist intellectual who had been exposed. He told the journalists that the picture was authentic, that I regularly declared any metaphysical pictures to be fakes because, according to him, I was angry that these pictures fetched high prices on the American market. This repetition of the phrase 'high prices on the American market', when it refers to me and to other well-known painters, is a remarkable legend which I have been hearing for a long time. In fact, Monsieur X—— stated, in exceedingly offensive terms, that the picture was authentic. I then wrote him a second letter stating that I would give the photograph of the fake, with the name of the museum director and all the details, to the Italian and foreign newspapers and that if I did not receive an assurance that the picture had been removed from the museum I would continue to expose and denounce the operations of M. X——.

There was then another press conference in Paris and M. X—— stated that he had had the painting removed from the room where it was on view, not because it was a fake but because it was ugly. Such is the mentality and I would even say the logic of certain people who in Paris today have a hand in the business of modern painting. The director of a national museum buys a painting, paying for it, as all the directors of museums do, with taxpayers' money, exhibits it in his museum and, after five years during which it has remained on show, when the person presumed to have painted it tells him it is a fake, and when he sees that things are going badly for him, has it removed, but at the same time states that he is having it removed because it is ugly and not because it is a fake. In fact, the men who concern themselves today with the shameful business of modern art are truly the ones that such modern art deserves.

Now it should be known that, together with M. X—— at the Musée National d'Art Moderne in Paris, there also functions

M. Jean Cassou, a high priest of modernistic freemasonry. This highly esteemed gentleman is often invited to Italy, with solicitude and respect, to supervise the awards of the various Marzotto prizes and others of the same kind, offered by would-be Maecenas figures and of which the only result is to accelerate the progressive ruin of art.

During the scandal of the fake de Chirico exhibited at the Musée National d'Art Moderne in Paris I discovered once more how little is done in Italy to maintain our prestige abroad and to defend our interests. Imagine what would have happened if in Italy a large piece belonging to the Paris school, for example a Matisse or a Braque, had been treated as I was treated in Paris by M. X——: imagine that it was discovered how an Italian museum had exhibited a fake bearing a forged signature, after the alleged painter had made his justified protest. I think that the least thing that would have happened would have been a diplomatic incident. The French ambassador in Rome would certainly have intervened with the maximum firmness to protest and to demand full satisfaction for the artist of his nationality, and I am sure that the Frenchman would have obtained complete satisfaction with many excuses and apologies on our part. On the other hand, in my case, nobody made a move, least of all our ambassador in Paris who would certainly have known from the French press the facts which were certainly pointed out to him, also by our cultural attaché in Paris. During the scandal of the fake de Chirico at the Paris museum, I met one evening at a concert a well-known personality from our political world, a person who is also head of a party, and I complained to him about the offensive attitude assumed towards me in Paris by the director of a museum. This well-known personality, who probably knew everything already, stood listening to me with the amused expression of someone listening to some romance, and when I had finished he patted me on the shoulder in a familiar way and then, in tones of good-natured irony, said, 'Well, dear Maestro, we will now declare war on France!' And this is how Italians of worth are sustained and defended in Italy today.

Now I must go back about two or three years and recall with sadness a great sorrow which struck me early in May 1952 : the death of my brother Alberto Savinio, which occurred during the night of May 4th and 5th of that year. My brother had already been ill with heart trouble for some time, but I did not know that it was so serious, and here I believe it my duty to say that the doctor who was looking after him should have warned me about the seriousness of the illness which was undermining him. The doctor knew of my existence and also knew me personally; he knew that I was the elder brother and my financial situation was better than my brother's. As a doctor he certainly knew how much physical and mental rest and quiet are needed by people with heart trouble and how fatal hard work, preoccupations, anxiety and worry can be for them, especially in serious cases. He should, therefore, have warned me and told me how serious the illness was. I could have helped my brother, morally and materially, and perhaps in this way could have prolonged his life. During the last months of his earthly existence Alberto Savinio lived a life of intense hard work, I should say super-intense, for he worked intensively all his life. Great men hardly ever receive what they deserve, but they usually receive at least part of what they deserve. My valiant brother did not even have the hundredth part of what he deserved. He was a writer of enormous power and depth, he wrote books which nobody has succeeded in writing so far, but if you go into all the bookshops in the towns of Italy you will never see a single one of his books displayed, while you can see whole rows of French books all of which put together are not equal to one page from one single book by my brother. He knew the treatment that was in store for him by the men of our time when he was no longer one of them. Stupidity, jealousy? . . . . a little of both, but especially the latter, personified by that ugly woman with the green face and the crooked mouth who can never tell the truth.

I rushed to his house in the middle of the night after a telephone call from my sister-in-law and saw him lying on his bed; his right arm was folded and his right hand rested on his chest, while his left arm was stretched out alongside his body. My sister-in-law Maria had certainly arranged the body in this way, with care and sensitivity and thoughtfulness, since if she had placed his left hand on his chest it might have looked as though he were trying to repress the palpitations of the organ that had killed him. The expression on his face was serene and I remembered the expression on my father's face as he lay on his death-bed; the expression of a man who, weary from the long and trying journey of life, is content to rest at last in the arms of kindly death. Only my brother still had that slightly ironical and contemptuous smile that I knew and which was also the smile of an exceptional man *who knows*. My brother was also a painter and a

musician. His greatest strength, however, was that of writer and
poet; as a poet he has written magnificent verses of a truly remarkable
lyricism, metaphysical quality and pathos. I only need quote this
epode from his book *Tragedia dell'infanzia* :

Be silent and rest : here ends the song
Of your life. The faint-grown echo
Of the ancient lament returns later
In this brief pause when the enchantment
Dies away. Turn your face to the serene
Peace in which the Siren's song
Loses its magic.
Daughters clearer than Piety : hopes.
Close-veiled companions, go into exile
Before you reach the shore you invoke.
In your shadow, faith, recollections,
All is vain. Vain the sigh and the light
In the high solitude of the god
In whom hope revives again in hopelessness.

Tranquil departures, pleasant return
Of the seasons; innumerable skies
And endless movement of veils
Over the brief magic of cities.
Wandering winds and stricken air
Over the heavy mountains, and as you remember them,
Faithful lingering of sunsets and slow
Journeys of clouds, the exploding
Dawn and tranquil, serene
Ecstasy.

The sky of human destiny thundered
When fate conquered you.
Only you were not bowed by Death
As you thought.
No voice, immeasurable frost
Covers the silent sleep of the sea
And in the arched night the noise

Of the stars and the deep breathing of the sky.
Lofty afternoons, nights full of sighing,
Extreme destiny has taken from you
The most dead, the faceless hour,
The most silent among the silent.
O night that is yours, affection gone and the heart
Deprived of stars, darkness soothed,
Love is given to you without tears,
Naked and more beautiful in the starry night.

Since memory hurts you more,
Hope to have no hope : nothing else can help
Down here, nor memory, nor voice.
The weeping of the ghosts begins again.
The cycle of return is closed : the dry wood
Is silent and the body bowed, weary
In the bosom of everlasting peace.
The heart is closed within time, throughout
The white, soothed and scattered air is the trace
Of the passing of hours.
The wandering face of the sun will never
Shine again over the colourless earth ;
No voice will come from those returning,
Nor hopes repeating : 'again'.
Dead at the feet of the giants
Lies the unfinished dream of Dawn.

Different from our bards of Italy and France! . . . and of other
countries too! . . .

He was less powerful and profound as a painter than as a writer,
but all the same he still left extraordinary works behind, especially
a series of portraits, which were highly impressive through their
interior and exterior resemblances. Some of these portraits, and
especially the portrait of our mother, can stand on the same level
of expressive and plastic power as some of the best works of Dürer.

As a composer he was more on the level of modern music, although
from that point of view he was also superior to what is being done
today. But so far as his musical production was concerned, the
boycotting method of the modernists has been in operation and still

is so to the fullest extent. The freemasonry of the modernist music-lovers insists upon at least a little, but increasingly more, of modern music at every concert; no composition by Alberto Savinio ever figures in a concert programme.

On the day of the funeral many intellectuals, journalists and writers, more or less friends of my brother's, came to pay him their last respects. But so far as officialdom was concerned, there was very little; a brief visit from the deputy mayor Lupinacci, before the funeral, and a wreath sent by the Ministry or Office of Entertainments. That was all.

On the other hand, when the Picasso exhibition opened a few years ago at the Gallery of Modern Art in Rome the President of the Republic, Einaudi, came personally, with all his suite, to open it; and to think that Picasso did not even condescend to put in an appearance, which was a stupid lack of courtesy towards the leader of the country which was giving hospitality to his works. For this offensive discourtesy on the part of Picasso we have to thank the usual consortium made of up Signora Bucarelli, Professor Lionello Venturi and their friends and allies, since it was apparently they who under the leadership of Professor Venturi persuaded the President of the Republic that he should attend the private view of the exhibition. Again, a few months ago, when Vincenzo Cardarelli died, President Gronchi sent a telegram to the dead man's sister, but at least this was a case of an Italian poet. On the other hand, when my valiant brother died, in spite of the enormous value of his work, not even a clerk on the city council sent two lines of condolence to his widow, the faithful and courageous Maria. I repeat, in Italy there is a mentality and a type of behaviour which perplexes even the least pessimistic and those who are the most short-sighted from a moral point of view.

Among the people who came to pay their last respects to my dead brother were some, such as Leonida Repaci and De Benedetti, whom I did not know and I did not speak to them; but in those circumstances and having actually met me by my brother's death-bed, close to his body, they could have extended some sign of greeting. This shows the little politeness possessed today by certain of our intellectuals. Repaci, Bellonci, Falqui, Dino Terra and others displayed much zeal, either in carrying the coffin and placing it in the funeral carriage, or in going with the cortège to church and even to the cemetery. But later not one of them lifted a finger to arrange even the most modest prize in memory of Alberto Savinio, or to have one of his writings published in the cultural page of a daily paper. Articles signed by Emilio Cecchi, Carlo Belli, Bellonci and others were published; most of these articles, however, revealed a lack of intelligence, a lack of temperament and sometimes even bad faith and falsehood. The most intelligent and level-headed piece was one written by Dr Fausto Bima, an article which came out in the *Giornale d'Italia* on May 7th, 1953, on the occasion of the anniversary of the day on which Alberto Savinio died. I transcribe this article in its entirety because it deserves it.

Here is the article by Fausto Bima:

It is a year since Alberto Savinio left us. During the days which followed his premature death there was much talk about him. People spoke of him with enthusiasm, in unqualified and unanimous agreement, with a generic and uniform praise based on commonplaces, tacked on to a superficial and conventional biography. We witnessed, therefore, on one side a noble competition between vaunted displays of friendship, and on the other a sudden, tardy recognition. We had the impression that people were trying to analyse him and talk about him with instant praise, to exhaust the argument, to salve their consciences and then mention him no more. This is what happens to overstrong personalities, to men who walk alone, who exercise independence of judgment, that terrible and inexorable weapon, that instrument so unusual in a conformist and comfortable country like ours.

With the same seriousness and commitment with which Savinio approached each piece of work, even an ephemeral piece of journalism, with the same concern for writing something definitive, for formulating judgments which we will not renounce, either through exaggeration or understatement, let us try now to settle accounts. Let us try to do so without letting ourselves be influenced by him and by what other people have written.

Some of his works, through their dense and delicate fragmentation, have led those who look at them superficially to mention the commonplace of Stendhalism.

In reality Stendhal is a man of the north, a lively, ingenuous

man of genius, eternally bitter, an impulsive man who wants
to be heard. Sometimes he anticipates the tastes and judgments
of succeeding generations, but he remains anchored to detail.
Savinio, on the other hand, is a mature Mediterranean type,
with an innate sense of universality. He seeks out the basic
elements of our time and elaborates them in his imagination,
transmuting them into works of art; but he enjoys concealing
himself in them like a sylvan diety, behind the fruits of his
genius.

Today therefore Man in born again from the entire work of
Alberto Savinio; Man in his robust entirety.

Savinio, this last humanist, with his mighty mind, understands, perceives and embraces everything; from philosophy to
music and painting, from prose to poetry, from literature to
criticism, from the principles of science to politics. He was a
man through whom all the voices of the cosmos vibrated in
sympathy, and during the course of his life he was almost
concealed within his individual works.

Anyone, therefore, who puts the emphasis, as some have done,
either on a contingent aspect, a temporary pretext, surrealism
for example, or on one form, literature, of Savinio's activity,
would be committing a grave error. If among his individual
activities something will be less important, and other things,
with the passing of the years, will appear more comprehensible,
more contemporary, the thing which counts is that the literature,
painting and music will become integrated in one harmonious
composition in which a single Man has manifestated himself in
the admirable fullness of His superiority and His human dignity.
This polymorphism, and choice, sometimes with rapid and
essential cuts, sometimes with unpremeditated foreshortening
and construction, in a snobbish, absent-minded and superficial
society like ours, has meant that many people, I would say too
many, dismissed Alberto Savinio as a talented magus-figure
producing *divertissements* and pastiches and he was only
admired as such. These people mistook the bizarre nature of His
genius and His highly personal inspiration, which in reality
were only means and pretexts, for the real aims of His art. The
writings, through their intrinsic nature, are the works which
reveal his thought most clearly, and since Savinio's prose often
comments on and clarifies his painting and his music it seems

to me that by referring to these writings we may be able to reach some conclusion about his entire work.

In 1941 a radically new voice came almost secretly into the polite, severe and, let us admit it, unexciting scene of Italian literature, through an attractive book, as tersely written as the best prose of Voltaire, flavoured with Attic salt, like Lucan, lyrical, metaphysical and ironic; I mean *L'Infanzia di Nicasio Dolce Mare*.

With Savinio's book irony—this unacknowledged element in our literature—of a serene, profound and well-balanced type, classically perfect, forced the doors of the literary citadel, which remained closed within the traditional bastions of a serious and conformist academicism.

Panzini, not with irony but with witticisms, had already tried to bring down the massive walls of heavy seriousness within our literature. Panzini's good-natured, superficial smile seemed to ask forgiveness for its own boldness and it was succeeded by the smile which belonged to neo-classical painting, the almost tragic, detached, remote, liberating smile of Savinio's irony; the same smile that he painted in his portraits, the same smile which flowers and ripples in his music, the same eternal smile with which Death has left us a memory of his last image.

Savinio knew Panzini's work; during the last part of his life Panzini's books formed his bedside reading. We can, however, state with definite knowledge that Savinio was not influenced by Panzini and did not take his inspiration from him. Furthermore, Savinio, throughout all his activity, relied only on himself (hence his tendency towards autobiography, just as his brother, Giorgio de Chirico, tends to paint self-portraits), deepening and transforming the experience and the world of others into a world that was unmistakably his.

Another element which might appear to be in complete contrast with the irony, and also one rare in our literature, is a profound romanticism, like a remote and constant counterpoint, expressed with a northern type of eagerness, with a vein of lofty humanity, with an earnest aspiration towards a better world.

Casa la vita and *Alcesti di Samuele* are the clearest and most obvious examples of this pathos, this sensitive poetry which on some pages reaches a highly elevated tone and a great completeness of expression.

But even in his earlier works such as *La casa ispirata*, *Tragedia dell'infanzia*, *Angelica o la notte di maggio*, we can find these strange and profound aspects of Savinio's work.

It might seem as if in Savinio's work there were two elements in apparent contradiction to one another. On one side this romanticism and faith in progress, on the other irony and scepticism of a pre-Socratic type. But this is not the case : for Savinio irony and scepticism are conditions necessary to the serenity and equilibrium of man, who can and should look before him with moderate faith in progress, with a pure heart, with expectation. As a result Savinio's work is also a vehicle of social education, an invitation to individual dignity and understanding, leading to a new and better society.

To conclude, so far as we can conclude today without the perspective of time. A body of literary work, like one of painting or music, has a succession which is not ephemeral, inasmuch as it expresses or sometimes anticipates the feelings of a society or a world which cannot be expressed. Savinio thought with the mind of a European. He was at the same time an illuminist free-thinker of the seventeenth century and a fighter for liberty today, against the conformists, whatever their nature or colour. It seems, therefore, fairly easy to understand how in the conditions created by the environment of our country his work was bound to come up against a worldly condition of insensitivity to these new voices. Perhaps Savinio tried to be bizarre sometimes and sometimes persuasive in order to attract attention not to himself but to those concepts which he regarded as important for the improvement of mankind.

In spite of a few juvenile manifestations in music and literature, Alberto Savinio was not precocious. He was too contemplative, too profound, too much his essential self and as a consequence of this maturity Savinio could not be popular in his time.

Savinio's work will continue to find more and more admirers as the condition of humanity gradually resembles what he hoped for. What remains to be said further? Nothing, I think. Let us wait for time to be gallant; because Savinio, as I have already said, made his own commentary on himself, in all respects, even in death.

The night when Thanatos took him into his arms I found

some notes which had been written a few hours earlier, for the finale of the libretto for one of his musical works.

The words of these notes could also be his epitaph : *'He was a man—do you remember?—Good-bye! Man!—Where is he? He's disappeared!*

'No. He is us.'

18

Afterwards, all those intellectuals who had been more or less friendly with my brother and who were so attentive on the occasion of his funeral, did nothing, and did nothing else whatever to keep Alberto Savinio's works alive in the memory of the public. Some of them, such as Enrico Falqui and Goffredo Bellonci, who edit the cultural pages of our well-known daily papers, could on rare occasions publish something by my brother, for these pages are nearly always filled with extremely boring and tedious writing that nobody reads. My brother left many interesting pieces of unpublished work, each one more interesting than the last, but there was never a reminiscence of him, not even a reference to one of his thoughts, not even one of his remarks, not even a mention of his name. Do you ask me what the reason was? . . . There are various reasons, and Fausto Bima has already written about this phenomenon. But I feel and think with absolute certainty that the principal one is the superior strength and superior personality in Alberto Savinio's work which stands out among the best of what is being done today and also among the best of what was done yesterday. And this is something that causes considerable annoyance and is also the reason that when I appear with my paintings, my lectures and my writings, people always try to be either malicious or silent, but mostly they are silent.

In order to understand certain attitudes on the part of certain critics and certain publishers, both Italian and foreign, one must know that publishers and critics are often writers themselves, which in this case explains why some writers and poets of value are not published or are published inadequately and their books are not displayed in bookshops. Even if the publisher is not a writer himself he is always surrounded by the so-called readers who are always a kind of grey eminence; they in their turn are more or less failed writers and instinctively, subconsciously and automatically they feel the need to place anything of real value in the shade. The greater its value, the more they place it in the shade and they advise the publisher instead to take on everything mediocre, deprived of true value, boring and commonplace, suiting the temporary fashions and so-called 'tastes' of the public, tastes which only exist in theory. In talking of 'failed' writers as of 'failed' artists, it should always be remembered that by 'failed' I do not mean unknown, or little known, just as I am not referring to a lack of commercial success; a writer like an artist, can be very well known and earn a lot and yet *be a failure*; in this case he feels that what he does has no value and does not deserve what it earns, and in this way he can never be a serene, happy man who is sincere in his judgments. I, who am the non-failure *par excellence*, have never felt envy for anyone, even when I was unknown or little known and earned little or nothing. Naturally when I find that an individual of no value is praised in the press and pockets lots of money, I am angry; but this is not envy, it is a sense of justice. In the same way I am angry when I see artists of value neglected. In France this happened with Edouard Vuillard and André Derain and with a magnificent poet named Vincent Muselli. So far as Vuillard is concerned, I should say that in France he has not really been neglected because his paintings sell and are expensive; but he does not have the place he deserves; he is much less talked about than Bonnard, although Bonnard is infinitely inferior to him. Vuillard had a very deep understanding of many aspects of men and things and has expressed in a way I would call almost meta-physical certain aspects of Paris and certain aspects of Parisian interiors, the mysterious atmosphere that is sometimes assumed by people in a room, seated at a table or on a divan, by the light of a lamp. But he has not been understood, and yet in France there has been and still is much more talk about Bonnard than about Vuillard. In Italy our critics, and in general all those who take an interest in things to do with painting, remain faithful to the old method, which consists in following in a humble, provincial way and repeating parrot-wise all that is said and done in Paris; when they mention Vuillard, they are very cautious and tepid; this was particularly evident when Vuillard's works were exhibited at the Palazzo Reale in Milan. As for Vincent Muselli, here are two short samples of his magnificent and truly *poetic* gifts: *Evening* and *This Grey Garden*.

> The leaves are only ash and rust.
> The day is dead, the sky emptied of birds;
> Already the moon rises, already the quarrelsome
> Voice of the frogs disturbs the reeds.

> This grey garden, clad in spiders,
> These dead trees, these birds grown so old,
> These fallen walls, these faded wings
> And the desert of these gloomy places,
> Dust, O days: patient prey!
> What pure nothingness sleeps in this shelter!
> Sorrow too dear, delight too exquisite!
> We shall return to this grey garden.

Vincent Muselli was (I say 'was' because I think he died a few years ago) a great poet, far superior to all the Paul Valérys, Paul Claudels, Paul Eluards and other pseudo-poets of the same ilk. But precisely because he was a man of worth and an authentic poet he has been put in the shade and boycotted by the freemasonry of the mediocre, the modernists, the snobs and the envious.

Sometimes I ask myself, I say I ask myself rather than I wonder, as so many people today say and write, including even writers and literati. In fact one must not forget that the verb 'to like' is used, in the conditional, when one intends to say that one requires something, for example: 'I would like you to give me a hundred lire', 'I would like you to give me a match', because it is understood that I would like to have a hundred lire, or that I would like to have a match. On the other hand, when one is waiting for an answer, one has to use the verb 'ask', for example: 'Can I ask you how old you are?', 'Can I ask you what time it is?' So I sometimes ask myself the reasons why in Italy there is so much love, so much devotion, so much shameful kotowing to everything that is French or rather everything that comes from Paris, since it is clear that the France which today makes both our intellectuals and the less reputable part of our public swoon with love and admiration, is certainly not the

France of the school of Avignon, or the France of the great architects who built the châteaux of the Loire or the cathedrals of Chartres and Rheims, who built the palaces of the Tuileries, the Louvre and Versailles and other masterpieces which are as far removed from the buildings of Le Corbusier as Peking is from Rome. Nor is it the France of the great sculptors such as Jean Goujon, Houdon and Carpeaux, or the France of the great writers and the great poets like Montaigne and Rabelais, or that of Corneille and Racine, nor is it the France of that magnificent *pléiade* of painters, sculptors, carvers and craftsmen who in the eighteenth century elevated taste and mastery to the nth degree, or the France of the great nineteenth-century painters, from David to Courbet, and not even the France of the great novelists who flourished in the second half of the nineteenth century, like Flaubert and Guy de Maupassant, no, dear reader, the France that makes the mouths of certain Italians, and especially the intellectuals, water today, and does so in a way that makes them wet their pants with emotion, is the France of the shapeless and misshapen painting, kept going purely for financial reasons by the Parisian dealers whose aims are not even French. It is the France of the costive and presumptuous writers like those who appear in the *Nouvelle Revue Française*, it is the France of the Sartres and Cocteaus and all those funambulists of art and literature who have one single purpose : to make a name for themselves with their minor talent and earn money with little effort. This hysterical love which exists in Italy for our so-called Latin sister is not even justified by reasons of material interest, since in Italy dealing in modern French painting is almost non-existent, and so far as books are concerned they are seen, it is true, but they certainly do not sell quickly, nor is it possible to earn large sums from their sale; many more of them can be seen in Switzerland, Belgium, Greece, Turkey and the countries of South America.

Even here all this modern France, of which I spoke earlier, is publicised as though our very existence depended upon it. It is sufficient to quote as an example the fact that in Rome there is a daily paper whose cultural page is devoted to Paris. You can see endless photographs of Cocteau, Picasso and other big leaders of the Parisian intelligentsia; very long and very tedious articles are published concerning the sordid doings of the modernist painters of Paris and the critics and organisers of exhibitions, while gossip of all kinds is reported about the existentialist cabarets and the fashions that come and go on the Left Bank of the Seine. I say that instead of these boring, inane things it should be possible to print interesting articles full of life and wit and that at one time these would have been written by Italian authors. I have just mentioned the daily paper which in Rome dedicates its page about the arts to the cult of contemporary Paris, but, out of a sense of fairness, I must say that just today I have seen in an old and important paper in the capital a large photograph on the arts page showing Jean Cocteau, a member of the French Academy, and therefore 'immortal', roosting on scaffolding in front of a vast extent of canvas or board, it was not very clear what he was doing, but he was working very hard, in Picasso-like style, for some modernist church or other, drawing drooping or distorted Madonnas and squinting Infant Jesuses. Through the machinations of a few zealous high priests devoted to the ruin of art, and a few ardent paladins of all modernist ugliness, especially that originating from Paris, modernism is in process of tainting the Catholic churches. Modernist dictatorship has also laid its destructive claw on the things of God. What fine liberty! To force the poor faithful who go into a church to meditate in prayer as they think of their own woes, to force them, I say, to find themselves in front of so many unpleasant paintings or bronze casts which, instead of inspiring peace and tranquillity of mind or spirit, lead to thoughts of flight, desperate flight, a flight by any means and towards any place, provided it is as far away as possible, where one cannot see all that dehumanised, depressing and repulsive stuff.

The major contribution to this beating of the big drum on behalf of France today is made by our booksellers and publishers. Just recently a well-known publisher in Milan published a thick volume on Cézanne; the same firm, I think, that published a thick volume on Gauguin, who is a forgotten pseudo-master and whom they have been trying to relaunch for some time. Automatically a bookshop in the Piazza di Spagna would arrange in one window a kind of little scene, a sanctuary, a *sacrarium*, a kind of strange *crèche* where could be seen several copies of the volume dedicated to the pseudo-master of Aix-en-Provence, scattered in simulated disorder, and then in the middle of the window a little easel carrying a reproduction in colour of an extremely ugly landscape by Cézanne, ugly, stunted and childish, a landscape in fact which any painter worthy of the name would have been ashamed to have painted, even at the age of eight. Beneath the 'masterpiece', there would hang, fastened to the easel,

a length of red velvet, and as though all this were not enough there
was also a kind of little tablet, or painter's palette, covered with a
few dull, dirty and faded colours, just like the colours in Cézanne's
paintings; there were also a few tubes which had been half-used.

This grotesque method of window-dressing is not even an inven-
tion of ours but an American importation. I recall once seeing in
New York, in the window of a smart furrier in Fifth Avenue, among
minks and ermines, a whole arsenal of rifles, harpoons, ropes of all
thicknesses, in fact all the equipment that is generally used in
whaling; but to be truthful, I must say that these surrealist window-
displays in the land of dollars and canned foods are arranged with
more verve and taste than they are in Italy, which was the cradle
of the Renaissance. Now, still apropos the volume on Cézanne,
published by the famous firm in Milan, can you imagine a well-
known bookshop in Paris devoting a whole window to showing you
a book about an Italian painter, shall we say Giovanni Fattori?!
A book published by a well-known French publisher—and the
volumes scattered in the window would be surrounded also by toy
soldiers and little horses made of lead and tiny gun-carriages, to
recall the work of the famous Leghorn painter . . .

Then I ask myself why that large publishing film in Milan should
use its energies to print a volume on Cézanne. Perhaps the publisher
thought he should educate our public? I do not think so, for the
publisher, however little or badly informed he is, certainly ought to
be aware that the Italians today know Cézanne much better than
the Parisians do. In fact here among us the pseudo-master of Aix-
en-Provence is much better known than he is in his own country.
Also, everyone who is concerned with modern painting today knows
that in France hardly any books about him are published now, and
this is why. When the nefarious Vollard launched Cézanne's big
daubs, thus playing on mankind the most fantastic joke possible, so
far as painting is concerned, many, so many books about this hideous
painting were published, monographs, biographies, essays and short
works of all types and varieties, that the critics and art historians
have now exhausted the whole repertory of foolery, idiocy, lies and
commonplaces that they usually employ when talking of modern
painting. That Milan publisher who was so devoted to the ugly
painting of present-day France, would have done better to publish
a large book with fine reproductions and a clear, intelligent text,
about a few of our artists of the last century; for example on

Giovanni Carnovali, Giacinto Gigante, Fontanesi, Gaetano Previati, Vincenzo Gemito or Filippo Palizzi, artists who were capable of showing the way to all the Cézannes of France and Navarre, taking hold of their noses between their forefingers and middle fingers, crooked and pincerlike, as the *carabiniere* takes hold of Pinocchio in Collodi's classic and famous book.

This illustrates the methodical soft-pedalling of Italian values, and the no less methodical build-up for everything that comes from Paris and is done in Paris, which continues without interruption. Even yesterday we were shown on television a saleroom where paintings donated in France were being auctioned to help the victims of the Fréjus disaster.[1] On two consecutive occasions they announced the prices reached by a few painters of the school of Paris. It was clear that the gathering of French dealers, who make a profit out of everything, were aiming for the usual astronomical and uncontrollable figures in order to increase the urge, especially outside France, to acquire French paintings. We heard the figure of twenty million mentioned, but the day before the same pictures were quoted at seventeen or even fourteen million; others, however, were quoted at five million the day before, and the day after, truthfully, the five million had become fifteen million. And here, with naïve stupidity, we are ready to swallow the push and the bluff of the Paris dealers who, very probably, regard us as a pack of cretins in the clinical sense of the word.

Do you want to have some idea of how artists of value are treated in Italy? Know then that I submitted five pictures to the eighth Quadriennale exhibition in Rome. Since I was afraid of being badly hung I had stated as a condition that I myself would select the wall where I wanted my pictures to be placed. My terms were accepted and in fact the pictures were hung on the wall I had chosen. But something was fated to go wrong; in fact, when the exhibition was opened I noticed that my wall was the *least well lit* in the room where I was exhibited. I pointed this out to the secretary, Fortunato Bellonzi, requesting him to add a light to those which were already placed on the ceiling of the room. I was not asking for my wall to be *better* lit than the others, I was only asking for it to be *as well* lit as the others. But I achieved nothing, and I think that if instead of my pictures there had been pictures by Picasso, and if Picasso had asked in person for an extra light, the secretary Bellonzi would have had reflectors and lights brought from the Ciampino airport and they would have arrived escorted by the entire Ministry of Public Education flanked by outriders on motorcycles, with the entire municipality at their head, and that the procession would have been led by standard-bearers brandishing red banners and Spanish banners and by the city band playing communist songs alternately with songs from Franco Spain.

But I must say that something much more characteristic and worthy of note, so far as the disguised hostility and obscure, deceitful attitude towards me are concerned, could be seen four years ago at the seventh Quadriennale. On this occasion a kind of Valhalla was arranged in the *salon d'honneur* in the Palace of Exhibitions, where the paintings of a few Italian painters, living and dead, were shown. The secret and surreptitious aim of this noble manifestation was still that of attracting people's attention towards what, according to the modernists, *I did first*, towards my so-called *first manner*. According to what was stated in the announcement and regulations for this seventh Quadriennale, for this Valhalla of the Italian masters, there had been a rigorous selection of works highly representative of Italian painting and sculpture carried out during the period 1910–40. But the works of mine that were shown stopped at 1927 and it was I who placed the 1927 canvas there. The organisers, with exquisite deceit, were very careful not to invite me to exhibit works from the years following, until 1940, in spite of the announcement and the regulations in the catalogue. As though all this were not enough they brought from the United States, with the help of the Museum of Modern Art in New York, a few metaphysical paintings, without even asking my permission; this was rather like the action of the worthy Biennale committee eight years earlier when the famous Exhibition of Metaphysical Painting was arranged. But the thing more deserving of note, and also more diverting, was that there was *no* money prize, not even a prize of a thousand lire : the reason was that if there had been a money prize, on this occasion, they could not have done otherwise than give it to me. This would have been the limit, as the Supreme Soviet of the Quadriennale realised, and thus instead of money prizes there was a wide and generous distribution of handwritten diplomas, a distribution that was carried out personally by the Honourable Segni.

Let us return once again to that fatal year 1952, which represents for me an immensely sad moment in my life, because it was the year in which I lost my valiant and unfortunate brother. At that period

I had on several occasions made important designs for scenery and costumes for ballets which were performed at La Scala in Milan and the Teatro Comunale in Florence. On account of their quality and scale the scenery and costumes I executed for Boito's *Mefistofele* were very important. But I was aware of a kind of concealed spite which actually originated in certain circles of La Scala itself. I remember that after the première of *Mefistofele* a Milan newspaper published a stupid and spiteful article signed by Costantini—he is now dead—who once played the futurist painter and then devoted himself to art criticism. I realised at once that this article had been written at the instigation, or rather the insistence of those gentlemen who occupy a crucial position at the greatest lyric theatre in Italy. As though the spite of some senior and junior officials at La Scala were not enough, they received support from an elderly English lady who, I believe, lived in Florence, but I forget her name. It appears that this dear lady, who was a friend of the bass Rossi Lemeni, demanded in dictatorial fashion that during the prelude Rossi Lemeni should not wear the red gloves that were part of the costume imagined by me; then, in the classical Sabbath scene, I don't know why, the same Rossi Lemeni removed from the head of the tenor Tagliavini a very beautiful plumed hat which the latter was wearing and which completed his costume. He turned it into a flying-saucer and threw it in a parabola-like arc behind the scenes. What were the reasons for this hostility? . . . Always the same, dear reader, because my sets and costumes were finer than those usually seen at La Scala. But I should say that the principal people responsible for this wave of hostility were actually the directors of La Scala who, as often happens in Italy, have no respect for people of value coming from our country. If, let us suppose, at Covent Garden in London, a very well-known British painter had designed scenery and costumes, the directors of the theatre would certainly not have allowed ex-traneous people to attempt any modification of the work of the British painter. The principle is always the same : to support and push forward not only the mediocre but especially the nonentities, and at the same time put in the shade and boycott those who have the grave defect of being artists of value. I have noticed this not only in my case but also in the case of some worth-while designers of scenery and costumes like the Italian lady Signorina De Nobili, who lived and works in Paris, and who carried out scenery and costumes for a production of *La Traviata* directed by Luchino

Visconti, and I also observed it in the case of a young Frenchman who designed some very beautiful scenery for a ballet entitled *Cinderella*, with music by Prokofiev.

At the Teatro Comunale in Florence I was treated a little better. Only once, but in this case the Teatro Comunale had nothing to do with it, only once, as I say, when I designed scenery and costumes for an opera entitled *Ifigenia* by Ildebrando Pizzetti, I noticed on the part of Maestro Pizzetti, especially at the last rehearsals and at the première of the show, a spiteful and hostile attitude towards me. Then on the evening of the première, after the show, Maestro Pizzetti arranged a splendid reception at a large hotel in Florence to which everyone who had participated in the production of the opera *Ifigenia* was invited. The only one who was not invited was I.

All this, however, did not prevent a continual increase in the number of people who felt favourable towards me and valued me. Their number increases, because men of good will, whose souls and minds are not blackened by the poisons of envy, have intuitive understanding of the rhythm, the well-timed advance of my skill in painting and of my high qualities as a man of superior intellect. Sometimes, when I say to someone that I feel I have made progress, that I feel I have gone even further along the precipitous, difficult and wearisome path of art, he looks at me with an expression that is half-astonished, half-amused, and exclaims with a laugh, 'But you're joking, dear Maestro! You're talking about progress as though you were an earnest little schoolboy who's hoping to get a better report. Our dear Maestro is always ready for some fun!' And then there is more laughter to end the remarks about what he believes to be a kind of *boutade* on my part. Instead, I am telling the truth. Every artist worthy of the name is driven by all his strength towards progress, that is towards perfection. Perfection, supreme goal, unattainable ideal, which shines like a lighthouse beam over the stormy seas of art and urges the true artist to work continually better, to be continually more satisfied. In fact, the wish for perfection is like the wish for happiness, for supreme happiness, which is a mirage, at least in the adventure of our life. One thinks of Titian who began to study anatomy when nearly a centenarian, under the influence of Michelangelo, whose works he had seen in Rome, and at the same time collected all the information which reached him about the work of the Flemish painters, in order to improve his priming and the fluidity of his oil or dry tempera, and to improve his oil varnishes.

One thinks of Goya, who, exiled, extremely old and ill, in Bordeaux, would paint as he sat up in his bed and in the evening would show his day's work to the friends who came to see him and ask them if they thought he had made progress, and Renoir put the same question to the people who looked at the paintings he did with his brush tied to his hand which was deformed with arthritis. And at this juncture I recall the true and beautiful words which Baudelaire placed at the top of one of his little poems in prose : 'Unhappy the Man, but happy the artist obsessed with a desire for perfection.'

The last time that I worked for the Teatro Comunale in Florence I designed scenery and costumes for the opera *Don Chisciotte* by Maestro Frazzi. The scenery was very well executed under the intelligent direction of the architect Professor Caliterna. It was on this occasion, however, and precisely at the Teatro Comunale in Florence, that I saw my brother Alberto Savinio for the last time but one. While the sets for *Don Chisciotte* were being made he was doing the sets for Rossini's *Armida*, and I think he was also producing the opera. I remember him at one rehearsal of *Armida*; it was late at night and I thought he looked tired. In designing those sets and costumes he had shown all the zeal and ardour he always put into anything he did. His wife Maria and his son Ruggero were also there. At a certain moment while the rehearsal of *Armida* was proceeding, I saw him walking slowly towards the last row of seats at the back of the pit and sit down alone. I certainly did not have a premonition that his end was so near, that I was seeing him for the last time but one on this earth, but as I looked at him, sitting alone and tired in the middle of that row of empty seats, I felt a quiver of sadness go through me; I felt the need to go and sit next to him, to break down that strange modesty which held us back from any sincere admission, any freely expressed emotion. I felt the need to sit down beside him and say many things to him, to talk with him about our mother, to recall so many memories of our past life, and lastly there came into my mind one of his magnificent stories entitled *Mia madre non mi capisce* [My Mother Doesn't Understand Me], from the book *Casa la Vita*, in which he describes how he found our mother dead and metaphysically transformed. I thought again of the final piece of this extraordinary story which runs as follows :

Nivasio went up to the little hen, leant against her and tried at the same time to make himself very, very small. He succeeded.

And in the darkness of that room, which he thought he did not know, although it was the bedroom where he had come into the world, Nivasio gave vent in silence to the tears repressed for so many years and the weeping of a whole lifetime.

Thus, like Nivasio, I too felt the need to go and sit by him, he who was sitting all alone in the middle of that row of empty seats, looking wearily and distantly at the stage sets and the gestures of the singers. And I too wanted to go and sit down near him, to give vent in silence to the tears repressed for so many years and the weeping of a whole lifetime. . . .

But, as happens in cases of this sort, I did nothing. I remained seated where I was, while on the stage Maria Callas, her eyes immeasurably elongated, like those of an Egyptian goddess, trilled in masterly fashion, and from the orchestra pit rose the rhythms of the genius Gioacchino Rossini.

Precisely the next day, while I was waiting for someone in the theatre office, I saw my brother pass along the corridor. He looked at me and greeted me, saying 'Au revoir'. I answered him, 'Au revoir'. A few days later, in Rome, in his apartment in the Viale Bruno Buozzi, I saw him again stretched out on his little bed, reposing in the arms of kindly death. His face was entirely suffused with an expression of calm serenity and a barely perceptible smile of intimate and peaceful joy, kind-hearted irony and perhaps also sadness, compassion for those whom he loved and had left behind, could be seen on his lips.

Yes, brother, au revoir. This greeting that you gave me, the last time in this life, in the office of the Teatro Comunale in Florence, echoes in my mind. You were leaving for the other shore, leaving me alive at the frontier of Time and I do not know what kind of labyrinth the streets constitute, on the other side of your wall. In this adventure of life, as long as I live, I shall continue to work as well as I possibly can and do what I know I should do, and when the hour of my destiny strikes, it is there, very far away, or perhaps very near, it is there, beyond all time and space, it is there, when all anchors have been weighed, it is there in the ideal world, that I shall meet you and say to you, 'Brother, here I am!'

We are now at the end of the year of grace, 1959. And in the same way after almost fourteen years, as at the end of the year 1946, I cannot say that the spectacle offered by humanity is likely to inspire great optimism. At that time the war was barely over and we hoped that in the years to come many things would be changed; instead, nothing has changed. That great thermometer, or barometer, which indicates the degree, as is usually said today, of civilisation of an era and a people, that is, in fact, art, tells us that the situation is even more disastrous than it was fourteen years or so ago, since on one side there is a continual increase in ignorance, impotence, bad faith and stupidity, and on the other the same increase in indifference, confusion, conformism, amorality, and naturally, stupidity again.

So far as progress in civil affairs, morality and humanity is concerned, things are very bad. Just recently, in fact, news has appeared in the press about the re-emergence of Nazism and anti-Semitism. Apropos the phenomenon of anti-Semitism, which among all phenomena involving racism merits a separate study, I should state various truths which nobody has stated so far, not even those illustrious gentlemen who have recently given thought to such phenomena. I mean the gentlemen of UNESCO. These truths which I am uttering are truths which nobody has revealed before, just as I revealed the real causes which have led to the birth of modernist painting. Concerning the contemporary phenomenon of anti-Semitism, which during the rule of Hitler reached the peak of criminality and sadism, I should say the following : this sad, stupid, inhuman, uncivil and criminal phenomenon is due in the first place and more than anything else to the *attitude of the Jews themselves*. For centuries they have adopted the method of concealing the fact that they are Jews, of not speaking of Jews, of acting more like Catholics and Protestants, of regarding with nostalgia all those who have titles of nobility, those who profess themselves to be apostolic Roman Catholics, those who have hanging on the walls of their houses portraits of forbears with armour, crests, shields, swords and daggers. In fact, those who always place themselves in a *state of inferiority* before the non-Jews and above all before the non-Jews of Europe, whether they are Spanish, Italian, French, German, Russian or anything else. This attitude, not only metaphorically speaking, which is that of a whipped dog and has been assumed, as I have said, for centuries by practically all Jews, arouses in many individuals that deep, animal-like instinctive cruelty which lies dormant in every individual and is only kept silent in the mind and

222

spirit of those men who through intelligence, and also through kindness and generosity, through a sense of justice and through moral and
civil education are somewhat different from the rest of mankind. The
man who does not possess these qualities can always give proof of
animal instincts, which in certain cases can reach the height of
criminality just as, precisely, what happened throughout Hitler's
activities during the Nazi period. The thing that encourages and
helps the development of such evil instincts is also the certainty of
non-reaction; and not only on the part of the Jews but on the part
of many of those who are not Jewish, who do not admit that they are
anti-Semitic or racist and remain silent for the sake of a quiet life.
What is strange is that in spite of the existence of the State of Israel,
where the Jews have shown proof of great organisational powers, and
civil and military strength, this spirit of resignation, this inferiority
complex still exists. The inhabitants of the State of Israel feel no
need to react against the unpleasantness of the anti-Semites and the
racists. A year ago, I met a journalist from Tel Aviv, the correspon-
dent for an Israeli paper who had interviewed me on questions
relating to the state of painting today. At one point I spoke to him
about the racist phenomenon and about anti-Semitism in general,
but I noticed at once that he preferred not to speak about these
things and tactfully I changed the subject.

In spite of the atrocities committed by the Germans during the
Nazi period, in spite of the six million Jews murdered in the Nazi
concentration camps, I did not find, even in the young people of
the State of Israel, young people in whom the warlike spirit had
developed to the point of creating entire battalions even with girls
and young women, armed to the teeth, in none of these young people
could be seen a word or a gesture of protest, reaction and accusation
against the persecutors of their race. Thus one day, not long ago, I
read in a newspaper that a spokesman for Israeli youth in Tel Aviv
had declared that today the youth of Israel, in their country, wanted
above all to work and 'forget the past'. This type of behaviour
naturally encourages the hooligan delinquency of the anti-Semites
and racists. They know very well that no Jew will come to them and
say: 'Are you an anti-Semite, are you a racist? Take two fine slaps
on the face and a kick in the stomach and that will change your
ideas!' Anyone who invites trouble gets it. All in all, it should be
said that following the revival of Nazism and racism which have
been in evidence recently, the elderly President Adenauer has shown

himself to be more energetic and virile than the well-armed warriors of the Israeli army.

It should also be noted that these forms of anti-Semitism, this desire to unmask the Jew and accuse him, are practised by people who certainly at bottom have nothing against the Jews. In this way if a Jew earned, say, ten thousand lire, someone will immediately say, 'There you are, he's a Jew, he knows how to further his own interests', etc.; but if someone who is not a Jew, an Aryan, as used to be said during the period of Mussolini's racism, earned ten million, nobody says, 'Oh, yes, he's an Aryan, he's earned ten million, he knows how to further his own interests', etc. This type of thing is considered normal and usual. I still say and repeat that the attitude of an animal who runs away, and hides, an attitude which the Jews have had for centuries, is the principal cause of anti-Semitism, since it awakens in some people the animal and criminal instincts which slumber more or less within every individual. It is the bestial need of some stupid and malignant people which drives them to attack, offend, persecute anyone who runs away and anyone who hides, and in this those stupid and evil-intentioned people are encouraged by the fact of knowing that they are not risking anything, since they know that the individual against which their malignancy is manifested will never turn round and insult them and threaten them as they deserve. Anti-Semitism is not only a phenomenon of sadistic evil, but also one of great cowardice.

The Jews are not lacking in physical strength and courage. I remember how many Jewish soldiers, during the First World War, carried out acts of heroism and how many died valiantly on our front. Also in the field of athletics, especially all-in wrestling and boxing, the Jews have had and still have valuable champions. Nonetheless, the sense of resignation and the feeling of inferiority persists within them. Friedrich Nietzsche, in one of his books, devotes a very moving and utterly true chapter to the Jews; he speaks precisely of those men who for centuries have lost the habit of carrying arms and armour and who gave us the man most worthy of love ever known : Jesus Christ. This extremely fine chapter by Friedrich Nietzsche about the Jews was certainly not read by the Nazis, since they, interpreting in a stupid manner the meaning that the author of *Thus Spake Zarathustra* gave to the word superman, regarded Nietzsche as a precursor of Nazism and a prophet of the reign of the hooked cross. Anti-Semitism will end only when the Jews stop hiding and assuming the attitudes of whipped dogs and will say in a loud voice and to everyone's face : 'I am a Jew and I am proud of it !' And when they respond with courage and energy to provocations, attacks and offences, and pay people back in their own coin. That is the truth about this painful contemporary phenomenon which, as I have already observed, nobody has yet been able to express, not even the 'great men' of UNESCO.

Now, in conclusion, let us speak a little more about myself. The thing that is especially characteristic of me is an unquenchable thirst for progress that continually preoccupies me. As a result I am precisely the opposite of nearly all artists today who, as can be seen, do not advance by even one millimetre every ten years. Painters whom I have known for a long time still continue to do the same things, and if someone changes the subject-matter of his painting he does so, not in an attempt to improve the quality of his own work, but simply in order to improve his own situation, in order to sell more easily, to make the critics and intellectuals more favourable towards him, while in fact the change concerns only the subject of what he does, and the aim he wishes to achieve is in no way an ideal aim and has nothing to do with true art.

Yet the Biennale and Quadriennale exhibitions, without counting other more or less official shows, and those organised by dealers and pseudo-dealers, always with aims which have nothing to do with art, all these shows, as I say, follow each other and resemble each other with exasperating monotony. You never see any one of the exhibitors prove that he has made any progress or has done better than he did earlier.

My case, on the other hand, is different, I would say unique. If you think of all my exhibitions from 1918 until today you will see continual progress, a regular and persistent march towards those summits of mastery which were achieved by a few consummate artists of the past. Naturally, in order to see and say all this, one must have, in addition to my exceptional intelligence, so far as true painting is concerned, one must also have my mighty personality, my courage and my ardent desire for truth. As a result it is necessary to be precisely the opposite of so many gentlemen who concern themselves with art, as for example Signors Lionello Venturi, Carlo Ragghianti and Marco Valsecchi, to quote only three, and from our country, but in every country there are whole legions of Venturis, Ragghiantis and Valsecchis.

Observing with a clinical eye the spectacle offered to us today by the humanity of our country, as in the rest of the globe, we remain astonished by the enormous quantity of things which are badly done, from useless speeches, either tending to distort truth, to vast amounts of conformism, indifference and above all stupidity, which the public in every country today displays.

Yesterday, in fact, I watched on television the third and last evening of the Festival of Song at San Remo. Observing the public one could see so many expressionless faces which were trying all the same to appear happy, content and satisfied. The men were in dinner-jackets and the women in evening dress; one immediately realised that all these people in the world of song and music, art generally, were highly indifferent to it and probably began by understanding little or nothing about it. What brought them there and made them come together there, in that hall, was the need to be fashionable, the need to don their clothes and jewellery, to look at each other, to gossip and make malicious remarks, to give themselves importance, to seem young, rich and satisfied. They had come from many cities in Italy, but probably most of them came from Milan, and for them it was the same thing to hear one of Schubert's songs sung by Tagliavini or Tebaldi, or to hear a kind of monotonous and tedious recitation, sometimes whispered *sotto voce*, or yelled with the voice of one condemned. . . .

Watching this transmission I thought that, so far as the Festival of Song is concerned, one is present at the same phenomenon as abstract painting. Like abstract painting, which is more than half a century old and is supported and presented, either through ignorance or bad faith, by the modern critics, as a typical expression of the torment and anxiety of our era, so are the monotonous songs in which one word is not sung but yelled and repeated on the same note innumerable times; people try to present them as an ultra-modern phenomenon which is also half a century old or a little more so. I remember that in Paris, on the eve of the First World War precisely, a singer called Frakson was causing a furore : he would sing, or rather yell his songs, accompanying himself on the piano. His method consisted of singing as he sat at the piano and accompanying himself, but with his face always turned towards the public, staring like someone seeing hallucinations or undergoing hypnosis, at one or other of the spectators in the front row. He would yell out his songs, repeating the same word as though he had been stricken

226

with madness and ending with a yell like a ferocious jackal. The
final yell had hardly died away when a deafening roar of applause
would break out; the audience seemed delirious; but I think that
this deafening applause expressed rather more the delight of the
audience that their long torment was over, as in fact must happen
during the Festival of Song and also at symphony concerts, especially
when the symphony is particularly long.

It is certain that with abstract painting and in general with
modernist painting, as with Festivals of Song and in general with
modern and duodecacophonous music, we are very far from the
moral atmosphere of the Athens of Pericles, the Rome of Julian II
and the France of Louis XIV.

So far as the human atmosphere of our time is concerned, we are
present today at the shameful spectacle offered by America, regarded
as the liberal and democratic country *par excellence*, with the
incredible working of American justice concerning Caryl Chessman
who has been waiting for twelve years to go at a moment's notice to
the electric chair.[2] This reminds me of another tremendous and
similar case which occurred also in America about thirty-two years
ago : the case of two Italians, Sacco and Vanzetti. What is incredible
in the cases both of Chessman and Sacco and Vanzetti is that in
neither case was there irrefutable evidence of homicide, and as is
known in every country where there is a death penalty, only
assassination is punished with the maximum penalty.

In order not to think of so much amorality and stupidity or of
so many horrors I seek refuge more than ever in work and in that
sacred temple where two gods hold each other by the hand : true
poetry and true painting.

The Technique of Painting

The Technique of Painting

The one cause of the decadence in painting today is the total loss of skill, *technique*. Today, the words skill and technique, through the activities of the modernists, have come to stand for very little, something which is definitely not fit to mention. These grotesque myths created deliberately by the modernists to defend their position, myths such as 'spirituality' and 'inspiration' which, according to them, form the basis of all artistic creation, 'torment', 'anxiety' and other silliness and senselessness of this sort, spread abroad by intellectuals who repeat them, like so many parrots, in the belief that they make a good impression, appear up to date and above all intelligent, these myths based on lies and bad faith are the trenches between which the modernists hide themselves to disguise and conceal their ignorance and impotence.

One should not forget that the word 'technique' comes from the Greek *techne*, meaning art.

During a lecture I gave in Turin a few years ago I explained how all the decadence of painting, which has now become a real collapse, was caused principally by the great industrial development which took place in Europe about the middle of last century and led to the commercial production of artists' materials. In a relatively short time this commercialisation brought about the loss of all those principles and methods which, during the course of the centuries, had allowed the development of the skill of painting and the consequent possibility of good work which brought about the emergence of the master painters and allowed the creation of so many masterpieces which we can still admire in the museums and the great private collections.

All art, or rather modern pseudo-art, is due to this fact, and all these tendencies, these so-called isms, from impressionism down to the more recent manifestations of abstractionism—which, however, we should not forget, is half a century old—are the consequences of this loss of skill, this incapacity to work well, to create a true work of art, this loss of grammar and language which have forced painters to seek new ways of deceiving other people and sometimes themselves in order to make both ends meet.

This is the pure and simple truth about the origin of contemporary painting. Anything else that has been said in reply to this proposition is absolutely false and its sole purpose is to conceal the desperate state of painting today.

There are today a few painters who have understood, or more or less appreciated, what I am saying. These are the very few painters who work seriously, and even if they do not create masterpieces worthy of being signed by a Titian, a Rubens or a Velasquez, they can still execute dignified paintings, which everyone of good faith, sane in body and mind, enjoys hanging on the walls of their houses. For the most part, these very rare honest painters work in isolation; they earn enough, since every painter who paints a picture worthy of the name always finds, sooner or later, someone to buy it from him, but, as I have said, they work in isolation, they are not confined to a group, they do not constitute an international freemasonry with totalitarian activity, as the modernists do.

I have always been preoccupied with technique; I have always thought, as Albrecht Dürer also thought and wrote, that technique is everything in the creation of art. But it was especially from 1918 onwards, when I began to copy the works of the Old Masters in the museums of Rome and Florence that I began to delve deeply into the problem of technique. Since then I have never stopped and I have always continued to try, through experimentation and reworking things again and again, to give my painting an ever-better quality and in order to be able to work with ever-increasing confidence and freedom.

I will now set out my principal achievements to date. I will give suggestions and advice for serious painters, and I will also set out the true and actual methods which I have used in my experiments for many years with good, sometimes excellent, results.

The basis of all good painting, whether oil or tempera, or a combination of the two, is the priming.

Priming is the layer of material which is put on the board or canvas and constitutes the foundation of the picture. Today, since the commercialisation of artists' materials has placed on the market such a vast quantity of canvases crudely prepared with gesso or oil, true and proper priming has ceased to exist and it has even been totally forgotten. The canvases which are on sale today can be used, but on condition that they are used as though they were unprepared and only after they have been coated, before use, with true priming materials. By working directly on the preparation carried out by the manufacturer it is absolutely impossible to obtain good painting, and a more experienced painter, even an authentic, skilled one, would not succeed in obtaining a good result.

In connection with this I remember what an elderly painter-restorer once told me. He used to say that if a master from the golden ages of painting, let us say a Titian, a Rembrandt, a Rubens or a Velasquez, were to return to life today, wanted to paint something and went into an artists' materials shop, he would not find a single one of the items and materials that he was accustomed to use for painting; and thus he would finally buy a piece of paper, a pencil or some charcoal and would restrict himself to making a simple drawing.

Here now are some methods and directions for priming to put on the canvas, depending on whether one wishes to paint in tempera or oil.

PRIMING FOR TEMPERA

Take either unprepared canvas or else canvas prepared with gesso which can be found in the shops; if you take commercial canvas you must be careful to see that it is a completely absorbent canvas, and not semi-absorbent, as is sometimes found. If you take an unprepared canvas you must first cover it with a coat of isinglass diluted in tepid water and with this moisten some fine gesso, gilders' gesso. It is also possible to moisten it with Spanish white, and also with powdered white lead, usually called *biacca*. Before mixing the gesso or the white lead with the isinglass you must give the canvas a good coat of isinglass diluted in tepid water, with the addition of a few drops of glycerine or castor oil. When the glue is dry you should give it a coat of the same isinglass (always mixed with a little glycerine or castor oil) with a certain amount of gesso or white lead moistened with isinglass. So far as the proportions are concerned, it is not possible to give exact measures; all that is necessary is that this gesso, or white lead, dissolved in the isinglass, should form a more or less liquid substance, which flows easily beneath the brush; and it must be applied in rapid and even strokes, taking care that on the surface some parts are not more covered than others. When this second coat is quite dry the real priming is done, and you should proceed as follows.

In a cup or other vessel put the yolk of an egg and a spoonful of vinegar. Then with a stiff brush mix the egg and vinegar well together so that they make a kind of yellow cream. Then, still stirring with the stiff brush, add two small spoonfuls of crude linseed oil, a small spoonful of turpentine and a small spoonful of water.

Once this emulsion has been prepared, the canvas, which has already been prepared as set out above, is given two coats of the same emulsion thinned with water (one part emulsion to two parts of water); naturally the first coat is left to dry and then the second is applied. Lastly, still using the stiff brush, one part of white lead is moistened with one part of pure emulsion, that is without any addition of water. This must be well moistened until a kind of very liquid cream is obtained, which is then applied to the canvas in a rapid, even manner. One or two coats may be applied; if the grain of the canvas is fine or fairly fine only one coat need be given.

The final priming can also be applied by moistening the white lead with the following emulsion : one yolk of egg, a small spoonful of vinegar, two large soupspoonfuls of gum arabic (a large spoonful of powdered gum softened in two large spoonfuls of tepid water : the powdered gum arabic is placed in a cup and the two large spoonfuls of tepid water are added slowly, while stirred rapidly with a stiff brush). Finally a small spoonful of more or less liquid honey is added.

PRIMING FOR OIL PAINTING

The types of priming described below can be applied to two sorts of canvas for oil paint, either commercial canvas or unprepared canvas. The latter should first be given a coat of isinglass (as described in the preceding instructions), then a coat of zinc white moistened with heat-treated or even crude linseed oil, mixed with turpentine in the proportion of one part of crude oil to one part of turpentine (the zinc white moistened in the oil should form a kind of very liquid cream; let it dry well). The following types of priming can be applied : one part of powdered white lead moistened with Fat Oil (from Winsor & Newton) and virgin wax in the turpentine : grate the virgin wax with a penknife; put it in a cup and pour over it a quantity of turpentine equal in volume to the wax; cover the cup and leave it for ten or twelve hours. After this time the wax and the turpentine will have formed a kind of fairly liquid gelatine. Then place in a bottle equal parts of the Fat Oil and the wax and turpentine solution. Shake the bottle well and with this solution moisten the powdered zinc white and apply one or two coats of it to the canvas.

It is advisable to add to the zinc white a little powdered black, or red clay, because it is not easy to paint on an absolutely white surface.

Another more simple type of priming for oil painting consists in taking a commercial type of canvas for oil painting and giving it a coat of silver white, as found in tubes—the make I suggest is the Lucas silver white—and moisten it with spirits of turpentine, to which you should add a few drops of white spirit, which is a very strong drying agent and is sold in liquid form in shops selling colours and varnishes.

After this priming is quite dry you can, before starting work, apply a good varnish with dammar varnish thinned with turpentine.

PRIMING FOR EMULSION PAINT

The following priming can be applied to a commercial canvas for oil painting or to a canvas prepared first with glue and then with zinc white and prepared oil.

Put in a cup some prepared oil, the commercial sort of Winsor & Newton's Fat Oil, then add with a spoon some water in which a little isinglass or rabbit glue has been dissolved, or even water with a little lime. The water should be poured into the oil very gradually, almost drop by drop, and stirred continuously with a stiff brush. The proportions are : equal quantities of water and oil. When this water and glue, or water and lime, emulsified with the Fat Oil, has formed a kind of whitish cream, mix it with silver white for oil painting, from tubes. In this way you will obtain a fairly solid substance, but

you should be able to smear it on to the canvas with a brush, and use
it to give one or two coats of priming on the canvas. It is always
advisable to colour the priming lightly with a little black, red or
yellow clay.

Priming for oil painting can also be carried out on canvas for oil
paint, with oil colours, either with those in tubes or by moistening
powdered colours with linseed oil, crude or heat-treated, and by adding to such colours a certain quantity of oleo-resinous varnish. This
type of varnish is not on sale today, but it is easy to make it. This is
what you should do.

In a terracotta dish (small, medium or large, depending on the
quantity of varnish required) put one part of gum mastic resin or
dammar resin crushed in a mortar, until it is reduced to as fine a
powder as possible; add an equal quantity of crude linseed oil to the
powdered resin. Then put the dish over a very low flame, taking
care, if the dish is on a gas stove, that the flame does not touch the
dish; you must watch the heating process continually and stir the
resin into the oil with a little stick from time to time to make it
dissolve more easily. Then, when all the resin has been absorbed
into the oil, using the stick, take a little of this solution and let a
drop fall on something cold (a small piece of glass or metal or even
a smooth stone). With the fleshy part of the finger touch the drop to
test its density. If when the drop is spread in this way with the finger
it offers some resistance and presents an oily texture, then remove the
dish from the heat; if it spreads too easily, then return it to the heat
and let the oil cook longer. As soon as the required density has been
obtained place the solution in a bottle. If the varnish coagulates as
it cools down and forms a kind of gelatine, place the bottle in a
bain-marie and, when the varnish becomes liquid again, add a little
crude oil to it.

This oleo-resinous varnish can be used either for adding to priming
for oil painting or as a medium for painting. If it is used as a
medium, however, you should make certain, before using it, by
making a brush-stroke with colour strongly diluted with this varnish,
that the colour does not stick and the brush-stroke does not lose its
shape. If this should happen, then the varnish must be heated again
until it becomes thicker and a small piece of virgin wax should be
added to it.

The principle, the basis of all priming for oil painting is that it should be very thick; that it should form a thick layer of matter over the canvas; the thicker it is, the better it will be to paint over, whatever method of oil painting is used. It is also advisable to give a good coat of varnish (possibly *Damar* varnish from Lefranc) over the priming before painting.

Some Diluents for Oil Painting

Varnish and diluents for oil painting can have a base of resins moistened in distilled turpentine or else a base of resins moistened in oil, or emulsions of fat oil with water, amounting to half gum or lime, or fat oil with water, and gum mixed with egg-yolk.

Varnishes with a base of resins moistened in spirits of turpentine can be painted on, provided the colours are diluted with them on the palette and make it possible to produce painting of fine quality, glazed and transparent, recalling Flemish painting, especially that of Teniers and Rubens. Since these colours dry too quickly on the palette, however, it is difficult to work with them; this difficulty can be remedied by adding to the varnish a little crude linseed or poppy-seed oil. By dipping the brush in this varnish, diluting a colour and making one stroke on the canvas, you can immediately add another stroke on top of the first, which will show through the second stroke and will not be diluted by it. Naturally, the strokes must be very liquid. This is the basis of Rubens's painting.

With oleo-resinous varnish, which consists of a resin (dammar, gum mastic, colophony, rosin) moistened directly over heat in linseed, walnut or poppy-seed oil, with a small addition of virgin wax, painting can be done without the inconvenience of colours drying too quickly. I have already described earlier the method of preparing such varnishes.

Another varnish which produces glazed and transparent painting is made as follows. Into a cup put one part (a soupspoonful) of Venice turpentine. Venice turpentine is a kind of extremely dense viscous substance, made from pine and fir resin; it was much used by the Venetian painters of the sixteenth century who called it Abezzo oil. To the Venice turpentine add a soupspoonful of pure alcohol (90 per cent proof), then with a stiff brush moisten the Venice turpentine in the alcohol. When it is completely dissolved add, still moistening it with the stiff brush, a little honey; a coffee-spoonful or even less. Instead of the honey one can also add a little crude linseed oil.

Here now is another varnish which produces transparent and glazed painting. Put to dissolve in a *bain-marie* one part of dammar resin, ground into an extremely fine powder, and two parts of turpentine. Once these have dissolved in the *bain-marie* add one part of Venice turpentine. When this also has dissolved add two parts of spirits of turpentine.

This varnish is naturally not on sale today and probably everyone concerned with painting, even those with skill or technique, is unaware of it. It is a very important varnish and allows one to work rapidly, producing a fluid and solid material which is in particular very manageable. Even recently, when I visited, at the Rome Palace of Exhibitions, an exhibition of eighteenth- and nineteenth-century French paintings, which showed Italian buildings and sites in our country, I observed at length that famous painting by Fragonard which belongs to the collection at the Louvre and which was once said to be a self-portrait, while it is now considered to be a portrait of the Abbé de Saint-Non. On the back of the painting are the following words: Portrait of the Abbé de Saint-Non, painted by Fragonard in 1789, *in one hour*. Since the canvas measures 0.80 x 0.65 centimetres, Fragonard, in spite of his skill, must have disposed of a truly exceptional medium in order to carry out a portrait of these dimensions in such a short time and with such powerfully plastic results.

It is probable in fact that lead oxide varnish was used by the French and also the Italian painters of the eighteenth century. I have encountered in many paintings by the eighteenth-century French masters the qualities obtained by lead oxide varnish.

I found the method for making this varnish in a French book published in Paris in 1830, written by a painter called Jean François Mérimée; the title of the book is *De la peinture à l'huile*.

Mérimée says that he found lead oxide varnish in Italy, where it was called prepared oil. He could not discover the origin of this varnish, from which Mérimée deduced that it had existed for a long time and that it was probably used by Italian and foreign painters of the eighteenth century.

238

Mérimée defines the varnish as a greasy, plasterlike preparation and says that it resembles honey and sometimes semi-coagulated fat. Its principal quality is oiliness.

This is how it is prepared.

Place in a terracotta dish seven parts of crude linseed oil and one part of lead oxide. It is very important that the lead oxide should be reduced to a very fine powder, since in this way it blends more quickly with the oil. Sometimes commercial lead oxide, which almost always contains granules, should be pounded finer in a mortar or in some other way. The heat should be very low; if a gas stove is used the flame must not touch the dish; if an electric or charcoal stove is used it is better for the dish to be held at some distance above the heat. The oil should be continuously stirred into the lead oxide with a stick. This work must be done patiently, without any hurry, and it is strongly advisable, when the oil and lead oxide start to boil, not to stand with your face exposed to the steam which rises from the dish, and better still to place a light, damp cloth over your nose and mouth. Lead oxide is a poisonous substance; avoid touching your mouth during the heating operation and wash your hands as soon as the varnish is made.

When after a time you have the impression that the lead oxide is blended with the oil, take a little of the substance on the stick with which you have been stirring it and let a drop fall on something cold. If the drop condenses as wax does when it falls from a lighted candle, this means that the varnish is ready. Take the dish from the heat and let it cool. While it is hot you can also put a small piece of virgin wax into it; when it is cool this substance looks like fat which has gone cold at the bottom of a saucepan and it is more or less dark brown in colour. The best way of keeping it is to put it in tin-foil tubes, like those used for oil colours; it can, however, also be kept in a pot with a screw top. This varnish can be put on the palette or in a can and is diluted with crude linseed oil in order to make it fairly fluid.

The advantages of this emplastic oil are that brush-strokes of highly diluted colour do not run and do not lose their outline, and it is possible to make one stroke over another one without the second one cancelling out or displacing the first one. The principal quality of this varnish is its oiliness; it is the oiliness which allows each brush-stroke to cling to the preceding ones by a suction effect; it is the same phenomenon as that of *ventouses*.

Tempera Painting

'Tempera' is a word which was used rather vaguely by the old painters. Ultimately it meant 'paint, or colour, soluble in water'; therefore, if a colour placed on the palette is diluted with a brush dipped in water, then that colour is tempera; if not, it is oil. 'Tempera' comes from the Italian word *'stemperare'*, and means 'to make a colour by adding a liquid to the colour when it is in powder form and moistening it with this liquid'.

I shall now give a few instructions for making tempera. These are methods with which I have been experimenting for many years, which I have used and am still using today.

THIN TEMPERA

Place in a cup some pieces of joiner's glue, the so-called fish glue [isinglass]. Cover this with water and leave it for twenty-four hours. After this time some of the glue will have dissolved in the water which has become sticky. Place four soupspoonfuls of this sticky water in another cup; then add a small coffeespoonful of vinegar, or a few drops of carbolic acid; but vinegar is better; and add also a small spoonful of honey. If these substances are put into a bottle, shake the bottle well to bring about an emulsion; if not, mix them well in a cup by stirring with a stiff brush. This emulsion can be used both for moistening colours in powder form and as a medium for diluting them on the palette.

ANOTHER THIN TEMPERA

The same as the previous one, except that instead of joiner's glue it is possible to use gum arabic, which is made by stirring with a stiff brush one part of gum arabic to two parts of tepid water added to it gradually.

Tree gum can also be used, by placing a few pieces of tree gum in a recipient with water, and using this water when it has become sticky.

EGG TEMPERA (SEMI-OILY)

Place in a cup an egg-yolk, a small coffeespoonful of vinegar, two coffeespoonfuls of crude linseed oil, a coffeespoonful of spirits of turpentine, a small coffeespoonful of water and one of honey. These substances are placed in the cup by mixing and stirring them rapidly with a stiff brush. In this way you obtain an emulsion which slightly resembles a fairly liquid yellow coloured mayonnaise. Powdered colours can be mixed with this emulsion and it can be used as a medium to dilute colours on the palette.

So far as the canvas is concerned, it should be covered with gesso; and before painting, this canvas should be given two good coats of the above emulsion diluted with water, one part emulsion to one of water. When work is begun it is advisable to use the emulsion diluted with a little water, either for drawing with the brush or for sketching. However, for moistening the powdered colours and finishing the painting, especially where there are white or light coloured parts, where the impasto should be thicker, the emulsion must always be used undiluted.

Once the work is finished the painting can be varnished with dammar varnish and when it is dry it can be retouched with oil colours diluted in oleo-resinous varnishes. On the varnished surfaces, and also on the parts retouched with oil, touches can be added in tempera, especially with white on the light coloured parts, which gives the painting a rich and brilliant appearance.

The same tempera can be made more oily by adding, after the egg, three instead of two small spoonfuls of prepared rather than crude oil, and also a small spoonful of Venice turpentine plus the white of the egg. The white of the egg, however, must not be used in its natural state. First of all it must be placed in a separate cup and beaten well with a fork, the froth that forms on the surface should be removed, and when it has gone, or almost gone, then what remains at the bottom of the cup is added to the emulsion.

OTHER THIN AND SEMI-OILY TEMPERAS

Place in a cup two large soupspoonfuls of milk, two large soupspoonfuls of gum arabic prepared in the way described above, and a small coffeespoonful of honey.

A more oily emulsion can also be made by adding first an egg-yolk with the usual small spoonful of vinegar, then two or three coffeespoonfuls of crude or heat-treated oil.

Another method : with a stiff brush moisten together in a cup one egg-yolk, a small spoonful of vinegar, two small spoonfuls of crude linseed oil, a small spoonful of spirits of turpentine, a small spoonful of honey, two large spoonfuls of gum arabic (in the proportion of one large spoonful of powdered gum arabic moistened with two large spoonfuls of tepid water, according to the method already described).

Note carefully: all these emulsions can be used both for moistening colours in powdered form as well as for painting, that is they can be used as a medium or a diluent, and can also be used for preparing absorbent canvases and priming for tempera painting.

Here is another method which I have used several times and which produces a type of painting rich in quality, fluid and glazed in appearance, reminiscent of certain sketches by Rubens.

Take a canvas prepared with gesso, of the kind available in shops. Make two emulsions, the first as follows: one egg-yolk, a small spoonful of vinegar, two small spoonfuls of crude linseed oil, a small spoonful of spirits of turpentine, a small spoonful of water. After making this emulsion add to it eight small spoonfuls of water.

Make a second emulsion as follows: one egg-yolk, one small spoonful of vinegar, two small spoonfuls of crude linseed oil, one small spoonful of spirits of turpentine, one small spoonful of honey, two small spoonfuls of gum arabic (one of gum to two of water).

The canvas prepared with gesso is given two coats of the first emulsion and then two coats of powdered lead oxide, moistened in the same emulsion (proportions: one part of lead oxide to two parts of emulsion). Then two further coats of the first emulsion can be given again and one coat of the second can also be given.

The painting is done with powdered colours moistened in the second emulsion.

After painting with tempera, varnish with Damar varnish (from Lefranc). Finish again with oil colours and oleo-resinous varnish and also with tempera colours made with the second emulsion.

Conclusions

In the first place I should say that the technique of painting is closely linked to the artist's intelligence concerning the art of painting. And this particular intelligence can be extremely great, vast, as it was in the case of Rubens; it can be great as it was in the case of all the masters of the past centuries; it can be medium or slight as it was amongst us in the seventeenth century and even more so in the nineteenth century, especially in the second half; and it can also be non-existent, as almost always is the case in our century.

When a painter possesses this special intelligence, even when its extent is not great, then he immediately understands that what is being done today, independently of the subject, abstraction and so-called figurative painting, with its absolute lack of drawing, form and volume, is also, above anything else, something that is not in fact painting but simply powdered colours moistened with oil (whether this is done by a manufacturer of colours or by the painter himself is not important) and put on a canvas where, after a certain time, they dry through contact with the air.

Instead, painting is a weaving together, an intermingling, a skilful superimposition of colours which can be compared to those ancient Oriental carpets, so beautiful and so highly prized, which were not made by machine but patiently woven by skilful artisans.

When a painter feels and understands these things, then it becomes a pleasure for him, a kind of ideal play, of divine entertainment, to try and retry, to seek out and make continual experiments in order to make progress in his art.

Chronological Table

1896–1903 : Giorgio de Chirico draws a great deal, copying prints, photographs and sometimes working from life. He also draws portraits of his father and mother and self-portraits.

1903–1906 : In the Fine Arts department of the Athens Polytechnic he enters the drawing class and for two years makes copies in black and white of Greek and Roman sculpture. In the evenings he goes to a school for drawing from the nude, where he copies from life, still in black and white, figures of nude men. In 1906 he begins to paint, and for a year, still working at the Polytechnic, he draws from life heads of men and women and half-length figures. He also works at home : often taking his box of colours and going to paint in the country, near Athens or on the banks of the Gulf of Phaleron. Sometimes he also goes to the Piraeus, the port of Athens, where he draws steamers and sailing-ships and boats of all kinds.

1906–1911 : Following the death of his father he leaves Greece, together with his mother and brother. After passing through Italy he goes to Munich, Bavaria, where he attends the local Academy of Fine Arts, working there for a year and a half. But the atmosphere of the Academy does not satisfy him and during his stay at the Bavarian capital he takes great interest in German literature and philosophy, visits the museums and in the evenings goes to concert halls where concerts of classical music are performed. In 1908 he is in Milan. Still thinking of the paintings of Arnold Boecklin, which in Munich had impressed him with their poetic and narrative content and plastic qualities, he paints a series of pictures with a Boecklin-like flavour, portraits of his mother and brother and also self-portraits. Then he goes to Florence, where he visits the Uffizi and the Pitti Palace. He paints a few more pictures of a Boecklin-type flavour, but under the influence of the works of Friedrich Nietzsche, of whom he was at that time a fervent admirer, he begins that series of pictures which form a prelude to the metaphysical painting. In 1911 he leaves for Paris.

1911–1915 : In Paris he continues and develops his metaphysical painting.

1915–1918 : In 1915 he is in Ferrara. He continues metaphysical painting until 1918.

1918–1925 : In 1918, after demobilisation, he goes to Rome. He frequents assiduously the museums and especially the museum at the Villa Borghese. He executes various copies of Old Masters. At home he immerses himself in the study of the technique of painting. He paints portraits and self-portraits, compositions and paintings of fruit, fish and objects. He also paints pictures of inventions such as 'seated mannequin figures'. He executes scenery and costumes for Les Ballets Suédois which give performances in Paris.

1925–1930 : In 1925 he returns to Paris. He continues the series of realistic paintings and portraits, and the series of imaginative and invented paintings, such as 'seated mannequin figures', 'gladiators', 'horses of ancient times'. He also designs scenery and costumes for the Paris Opéra and for the Diaghilev ballet.

1930–1935 : In 1930 he is in Paris again, in 1931 in Florence. Having obtained other technical successes he paints a series of nudes and pictures of fruit. In 1933 he returns to Paris, where he continues technical research, often examining at the Bibliothèque Nationale old treatises about the technique of painting. He continues the series of portraits and compositions, and when commissioned by dealers paints works of metaphysical or inventive type.

1935–1940 : In 1935 he goes to the United States, to New York, where he remains for eighteen months. During this period he paints

a few portraits and pictures of various subjects. In 1937 he returns
to Italy and works in Milan; he works also in Paris. At the end of
1939 he stops in Milan.

1940–1945: After making designs for Covent Garden in London in
1939 he returns to Milan, where he works for two years on pictures
mainly dealing with realistic subjects. He also executes commissions
for portraits and paintings of metaphysical and inventive type. In
1942 he is in Florence; his production varies between paintings of
realistic style, reflecting his conquests in the field of technique, and
paintings in metaphysical or imaginary style. At the end of 1943 he
is in Rome, where he continues the same type of production.

1945 and afterwards: He still continues the realistic style of painting,
interspersed with paintings of metaphysical and imaginary subjects.
He also designs many sets of scenery and costumes for the Rome
Opera, the Teatro Comunale in Florence and La Scala in Milan.
He also carries out many lithographs, sculptures and illustrations
for books.

Translator's Notes

CHAPTER 3

1. Heinrich Schliemann (1822–90), the German-born archaeologist who discovered the ruins of Troy and Mycenae and later settled in Athens.

CHAPTER 4

1. Giovanni Segantini (1858–99), painter of alpine landscapes, peasant life and symbolic subjects.
   Gaetano Previati (1852–1920), painter of historical subjects and landscapes.
2. Arnold Boecklin (1827–1901), the Swiss-German painter, was one of the most important influences on the young de Chirico. In 1920, the latter wrote enthusiastically of the element of surprise, the metaphysical power and lyricism of his work, which combined 'the preternaturalism of the Italian landscape with architectural elements'. Boecklin specialised in mythological subjects, and spent his last years near Florence.
   Max Klinger (1857–1920), German painter, etcher and sculptor whose works, notably the *Paraphrase on the Finding of a Glove*, created a sensation in Berlin when he was young. De Chirico was impressed by his unconventional approach and wrote in 1920 that 'by combining in a single composition scenes of contemporary life and visions of antiquity, (he) produces a deeply disturbing dream-reality'.

CHAPTER 5

1. 'No, good sir, we haven't got such a splendid name.'
2. Does Hector wish to turn from me forever,/Where Achilles of the implacable hands/Carries out a fearful sacrifice to Patroclus?
3. Luigi Pulci, fifteenth-century Italian poet famous for his burlesque versions of chivalric romances.
4. A version of this incident is included in de Chirico's novel *Hebdomeros* (Paris, 1929; London: Peter Owen, 1968).
5. *Hebdomeros*, written in French, was originally published in France by Calmann-Lévy and republished by Flammarion in 1964.

CHAPTER 6

1. The Latin words *aquae calidae* mean simply 'warm waters'. In the novel

Hebdomeros de Chirico mentions 'those with liver trouble (who) care for themselves by visiting warm and cholagogue springs; *aquae calidae*; Ceasar, amorous and dyspeptic, surrounded with his legions, in the conquered valley'. This is one of the many autobiographical reminiscences in the novel which can now be identified.

2. Pierre Laprade (1875–1931), successful French painter, much of whose work was in the style of *fêtes galantes*.

3. Lionello Balestrieri was born in Sienna in 1874. His imaginary portrait of Beethoven won him a gold medal in Paris in 1900 and it became world famous. It hangs in the Revoltella Museum in Trieste.

4. The charcoal *Portrait of Guillaume Apollinaire* (1914?) includes a silhouette of the poet's head and shoulders presented with markings like those on a dummy target figure. The mark on the head was interpreted, notably by Cocteau, as foreshadowing the head wound suffered by Apollinaire during the last year of the war.

5. Constantin Brancusi (1876–1957).

6. Adolfo Wildt (1868–1931), Italian sculptor.

7. André Derain (1880–1954), the famous Fauve painter whose style gradually became more classical.

8. Max Jacob (1876–1944), the Jewish poet from Brittany who was later converted to Roman Catholicism. He is best known for his ironic prose poems, especially *Le Cornet à dés* (1918).

9. André Dunoyer de Segonzac (b. 1884), painter mainly of landscapes.

10. Luc-Albert Moreau (1882–1948), successful if undistinguished French painter.

11. Othon Friesz (1879–1949), French-born painter associated with the Fauves.

12. Usually called *The Rose Tower* (*La Tour Rose*). Painted in 1913, this picture exemplifies the painter's transition from the orthodox to the individual. The characteristic arcades, the equestrian statue, the long shadow, are already there; only the distant hills and the low cottages indicate the early date of the work. At one time it was in the Peggy Guggenheim Collection in Venice.

13. Paul Guillaume (1893–1934), the art dealer who supported most of the leading painters of the twentieth century, including Modigliani, Picasso and de Chirico himself. Guillaume was an expert on Negro art and also helped to assemble the famous Barnes Collection in the United States. His own collection in France was given to the State by his widow in 1960.

14. Giosué Carducci (1835–1907), critic, scholar and poet.
   Giovanni Pascoli (1855–1912), lyric poet and scholar of classical philosophy.
   Gabriele D'Annunzio (1863–1938), the prolific writer who knew European fame but is now regarded as decadent and dangerously close in thinking to the fascist movement.

15. Giovanni Papini (1881–1956), iconoclastic critic, sceptical novelist, famous for his egotistical arrogance.
   Ardengo Soffici (1879–1964), minor futurist writer and one of the first Italian critics of de Chirico.

CHAPTER 7

1. André Breton (1896–1966), the leader and spokesman of the surrealist movement, author of the two surrealist manifestoes, etc.

2. Cesare Lombroso (1836–1909), Italian criminologist who has been mentioned as a precursor of Freud in some respects. He became professor of forensic medicine and psychology at Turin.
3. Benjamin Disraeli's grandfather (Benjamin D'Israeli, father of Isaac) came from Cento, near Ferrara.
4. Corrado Govoni (1884–1965), lyric poet and novelist.
5. This portrait, painted in 1915, is thought by art critics to reflect Germanic influences. The long, lustrous finger-nails are clearly visible.
6. Filippo de Pisis (1886–1956), regarded as one of the 'metaphysical' painters when young, but his style became more impressionistic in later life.
7. A curious character with the same habits appears in de Chirico's novel *Hebdomeros*.
8. Carlo Carrà (1881–1966) was originally known as a futurist painter. De Chirico adversely reviewed Carrà's book on metaphysical painting, published in 1919.
9. The Latin reads: 'Thus is and will be the justice of the world.'

CHAPTER 8

1. Armando Spadini (1883–1925) originally worked in ceramics, went through a period of 'naturalist reaction' and was later regarded as an impressionist.
2. Mario Sironi (b. 1885) was associated at first with the futurists, and influenced at one point by de Chirico.
3. Among this group of mid- to late nineteenth-century German painters Wilhem Leibl was the leader of the realist school and Franz von Lenbach was official portrait painter to Wilhelm I and Bismarck.
4. Roberto Longhi, well-known art historian and critic.
5. De Chirico's younger brother was called Andrea, but when he began to compose music, write and paint he used the name Alberto Savinio.
6. Anton Giulio Barilli, the critic.
7. This famous café was the first to open in Rome after 1870, and it became a political, literary and artistic centre. In its 'third room' (*terza saletta*) spirited discussions would take place among professional politicians, artists and journalists.
8. Roberto Longhi wrote a book about Carlo Socrate (b. 1889), the 'mystical realist'. Giorgio Morandi (1896–1964), who was born in Bologna, was one of the greatest Italian painters of the twentieth century. Much of his work was grouped with that of de Chirico and Carrà as 'metaphysical'. He was one of the few Italian painters who never went to work in Paris.

CHAPTER 9

1. Vincenzo Cardarelli (1887–1959) has been described as a latter-day classic, carrying on the tradition of Leopardi, the famous nineteenth-century Italian poet. Cardarelli wrote many outstanding love-poems.
2. Emilio Cecchi (1884–1966) was an expert on English literature. Among the many Italians about whom he wrote were Pascoli and Spadini (*see* Chap. 6 *n* 14; Chap. 8 *n* 1).
3. This incident, described in almost identical words—without, of course, any mention of Derain—is included in *Hebdomeros*.

CHAPTER 10

1. These two reviews were important in the literary and artistic history of their period. De Chirico contributed important articles to both of them, and *Valori plastici* published his essay on the French painter Courbet in 1925.
2. For Leopardi, *see* Chap. 9 *n* 1.
3. *Ovunque* means 'everywhere'. *Quantunque* means 'although' and is normally followed by a subjunctive verb form, in this case *cantassero*. The sentence quoted by Cardarelli would normally mean 'Everywhere the birds were singing'.
4. Ugo Foscolo (1798–1837), the great Italian romantic poet who was born in Greece.
5. Emile-Jacques Dalcroze (1865–1950), the Swiss musician whose system of musical education was known as 'Eurhythmics'.
6. Marie Bashkirtseff (1860–84), a Russian girl who lived in France, wrote a famous *Intimate Journal*. She also painted, though not as well as she had hoped to do.
7. Capitaine Fracasse, the hero of Théophile Gautier's novel of the same name, published in 1863, a cloak-and-dagger story based on *Le Roman comique* (1651) by Paul Scarron.
8. This is presumably the *Self-Portrait* of 1923.

CHAPTER 13

1. 'Farewell bright glow of summers too short!' This line is from Baudelaire's *Chant d'automne* (Autumn Song) in *Les Fleurs du Mal*.
2. Victor Hugo's lines could be translated as follows:
    When November fills the blue sky with mist,
    When the wind whirls down a snow of leaves,
    O my muse, then you creep into my heart,
    As a shivering child comes close to the fire.

CHAPTER 14

1. *Protée*, with choreography by David Lichine.

CHAPTER 16

1. The red lily has been the symbol of Florence for several hundred years and Anatole France used the phrase for his novel about Florentine society, *Le Lys rouge* (1894).

CHAPTER 17

1. De Chirico's wife, Isabella Far, was the first to use the expression 'silent life' for what in English is called 'still life'.
2. The Court of Cassation is the highest appeal court in Italy.
3. Giuseppe Arcimboldi, the sixteenth-century Milanese master famous for his strange paintings which include monsters built up from fruit, vegetables, etc.

CHAPTER 18

1. In 1959 the Fréjus dam—in the South of France—burst, causing serious flooding and heavy loss of life.
2. The case of Caryl Chessman, who was accused of kidnapping, sexual and other crimes in the United States, caused an outcry. He was eventually executed in 1960 after seven interventions by judges or courts.

Bibliography

NOTE: This bibliography is not definitive, although it may appear much more comprehensive than previous bibliographies. For writings about de Chirico, readers should consult the following:

Lo Duca, *Giorgio de Chirico*, Milan: Hoepli, 1945 (*Arte moderna italiana*, No. 10); bibliography by Giovanni Scheiwiller, pp. 17–41.

Soby, James Thrall, *Giorgio de Chirico*, New York: Museum of Modern Art, undated (1955); selective bibliography, pp. 254–8.

Giorgio de Chirico, presented by Fortunato Bellonzi, Rome: La Barcaccia, undated (1961).

The article 'Al dio ortopedico', to which the author himself refers, can now be reread in:

Roberto Longhi, *Scritti giovanili*, Vol. 1, Florence: Sansoni, 1961, pp. 427–9.

For the sake of bibliographical accuracy and documentary completeness we have also included those articles which, although they appeared over the signature of Giorgio de Chirico, are attributed in these *Memoirs* to Isabella Far.

Vanni Scheiwiller

1914   'The Enigma of a Day', Farmington, Maine.

1916   'Hector and Andromache', New York.

1918   'Il Signor Govoni dorme', in Alberto Savinio, *Hermaphrodito*, Florence: La Voce. (Partial reissue, Milan: Garzanti, 1947, see p. 26.)
        'Zeusi l'esploratore', *Valori plastici*, I, 1, Rome (Nov.), 10.

1919   'Noi metafisici', Cronache d'attualità, Rome (Feb. 15).
        'Sull'arte metafisica', *Valori plastici*, I, 4–5, Rome (Apr.–May), 15–18.
        'Impressionismo', ibid., I, 6–10 (June–Oct.), 25–6. (Reprinted in *Bollettino della Galleria del Milione*, Milan, 1939.)

1920   'Paolo Gauguin', *Il Convegno*, Milan (March), 53–9.
        'Raffaelo Sanzio', ibid. (Apr.), 53–63.
        'Arnoldo Boecklin', ibid. (May), 47–53.
        'Classicismo pittorico', *La Ronda*, Rome (July), 506–11.
        'Gaetano Previati', *Il Convegno*, Milan (Aug.), 36–9.
        ' "Pittura metafisica" di Carlo Carrà', ibid. (Aug.), 55.
        'Max Klinger', ibid. (Nov.), 32–44.
        'Ottone Rosai', *La Toscana della Sera*, Leghorn (Dec. 14).

1921   Preface to the Catalogue for the One-Man Show held at the Arte Gallery, Milan.
        'Riflessioni sulla pittura antica', *Il Convegno*, Milan (Apr.–May), 201–6.

1922   'Une lettre de Chirico', *Littérature*, special number, 1, Paris (March 1), 11–13.
        'Giorgio Morandi', in the Catalogue of the Fiorentina Primaverile, Florence.

1923   'Pro technica oratio', *La Bilancia*, 1–2, Novara.

1924   'Courbet', *Rivista di Firenze*, I, 7, Florence (Nov.), 1–7.
        'Un Rêve', *La Révolution Surréaliste*, I, Paris (Dec. 1).

1925   'Vale Lutetia' (followed by 'Epodo'), *Rivista di Firenze*, I, 8, Florence (Feb.), 11–17. (Reprinted under the title 'Salve Lutetia', *Bulletin de l'Effort Moderne*, 33, Paris [March 1927], 7–12. 'Epodo' was reprinted in E. Falqui and Vittorini, *Scrittori Nuovi*, Lanciano, 1930, pp. 235–40, and in *1889, Per i 70 anni di Giovanni Scheiwiller*, Milan, 1959, p. 30.)

'Un Rêve' and 'Armando Spadini', *Rivista di Firenze*, II, 1, Florence (May), 14–17.

'Une nuit', *La Révolution Surréaliste*, I, 5, Paris (Oct. 15), 7. (Reprinted in Carola Giedion-Welcker, *Poètes à l'écart*, Berne, 1946, p. 201.)

Courbet, *Valori plastici*, Rome, 1925. (English trans. by M. Evans, London, 1937.)

1926   Catalogue for the Filippo de Pisis Exhibition at Le Sacre du Printemps, Paris (Apr. 23–May 7).

1927   'Statues, meubles et généraux', *Bulletin de l'Effort Moderne*, 38, Paris (Oct.), 3–6.

1928   *Piccolo trattato di tecnica pittorica*, Milan : Scheiwiller. (2nd edition, facsimile of the manuscript, ibid., 1945.)

1929   'A l'Italie', 'Lassitude', 'Odisseüs', 'Cornelia', 'Souvenir d'enfance', 'Sur la mort de mon oncle', in *Giorgio de Chirico*, Cahier 8, Antwerp : Editions Sélection, pp 27–9.

Hebdomeros, le peintre et son génie chez l'écrivain, Paris : Editions du Carréfour, 1929. (Italian edition, *Ebdòmero*, Milan : Bompiani, 1942; 2nd edition, published by the author, Rome, 1957. English edition, London : Peter Owen, 1968.)

1930   'Un giorno tu sarai qualcuno', *Poligono*, Milan (Feb.).

Preface to the Catalogue for the Exhibition of Puppets by Maria Signoretti at the Zak Gallery, Paris (May 9–22).

'Bambole', 'Personaggi', *Belvedere*, Milan (May–June).

'Saluto a Spadini', in *Omaggio a Spadini*, Rome.

1931   'Le fils de l'ingénieur', *Poligono*, Milan (March). (Already included in Waldemar George, *Chirico, avec des fragments littéraires de l'artiste*, Paris : Chronique du Jour, 1928, p. 39.)

'Maly Traktat a Malirské', in *Musaion*, Prague.

1933   'Bataille antique' (three poems in French), *Circoli*, Geneva (Jan.–Feb.).

1934   'Sur le silence', *Minotaure*, 5, Paris (May), 31–2.

1936   Preface to the Catalogue for an exhibition by Léonor Fini, at the Levy Gallery, New York.

'Aurore', 'Souvenir', 'Phileas Fogg', 'Nemrod', 'Antibes', 'C'est dimanche', *L'Italiano*, XI, 42-3, Rome (June–July), 138-9.

1938   'Barnes collezionista mistico', *L'Ambrosiano*, Milan (Feb. 16).

'J'ai été à New York', *XX Siècle*, Paris (March).

'Vox clamans in deserto' (I, II, III), *L'Ambrosiano*, Milan (March 16, 23, 30).

'Mystery and Creation' (text in English and French), *London Bulletin*, 6, London, 14.

'Deux fragments inédits', Collection *Un Divertissement*, Paris.

Hebdomeros (proofs of the Italian edition), Rome: Edizioni della Cometa.

1939   'Paola Levi-Montalcini', Turin : Edizioni Accame.

1940   'Une gita a Lecco', *Aria d'Italia*, 5, Milan (winter).

'Il signor Dudron' ('from the forthcoming novel'), *Prospettive*, Rome (May 15).

'Brevis pro plastica oratio', *Aria d'Italia*, 5, Milan (spring).

'Achille Funi', *Arte moderna italiana*, No. 4, Milan: Hoepli.

1941   'Perché ho illustrato l'Apocalisse', *Stile*, Milan (Jan.).

'Gregorio Sciltian', ibid. (Apr.).

1942   'Due prose', in *Beltempo, Almanacco delle lettere e delle arti*, Rome : Edizioni della Cometa, pp. 202-4.

'Considerazioni sulla pittura moderna', *Stile*, Milan (Jan.).

'Discorso sulla materia pittorica', *L'Illustrazione Italiana*, Milan (Apr. 26).

'I ritratti', ibid. (May 10).

'Le nature morte', ibid. (May 24).

'Miscellanea di alcune verità', ibid. (July 19).

'Gedanken des Herrn Dudron', *Italien*, Hamburg (Sept.).

'Discorso sullo spettacolo teatrale', *L'Illustrazione Italiana*, Milan (Oct. 25).

Ebdòmero, Milan : Bompiani (2nd edition, published by the author, 1957).

1943   'La forma nell'arte e nella natura', *L'Illustrazione Italiana*, Milan (March 21).

'Discorso sul cinematografo', *Cinema*, 166, Rome (May 25).

'Il tormento dell'arte', *L'Illustrazione Italiana*, Milan (July 4).

'Sulla pittura', *Pattuglia*, 7–8, Forlì.

1945   *1918–25. Ricordi di Roma.* Rome: Editrice Cultura Moderna.

'Une aventure de Monsieur Dudron', Paris: Fontaine. (Reprinted in *Pittori che scrivono*, Milan, 1954, pp. 89–96.)

Memorie della mia vita (Part I), Rome: Astrolabio.

Commedia dell'arte moderna, in collaboration with Isabella Far, Rome: Nuove Edizioni Italiane.

1946   'Une nuit' (1911–13), 'Une vie' (1911–13), 'Espoirs' (1911–13), in Carola Giedion-Welcker, *Poètes à l'écart*, Berne, pp. 201–4.

1952   'Pittura e modernismo', *Il Giornale d'Italia*, Rome (Aug. 3).

'Non reggono più le stampelle del surrealismo', ibid. (Sept. 28).

'S.O.S. dei modernisti', ibid. (Oct. 7).

'Cézanne e Van Gogh', ibid. (Oct. 30).

'Non Fisco ma Fiasco', ibid. (Nov. 21).

'Il virus modernista', ibid. (Dec. 11).

1953   'Made in France', *Il Giornale d'Italia*, Rome (Feb. 8).

'Il mistico zelo di certi espositori', ibid. (March 19).

'Lo snobismo contro l'arte', ibid. (Apr. 10).

'Nel I anniversario della morte di Savinio', ibid. (May 7).

'Il modernismo è arte borghese', ibid. (June 23).

'Un pittore senza "arie" ', ibid. (Oct. 21).

1954   'Il ratto di Derain', *Il Giornale d'Italia*, Rome (March 26).

'Pittori senza pseudo inquietudini', ibid. (Apr. 10).

'Controrivoluzione', ibid. (Apr. 24).

'Gli interessi della Nazione e il Festival del cinema', ibid. (Oct. 10).

'Biennale dittatoria', ibid. (Nov. 4).

1955   'Il caso Derain', *Il Giornale d'Italia*, Rome (March 23).

1958   'La Biennale di Venezia non mi incanta più', *Candido*, Milan (July 13).

1960   'Asta di quadri falsi a Roma e progetto di un museo per la pittura del 900', *Candido*, Milan (March 13).

'Psicoanalisi del modernismo', ibid. (July 3).

'Le vittime di una ostinata e perfida propaganda', ibid. (July 17).

'Settant'anni di progressivo crollo per l'arte', ibid. (July 24).

'Propaganda frenetica ma che perde le staffe', ibid. (Sept. 4).

'Continua in Italia il servilismo nei confronti della pseudo-pittura francese', ibid. (Oct. 2).

'Ecco che cos'è l' "arte" modernista', ibid. (Nov. 6).

1961   'Poesia e pseudopoesia. Scemenza mondiale ed esterofilia italiana', *Candido*, Milan (Feb. 26).

'I francesi vogliono istruirci', ibid. (March 26).

'Le grottesche menzogne di *Time*', ibid. (Apr. 9).

1962   *Dieci tavole dedicate all'IRI*, Rome : Edindustria.

Memorie della mia vita (Parts I–II), Milan : Rizzoli.

1964   Massa, Fioravanti Lionello, *Painting of Our Time*, Paris/Rome : International Centre of Art (with a contribution by de Chirico).

Stradone, Giovanni, *Giovanni Stradone*, Rome : De Luca (with an introduction by de Chirico).

Jacob, Max, 66
Jacobidis, 43

Kanzikis, 43–4, 126
Klinger, Max, 52

Laprade, Pierre, 65
Laurencin, Marie, 66
Lautréamont, 120
Legend of Joseph, The, 193
Lefevre Gallery, 140, 141
Leibl, Wilhelm, 90, 91
Lemeni, Rossi, 218
Lenbach, Franz von, 90
Léonce Rosenberg Gallery, 118
Leopardi, Giacomo, 107
Levy, Julian, 131, 133, 134
Levy, Pierre, 62
Locoff, Nikolai, 113, 114
Lombroso, Cesare, 75
London, 140–1
Longhi, Roberto, 44, 92–4, 95, 173, 185–6, 187

Manusso, 25–6
Marèes, Hans von, 90
Margherita Gallery, 158
Maroger, 128, 149
Mascagni, Pietro, 58, 59, 60, 61, 172
Mavrudis, 19, 20–1, 28
Mefistofele, 193, 218
Melli, Roberto, 96, 108, 109
Menzel, Adolf, 90
Meschini-Ubaldini, Signor, 175, 176
Messina, 145
'metaphysical interiors', 80
metaphysical painting, 94–5, 170, 184, 185–7, 217, 218
Milione Gallery, 137, 138, 139, 158, 179–83
Montano, Lorenzo, 99
Morandi, Giorgio, 93, 176, 185–6
Moreau, Luc-Albert, 66–7
Munich, 53–4, 57–9, 61, 90
Munich Academy of Fine Arts, 55–7
Musée National d'Art Moderne, 198–200
Muselli, Vincent, 211, 212

Museum of Modern Art (New York), 166
Mussolini, Benito, 111, 128, 144, 156, 159, 184

New York, 130–4
Newton, Eric, 188
Nietzsche, Friedrich, 16, 55, 61, 65, 224, 246
Nobili, Signorina De, 218

Obelisco Gallery, 195, 197
Ouistreham, 69
Oyster Bay, 133

Palazzo della Triennale, 127
Palazzo Ferroni, 125, 126
Pallini, Adriano, 82
Papini, Giovanni, 72, 91
Pascoli, Giovanni, 70
Péret, Benjamin, 121
Persico, Giovanni, 181
Picasso, Pablo, 64, 66, 71, 116, 170, 176, 193, 204, 213, 216
Pikionis, 124
Pisis, Filippo de, 80, 82–3, 126, 165
Pistono, 34–5
Pizzetti, Ildebrando, 219
Poveromo, 142–3
Previati, Gaetano, 52, 80.
Proust, Marcel, 120
Putz, Leo, 89

Quadriennale (Rome), 216–17

Ragghianti, Carlo, 225
Rallis, 31
Reger, Max, 57
Reinhardt, Max, 127
Renoir, Auguste, 220
Repaci, Leonida, 152–3, 204
Roilos, 31
Ronda, La, 88, 99, 100, 101, 106
Rosenberg, Léonce, 127
Rosso, Medardo, 155
Royal Society of British Artists, 188
Ruskin, John, 21